Canto is an imprint offering a range of
titles, classic and more recent, across a
broad spectrum of subject areas and
interests. History, literature, biography,
archaeology, politics, religion, psychology,
philosophy and science are all represented
in Canto's specially selected list of titles,
which now offers some of the best and
most accessible of Cambridge publishing
to a wider readership.

D1297381

SHAKESPEARE'S
PROFESSIONAL
CAREER

Shakespeare was a supremely successful accommodator. The story of his career as actor and playwright, which this book tells, shows the accommodation of his remarkable talents to the circumstances of his time: the social, political and professional life of Elizabethan and Jacobean England. It describes the development of this talent into genius. It also describes a background of theatrical rivalry, opportunism, service to noble patrons, and the sometimes involuntary involvement in political intrigue.

The book begins with Stratford-upon-Avon and investigates Shakespeare's likely link with the Earls of Derby, who were probably his first theatrical patrons. It goes on to detail the theatrical conditions that prevailed when Shakespeare first embarked on his profession. Year by year Peter Thomson recreates Shakespeare's writing career, showing how the plays mirror their times. The story reveals the precarious nature of theatrical survival, the constant threat posed by the withdrawal of noble or royal patronage, the spread of disease, the anxieties of war and the uncertain climate.

Peter Thomson's concern throughout is with the concrete details of the profession, setting out playhouse practices from the viewpoint of playwright, actor and audience. His discussion of the London playhouses incorporates the new evidence provided by the recent Rose and Globe excavations.

SHAKESPEARE'S PROFESSIONAL CAREER

PETER THOMSON
Professor of Drama, University of Exeter

CAMBRIDGE
UNIVERSITY PRESS

Published by the Press Syndicate of the University of Cambridge
The Pitt Building, Trumpington Street, Cambridge CB2 1RP
40 West 20th Street, New York, NY 10011–4211, USA
10 Stamford Road, Oakleigh, Melbourne 3166, Australia

© Cambridge University Press 1992

First published 1992

Canto edition 1994

Printed in Great Britain at the University Press, Cambridge

A catalogue record for this book is available from the British Library

Library of Congress cataloguing in publication data

Thomson, Peter, 1938–
Shakespeare's professional career / Peter Thomson.
p.   cm.
Includes bibliographical references (p. 200) and index.
ISBN 0-521-35128-6 (hardback)
1. Shakespeare, William, 1564–1616.   2. Dramatists, English – Early modern,
1500–1700 – Biography.   3. Literature and society – England – History – 16th
century.   4. Authors and patrons – England – History – 16th century.   5. Theater
– England – History – 16th century.   6. Actors – England – Biography.   I. Title.
PR2907.T48   1992
822.3'3 – DC20
[B]   91-27351   CIP

ISBN 0 521 35128 6 hardback
ISBN 0 521 46655 5 paperback

I could have written this book
for A, B or C, for D or R.
I anchor myself in them.
But, as things are,
I offer it to the University Funding Committee
And dedicate it
to my Exeter Drama colleagues.

Contents

List of illustrations   *page* xi
Preface   xiii
Acknowledgements   xv

1   Shakespeare and Stratford   1

2   Establishing a career: of patrons and provinces   23

3   Establishing a career: London 1590   52

4   A playtext and its context   79

5   Servant to the Lord Chamberlain: 1594–1603   105

6   Of Queen, Chamberlains, Admiral and King   145

7   Servant to the King: 1603–1616   162

Notes   189
Bibliography   200
General index   204
Index of plays   212

ix

Illustrations

1 Plan of Stratford (Shakespeare Birthplace Trust)   3
2 The Shakespeare coat of arms   21
3 The Careys, the Stanleys and the Howards – an
   inter-family tree   26
4 Portrait of Ferdinando Stanley, Lord Strange
   (The Earl of Derby: photograph by McMullin
   Associates)   38
5 William Segar's portrait of the Earl of Essex
   (National Gallery of Ireland)   39
6 A simple stage in the Boar's Head
   (C. Walter Hodges and Folger Books/AUP)   56
7 Edward Alleyn as Tamburlaine (By permission of
   the Syndics of Cambridge University Library)   61
8 Plan of the Rose Theatre excavations in 1989
   (Drawing by Kate Thomson)   70
9 Reconstruction of the Rose
   (C. Walter Hodges and Museum of London)   73
10 Locations of the London playhouses   76
11 A section from the 'bad' Quarto of *Hamlet*   86
12 Daniel Mytens' portrait of the Lord Admiral
   (National Maritime Museum, London)   91
13 Richard Tarlton
   (By permission of the British Library)   102
14 The dedicatory note to *The Rape of Lucrece*
   (Bodleian Library: Arch. Gd. 41(1))   107
15 Will Kempe's morris dance
   (Bodleian Library: 401.62 Art (12))   111

16 Section from Visscher's *Londinium*
(The Guildhall Library: photograph by Godfrey
New Photographics) 127
17 The Boar's Head re-designed as a permanent
playhouse (C. Walter Hodges and Folger
Books/AUP) 131
18 John de Critz the Elder's portrait of the Earl of
Southampton (In the collection of the Duke of
Buccleuch and Queensberry) 138
19 The Procession portrait of Elizabeth I
(S. Wingfield-Digby) 147
20 Daniel Mytens' portrait of James I
(National Portrait Gallery, London) 183
21 Section of Hollar's *Long View of London*
(The Guildhall Library: photograph by
Godfrey New Photographics) 185

Preface

This is not a book about Shakespeare but about Shakespeare's job. Even in his lifetime, he was uniquely successful, but part of that success was the outcome of his ability to accommodate his creativity within the confines of London's emergent professional theatre. It was neither common nor unknown for a country boy to make good in that bustling world, and it is certainly of interest that Shakespeare never rejected Stratford. Chapter 1 gives some account of his life there. The rest of the book aims to place his career in its historical and theatrical context. In order to do that, I have written more about the theatre's aristocratic patrons (in chapters 2 and 6) than is common in books of this kind. The Stanley family, Earls of Derby, have served as my main example, not only because of their intrinsic interest, but also because their fortunes and misfortunes tell us much about one section of the audience to which every successful playwright had to address his work. Shakespeare was 'well-connected'. The Lords and Ladies of his plays were not wild guesses from the wrong side of the track. I found myself intrigued by the discretion and diplomacy required of a playwright who elected to deal with recent English history in front of audiences that included direct descendants of the leading players in the power-game. Who were these men who legitimised England's first professional actors?

From the Stanleys, I have turned to the provincial life of the Elizabethan player and then to the new theatrical structures of the metropolis. Chapter 4 attempts to establish some of the ground-rules that dictated theatrical conduct in the London of the 1590s and how Shakespeare expanded those rules. It stands at the book's centre. The remaining chapters place Shake-speare's career against the background of the two contrasting reigns during which he lived, wrote and died. It has been an important part of my endeavour to hold in balance Shakespeare as 'typical' and Shakespeare as 'exceptional'. History has accorded him a supremacy that he seems never to have asserted for himself. That, too, is intriguing.

Acknowledgements

Those who have granted permission for the reproduction of illustrations are named at the relevant place. Our thanks to them. My particular gratitude goes to David Wiles for generous letters, to Dorrian Lambley for opening my eyes about the end of chapter 4 and to Leslie Read and Christopher McCullough for constructive conversation. The picture research for this book was undertaken by Cathy Turner, whose eye for detail saved many a slip. She has been an exemplary collaborator. And if I seem to take the support of my family for granted, that is because they allow me to.

CHAPTER I

Shakespeare and Stratford

The first volume of the Stratford-upon-Avon Parish Registers records ten baptisms in January 1564, seven in February, none at all in March and four in April. The last of these, dated very clearly 26 April, lists 'Gulielmus filius Johannes Shakspere'. It is assumed, though not known, that he was born on 23 April. Twenty-one baptisms in the first four months fits well with an average annual birth-rate of about sixty in the small market town. Stratford had been granted its first charter of incorporation, signifying its recognition as a single community, in 1553. By 1564 it contained upwards of 400 houses as well as 1,000 elms and forty ashes. Despite the regular visitations of bubonic plague, the population of England increased by a third between 1545 and 1603[1] and virtually doubled, from about 2.2 million to about 4.2 million, in the century that separated the accession of Henry VIII (1509) from the accession of James I (1603).[2] Half the population was aged under twenty,[3] a dominance of youth whose implications are only now being fully explored by social historians. Almost a half of any sixty children born in Stratford might have reached adulthood. From a study of London's St Botolph's parish records in Shakespeare's day, Thomas Forbes concludes that 'of every one hundred babies born ... about seventy survived to their first birthday, forty-eight to their fifth and twenty-seven to thirty to their fifteenth',[4] but the climate of Stratford was much kinder than that of an overcrowded parish in the overcrowded metropolis. Even so, only one of Shakespeare's four sisters survived childhood. His three younger brothers were hardier, though none outlived him. Tudor mortality rates indicate a life-expectancy of about thirty-five to forty years, higher than in most of the countries in early modern Europe.[5]

John Leland visited Stratford in about 1530, during his quest for English antiquities, and found it 'reasonably well buyldyd of tymbar', and, forty years later, William Camden called it a 'handsome small market town'. Fire was a constant danger in Tudor England's timber towns. Chester was devastated in the year of Shakespeare's birth, and Stratford suffered major conflagrations in 1594 and 1595, with 200 buildings wholly or partially destroyed and 400 people thrown on relief, and another in 1614, when over fifty houses were burned. The plague, on its sporadic provincial outings, spared property but not people. When Shakespeare was about three months old, the summer's first plague-death in Stratford was recorded. Two hundred of the town's total population of at most 1,500 would be dead by December.[6] London had lost nearly a quarter of its population the year before and England's second city, Norwich, would lose nearly a third in 1579.[7] One major epidemic and a few lesser mortality crises would be within the average experience of a Tudor Englishman, wherever he lived.[8] There was a minor outbreak of plague in Stratford in 1578, excessive mortality in 1587, due to 'the burning ague', and in 1608, due probably to smallpox. A quick way to recognise a mortality crisis is to set the number of baptisms recorded in parish registers against the number of burials, but what no measure can determine is the steady contribution made by malnutrition. Grain prices rose by about 400 per cent during the sixteenth century, whilst the wages of urban and agricultural labourers rose by only 170 per cent.[9] If harvests failed, the effects were catastrophic. Stratford's 'burning ague' of 1587 followed the bleak harvest of 1586. Wheat prices nationally had risen by forty-two per cent against the average rise for the previous thirty years. The Midlands were particularly hard-hit. Wheat in Warwick cost seventy-four per cent over the average and in Stratford eighty-two per cent.[10] Whatever the 'burning ague' was, it was surely hosted by hunger. The worst crisis came with the succession of failed harvests after 1594. By 1597, famine conditions were making the decisive contribution to burial rates

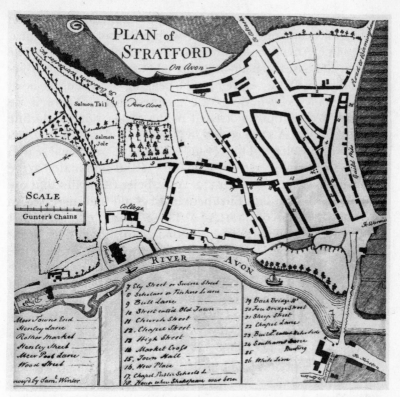

1 Samuel Winter's eighteenth-century plan of Stratford shows the pattern of streets that Shakespeare would have known; three running parallel to the river are met at right angles by three others, whilst Church Street curves sharply into Old Town at its west end.

fifty-two per cent higher than in the five-year periods either side. The poor, whose diet had steadily deteriorated through the sixteenth century, were starving to death in 1597, and if contemporary commentators are surprisingly reticent, it is all too probably because the ravages of malnutrition were so familiar as to be inconspicuous.[11] As Brecht was to observe, 'who mistrusts what he is used to?'[12]

In its response to poverty, Stratford was typical of Elizabethan towns. The levying of an obligatory tax for the relief of the poor raised too little money, there as elsewhere, to meet all circumstances. For example, the Corporation issued a petition in 1601 on behalf of the 700 poor within the borough,[13] whilst, in the same year, Stratford magistrates complained of the time spent in alehouses by near-destitute labourers 'when their wives and children are in extremity of begging'.[14] Then, as now, poverty had its own desperate compensations. There is no doubt that conditions worsened in the 1590s, but the decline was not sudden. A 1570 census in Norwich had identified 2,300 paupers in the city.[15] This census was part of a national search for vagrants that lasted from 1569 to 1572 and culminated in the notorious vagrancy acts of 1572. A. L. Beier calculates that the 15,000 vagrants of late Elizabethan England had increased to 25,000 by the reign of Charles I.[16] These 'masterless men', most of them forced to migrate by economic hardship in their home parishes, were generally unwelcome wherever they arrived. The village of Helperby, north of York, was said to derive its name from its eagerness to get rid of an old vagrant woman who had collapsed inside its boundaries and might, therefore, claim poor relief from the inhabitants. 'Help her by!' was the shout. The derivation has no historical justification (Helperby appears in the Doomsday Book), but such legends were buttressed by contemporary practices. The invalid Catherine Boland was, for four months in 1582–3, carted back and forth between Leicester and a Northamptonshire parish while local burghers disputed her birthplace. A Southwark pauper-catcher (like Dogberry, an ill-paid appointee of the Corporation) ordered that an old man 'not able to go, stand or speak' be deposited over the border of a neighbouring parish in which he had been previously lodged.[17] There is no convincing evidence that these displaced persons constituted a threat to public order, but the authorities believed them to be so. Beier suggests that we can recapture the contemporary force of the words 'rogue' and 'beggar' if we think in terms of today's equivalents, 'anarchist, terrorist, or (in some western countries) communist'.[18] After 1572, arrested vagrants, particularly those making a repeat appearance in a parish, were often whipped and sometimes hanged as 'felons without benefit of clergy'.[19] Secular officials had rarely the funds or the will to provide the lodging and support that had been traditionally supplied by religious institutions before the dissolution of the monasteries under Henry VIII. The decline of hospitality is a repeated theme in late Tudor and early Stuart literature. For Donald Lupton in 1632, true hospitality is a fading memory:

It's thought that pride, puritans, coaches[20] and covetousness hath caused him to leave our land ... he always provided for three dinners, one for himself, another for his servants, the third for the poor ... we can say that once such a charitable practitioner there was, but now he's dead, to the grief of all England: and 'tis shrewdly suspected that he will never rise again in our climate.[21]

For Lupton, the downward plunge of humane values was palpable. A major social and economic shift, fed by religious controversy and accelerated by the high cost of conflict with Spain, increasingly disrupted the patterns of life in country towns as the sixteenth century progressed, and the most pressing problems for local Councils and Justices of the Peace were those associated with poverty.

Prominent in the magisterial oligarchy that governed Stratford in the years following Shakespeare's birth was his father, John Shakespeare. The 1553 charter had called for a Common Council of twenty-eight members, fourteen of them aldermen, fourteen capital burgesses with a bailiff (a small-town mayor) elected annually from among that number. There were also various minor offices associated with the Council, typical of the inexorable spread of Tudor bureaucracy. John Shakespeare's first appointment was as one of four constables, sworn in 1558 to keep the peace, to deal with vagrancy and, if possible, to prevent fires from spreading. He had been born (c. 1529) and brought up in the nearby village of Snitterfield, where his father rented a farm from Robert Arden. This Arden belonged to a family of much greater prominence in Warwickshire than he himself was. Even so, it was a substantial step towards the minor gentry for John Shakespeare when, in about 1557, he married Mary, the daughter of Robert Arden. He was established in Stratford by then, having evidently preferred a seven-year apprenticeship as a glover and whittawer (dresser of white leather) to life on a Snitterfield farm. From constable he progressed to affeeror (assessor of non-statutory fines) and then, probably in 1560, was elected one of the fourteen capital burgesses. By 1565, he was an alderman and, in 1568, was appointed bailiff by his fellows. John Shakespeare's social aspirations led him at this time, when his first son was in his fifth year, to contemplate using his high office as the basis for an application to the College of Heralds for a coat of arms. His service on the Council continued, apparently untroubled, until 1576. In that year, a major hiatus in our knowledge of the Shakespeare family began. It will be treated in due course.

The outstanding architectural features of John Shakespeare's town were the Guild Chapel at the corner of Chapel Street and Chapel Lane, Holy Trinity Church in Old Town and the splendid fourteen-arched stone bridge, named after Sir Hugh Clopton who financed its building at the end of the fifteenth century. Bridges stood not far below churches in the hierarchy of man's achievements. An early fifteenth-century poem cele-brates the completion of a new bridge at Culham Hythe:

> Of alle werkys in this worlde that ever were wrought
> Holy Chirche is chefe ...
> Another Blissed besines is brigges to make.[22]

Clopton Bridge gave to Tudor Stratford an accessibility denied to its larger neighbour, Warwick. It carried into the town travellers from London, Oxford and Banbury. But roads in Warwickshire were notoriously sparse and ill-maintained. The great landowners had not yet developed the mercantile interests that encouraged massive expenditure on access highways; nor was the Avon navigable as far as Stratford until 1636. Of the seventy-three town plans in John Speed's *The Theatre of the Empire of Great Britaine* (1612), Warwickshire is represented only by Coventry and Warwick. Stratford served as a market town for its immediate region – the 1553 charter confirmed its weekly (Thursday) market – but was no Mecca. Its two licensed fairs (3–4 April and 13–15 September) were augmented by three more (Thursday/Friday before Lent, 14–16 July and 5–7 December) when the charter was renewed in 1610, additions which are their own evidence of success. Of the ten companies listed in the Guild Register during the fifty years that followed incorporation, the company of bakers was the oldest. Oddly, although Stratford was an acknowledged centre of the gloving trade, and although glovers were granted a prime site in the weekly market (by the High Cross at the corner of Wood Street and High Street), there was no separate company of glovers and whittawers until 1606. Nor was malting, already the town's principal industry in the sixteenth century, given company status. It is likely that many of Stratford's citizens, including both John and William Shakespeare, stockpiled malt surreptitiously during the end-of-century recession. A 1598 survey revealed that seventy-five of Stratford's householders had stores of malt on their premises, and this less than a year after the famine of 1597, when the corn used in malting might otherwise have gone to the making of bread. Philip Styles cites the local inhabitant who longed for the people's hero, the Earl of Essex, to visit Stratford and have the maltsters 'hanged on gibbetes att their owne dores'.[23]

Albeit on a modest scale, Stratford expressed the popular culture of the age. The 1547 attempt to suppress the annual Ascension Day Pageant of Saint George was probably unsuccessful, despite the strength of anti-Catholic sentiment in the town. A council that was prepared to contribute to a Whitsuntide Pastime in 1583 would have been strangely inconsistent to pay no heed to the townspeople's delight in the familiar spectacle of the fight to the death between hero and dragon, particularly under a Queen as eager as Elizabeth to incorporate the cult of Saint George in the Tudor myth. We can fairly assume that theatrical entertainments were a regular feature of the annual fairs. People travelled long distances to see plays. A Shropshire man, questioned as a vagrant at Chester's midsummer fair in 1577, explained that he had come because 'he heard of the plays here'.[24] Stratford's parish records mention payments to nineteen visiting companies between 1569, when John Shakespeare was bailiff, and 1587, the year in which it has often been argued that William Shakespeare left Stratford. As an addition, whose significance has only recently been appreciated, no country town was without its youth-organised festivities, some of which, having begun as rites of passage into adulthood, may have expanded into mere riot. The popular voice has been misleadingly silenced by writers whose primary interest is in literature. We are now invited to take account of a public theatre whose early life was not divorced from festive play nor even from resistance to authority.[25]

The young Shakespeare would certainly have seen some of the Stratford performances of visiting players. As bailiff, his father was the formal host of two of the most prominent contemporary acting companies, the Queen's Men at the Guild Hall in the early summer of 1569 and Worcester's Men in August of the same year, and if his eldest son was considered too young then, he was old enough to watch Leicester's Men in 1573 or Warwick's Men in 1575. Stratford is close enough to Kenilworth for its inhabitants to have been drawn to the extraordinary July festivities with which the Earl of Leicester greeted the Queen in 1575. The water-pageant, which was one of the outstanding features of the Earl's lavish display to the Queen he may have been hoping to marry, is impressionistically recalled by Oberon in *A Midsummer Night's Dream*:

> Thou remember'st
> Since once I sat upon a promontory,
> And heard a mermaid on a dolphin's back
> Uttering such dulcet and harmonious breath,
> That the rude sea grew civil at her song,
> And certain stars shot madly from their spheres
> To hear the sea-maid's music.   (ii.i. 148–54)

Open-air festivities, many of them directly linked to the Christian calendar, punctuated the half-year from 24 December to 24 June.[26] Shakespeare could have witnessed in Stratford itself rural rites of the kind recalled in the sheep-shearing feast of *The Winter's Tale*. The Whitsuntide Pastime, which the Stratford Council helped to finance in 1583, was not an isolated event. Perdita, conscious of her theatrical costume, is conscious also of her heredity as a ritual distributor of flowers:

> Methinks I play as I have seen them do
> In Whitsun pastorals: sure this robe of mine
> Does change my disposition.   (iv.iii. 133–5)

An inherent awareness of seasonal change is as unsurprising in an Elizabethan countryman as is the observation of the lunar month, but Shakespeare seems to have had a heightened response to performance from an early age. We have only the uncertain evidence provided by his plays to determine what he saw. Certainly he could have witnessed the Corpus Christi plays[27] in the still great but sharply declining city of Coventry as late as 1579, and either there, or in the special performance for the Queen at Kenilworth, the bawdy Hock Tuesday play, whose annual performance began in Coventry, in 1416. What we know is that the contemporary metaphor which invited a perception of the world as a stage exercised over him a peculiar fascination.

We know neither more nor less about Shakespeare's early life than we might reasonably expect. His father's career is better documented. We know that, in addition to holding a sequence of prominent civic offices, he was a substantial property-owner, a frequent litigant and, on occasions, a speculator on the edge, or even the wrong side, of the law.[28] He is likely to have sent his son to a petty school to learn his alphabet and catechism and then to the Latin-dominated grammar school in Stratford. There is a strong possibility that John Shakespeare himself was illiterate and his sons beneficiaries of the age's new educational priorities. Stratford paid its schoolmaster uncommonly well. It would not have been difficult, for example, to tempt the man who was probably Shakespeare's principal teacher, Thomas Jenkins, to leave the Warwick school where he was paid £10 per year and set up home in Stratford for an annual salary of £20. Each of the five teachers who might conceivably have instructed William Shakespeare was an Oxford graduate. Conscientious or not, they would have followed the normal practice of making Latin the language of the school. Ben Jonson's famous jibe that Shakespeare had 'small Latin and less Greek' is unhelpful and inaccurate. Jonson, who began to acquire his considerable learning at Westminster School with pride and some pain, was unready to acknowledge the similar acquirements of a country schoolboy, particularly if that immigrant to London was to be perceived as a rival poet. Shakespeare knew Latin well, and if he read Cicero through compulsion, he read Ovid with pleasure. There is affection mingled with mockery in the reminiscence of schoolroom encounters with Lily's *Grammatica Latina* in Act Four Scene One of *The Merry Wives of Windsor*.[29] We have no evidence that the Stratford boys performed or recited Latin plays, though that was a well-established custom in other schools. 'We send them to learn their Grammar, and their Terence', complains Censure in Jonson's *The Staple of News*, 'and they learn their play-books'.[30] The schoolmaster who has evidently concealed from Censure the wicked truth that Terence was a playwright had, no doubt, his real-life parallels. Whether or not he performed in any of them, Shakespeare knew the plays of Terence and Plautus.

He also knew the Bible with the kind of intimacy that results from assimilation as well as study. It is on the question of Shakespeare's religious education that we encounter a major biographical controversy. If we are to understand it, we must place it in both a historical and a local perspective. The English Reformation, precipitated by Henry VIII's failure to win the Pope's agreement to his divorcing Catherine of Aragon in order to marry Elizabeth I's mother, Anne Boleyn, had established an English Church without a secure practice of its own. The return to Rome, led by Catherine's passionately Catholic daughter Mary I, had ended with Mary's death in 1558, and the new Queen had wisely mixed tolerance with firmness in re-establishing a Church of England. But throughout her reign the new Church was under threat from two sides, the still-committed papists and the increasingly vocal group whose opposition to popish practices may be imprecisely defined as 'Puritan'. Patrick McGrath, a lucid historian of the conflicting pressures, has broadly divided Elizabeth's reign into four phases:

1558–70	The years of uncertainty
1570–80	The gathering storm
1580–90	The crisis (Papist challenge and Puritan onslaught)
1590–1603	The triumph of the establishment[31]

Shakespeare moved through adolescence to manhood as the national storm gathered towards crisis. By 1585, according to McGrath, up to five per cent of the population was Catholic and up to fifteen per cent Puritan.[32] There was good reason for Edmund Grindal, Archbishop of Canterbury from 1575 to 1583, to pray touchingly, 'May God at length grant that we may all of us think the same things'. Grindal was a leader of those who longed for reconciliation, but, outmanoeuvred from the start, he had by then been sequestrated by order of the Queen after his refusal to inhibit 'prophesyings'. This refusal has endowed Grindal with a historical reputation as a protector of radical Puritans, but this is to assume that the prophesyings were a vehicle for the conveyance of Puritan dogma. Grindal knew them for what they more typically were, meetings at which the widespread scriptural ignorance of local clergy could be exposed and corrected by the exegesis of experts. He was a true moderate whose wish was to heal the dangerous breach in English Christianity.[33] The schism seems to have been particularly deep in the Midlands. Coventry was a notably divided city, Warwick predominantly Puritan, though less so than Banbury, 'that Geneva of English provincial towns'.[34] Stratford, reputed to be a Puritan stronghold, offers contradictory evidence. John Shakespeare, who had married into a resolutely Catholic family, had self-proclaimed Catholics among his civic associates. The schoolmaster who preceded Thomas Jenkins and the one who followed him both renounced Protestantism after leaving their Stratford post. We may presume that they concealed their Catholicism from their employers, but we do not know how far it affected their pedagogy. Among local gentry, the Cloptons and Catesbys as well as the Ardens were Catholic, the Lucys of Charlecote and the Throgmortons vehemently Puritan. The enmity between Warwickshire's two greatest aristocratic families, the Dudleys and the Berkeleys, had its origin in religious opposition, and the Berkeleys were as protective of Catholic recusants as the Dudleys were of Puritan dissidents. Lord Henry Berkeley, whose main residence was at Caludon Castle, near Coventry, had been peripherally implicated in the pro-Catholic revolt of the Northern Earls in 1569.

Although easily quelled, this outburst of dissent was a sharp reminder to the Queen of smouldering religious discontent. In such an atmosphere, Lord Berkeley's wife was dangerously compromised by rumours that her brother, Thomas Howard, Duke of Norfolk, planned to marry Mary, Queen of Scots. Elizabeth I's counsellors feared that a match between the leading Catholic claimant to the throne and the Catholic leader of the great Howard family would constitute a direct challenge to the Protestant monarchy, and the Duke was pre-emptively imprisoned. Almost immediately after his release, he dipped his fingers in the Ridolfi plot of 1571 and was executed in 1572. Until the axe fell, he was the last Duke alive in England. The prudent Elizabeth created no new ones. Meanwhile the Berkeleys were to be reminded how the arm of retribution could reach round corners in Tudor England. Lady Berkeley was the dead Duke's sister, and so it happened that large tracts of Berkeley land in Gloucestershire fell forfeit to the Crown. To the family's fury, the Queen then saw fit to award most of her new estate to Ambrose Dudley, Earl of Warwick and Robert Dudley, Earl of Leicester, whom she loved if ever she loved any man.

National and local tensions, then, were having their effect on life in Stratford during Shakespeare's boyhood and youth; but it was probably John Whitgift's appointment in April 1577 to the Bishopric of Worcester, the diocese to which Stratford belonged, that had the sharpest impact on his immediate family. Whitgift's single-minded pursuit of uniformity frightened and antagonised both Papists and Puritans. His attempts to enforce church attendance were not always successful, but they were never ignorable. It was just before Whitgift's election that John Shakespeare's scrupulous commitment to local government suddenly ended, though not before Whitgift had begun his investigations of Midlands recusancy. A ten-year record of exemplary attendance at Council meetings was followed, after 1576, by ten years of absenteeism. That John Shakespeare's name was not removed from the list of capital burgesses until September 1586 suggests that he had won the respect of his colleagues. There is, indeed, presumptive evidence that they did their best to protect him. But what were they protecting him from? The simple answer – that he found his finances suddenly overstretched – is no longer accepted with confidence as an adequate explanation. To be sure, some of his dealings over the next decade support the view that he was short of ready cash, but others reflect a man of substance and property. Outstanding, perhaps because it is incongruous among so many family and financial documents, is the appearance of John Shakespeare's name on a list of recusants. This does not tell us whether he was Catholic or Puritan, since the pressure to conform applied equally to both parties. Edgar Fripp's endearingly detailed *Shakespeare: Man and Artist* (1938) declares John Shakespeare a stubborn Puritan and therefore a recusant. A rival tradition, stemming in part from the discovery in 1757, in the rafters of the Shakespeares' Henley Street house, of a Catholic profession of faith in the name of John Shakespeare, has gained greater strength in recent years. E.A.J. Honigmann's *Shakespeare: the 'Lost Years'* (1985) traces the effects of the father's Catholicism into the early career of the son. The argument here, in direct contradiction of Fripp, is that John Shakespeare was a stubborn Catholic and therefore a recusant. For the sceptical Samuel Schoenbaum, 'these interpretations have a romantic appeal, but John Shakespeare was a trades-man, not an ideologue'.[35] He would prefer to believe that John Shakespeare stayed away from church to avoid arrest for debt, but there are weaknesses in this uncontroversial position. The opposition of tradesman and ideologue is too facile, and the assumption that the sheriff's officers would have found it difficult to arrest a prominent glover in a small town, provided he steered clear of church and Council meetings, is puzzling. We may never prove that religious convictions lay behind John Shakespeare's change of life-style in 1576, but lingering doubts will continue to interest students of his son's plays. Writing from Kenilworth Castle in 1579, the Earl of Leicester complained to Lord Burghley that Whitgift was witch-hunting Puritans when 'Since Queen Mary's time the Papist were never in that jollity they be at present in this country'.[36] It is to Leicester's attempted persecution of the Catholic Ardens of Warwickshire that Peter Levi has recently turned to explain John Shakespeare's sudden withdrawal from public service after 1576. Leicester's real target was Edward Arden, High Sheriff of the County of Warwickshire in 1575, when the Queen came to Kenilworth. It was reported to the Earl that Arden, with dangerous accuracy, had referred to him as an upstart and an adulterer. The pay-off came in 1583, when Arden was hanged, drawn and quartered as a traitor and had his head stuck on one of the London Bridge spikes. Levi's suggestion that everyone with Arden connections, down as far as John Shakespeare, was caught up in the vendetta is not entirely farfetched, but it cannot be substantiated.[37]

Where is William Shakespeare in all this? The straight-forward answer is that we do not know. A parish register announces his baptism in 1564: a diocesan register in Worcester confirms his apparently hasty marriage in November 1582: and the Parish Register records the baptism of a daughter, Susanna, on 26 May 1583 and of the twins, Hamnet and Judith, on 2 February 1585. Assuming that he left school in 1579 or, at the latest, 1580, what happened next and how does it connect with his future success as a London playwright? In the absence of documentary evidence, there is ample room for speculation spiced with hearsay. Of the four comparatively plausible theories:

1   that he worked in an attorney's office in or near Stratford
2   that he was bound as an apprentice to his father or to some other local tradesman
3   that he became a page or minor official in the household of a nobleman
4   that he worked as a tutor or junior schoolmaster 'in the country'

it is the last that has been most strongly advocated in recent years. We may reasonably suppose that John Shakespeare would have liked his son to follow him into the family business, but his mind, or his son's mind, might have been changed if the business was failing, if it was felt prudent to send the firstborn out of the reach of Whitgift's 'discoverers' or if the Leicester/Arden feud was as virulent as Peter Levi proposes. The story that Shakespeare was, in his youth, a country schoolmaster is better based than many, since it reached John Aubrey by way of William Beeston, the actor-son of Shakespeare's former theatrical colleague, Christopher Beeston. It was developed with some style by Arthur Gray in *A Chapter in the Early Life of Shakespeare* (1926) and with a gritty attention to detail sixty years later by Ernst Honigmann; but the two accounts are literally miles apart. Gray has Shakespeare sent to the North Warwickshire town of Polesworth to complete his schooling under the patronage and in the household of Sir Henry Goodere and remaining as tutor to Goodere's son. The argument rests unconvincingly on topography, and Gray's theory leans towards plausibility only in providing, through the Gooderes, some connections between the Stratford of Shakespeare's boyhood and the London of his maturity. Old Sir Henry assisted the Stratford corporation in a number of delicate negotiations from 1570 to 1572 and was also familiar with the family of the Earl of Southampton, Shakespeare's patron. Young Sir Henry was an intimate friend of John Donne and Michael Drayton, a convivial acquaintance of Ben Jonson's and Gentleman of the Bedchamber to James I. Honigmann's argument is altogether more intricate. He calls it a detective-story and offers two initial clues: (1) the Lancashire birth and upbringing of John Cottom, the schoolmaster who succeeded Thomas Jenkins at Stratford in 1579, and (2) a bequest to 'William Shakeshafte' in the will (dated 3 August 1581) of Alexander Hoghton, a Catholic landowner from Lea, near the most stubbornly Catholic of all English towns, Preston.[38] The wording of this will leaves open the possibility that William Shakeshafte was one of a company of players in Hoghton's employ and bequeathed by him to his neighbour, Sir Thomas Hesketh, should his own brother, Thomas Hoghton, not wish to maintain them. Honigmann supports his case with a wealth of circumstantial detail and it is impossible to do justice to it here. It will be sufficient to record that the Lancashire connection, as elaborated by Honigmann, not only revives the claims of Catholicism in the Shakespeare family but also proposes a radical re-appraisal of the 'lost years' of the actor-playwright.

The outline is firm. In 1580, John Cottom, whether impressed by his pupil or generous in support of an endangered fellow-Catholic, commends William Shakespeare to Alexander Hoghton as an assistant teacher in his Lancashire jurisdiction. Under first Hoghton's and then Hesketh's patronage, the young schoolteacher develops his interest in the drama. This interest brings him naturally to the attention of the greatest of all the Lancashire families, the Stanleys. Both the head of the family, Henry Stanley, Earl of Derby, and his heir, Ferdinando, Lord Strange, are active patrons of the drama and the young Shakespeare is prominent enough to attract their attention. There follows an unexplained interlude in Stratford from 1582–5, during which Shakespeare marries and has his three children, and then, perhaps late in 1585, he takes the fateful decision to join Lord Strange's household as one of his company of players.

I have given Honigmann's version of the 'lost years' because it is better argued than any other and, in many ways, more challenging. It is pointless to speculate on the eighteen-year-old Shakespeare's marriage to a woman who was probably six years his senior and who seems never to have shared his professional life. The nobility could father bastards with comparative impunity, but for the Shakespeares, hovering on the borders of the gentry, Anne Hathaway's pregnancy made marriage necessary. Parenthood may have delayed Shakespeare's departure from Stratford, but it did not long prevent it. The old view, challenged by Honigmann, is that he made the decisive break with his home town in 1587, perhaps risking all by attaching himself to one of the several groups of players who visited Stratford in that year. The fact that such youthful improvidence does not tally well with the financial shrewdness of his later years cannot be taken to mean that he was incapable of it, but neither does it weaken Honigmann's case. It would have been plain silly for a young countryman, without proven credentials, to launch himself into the uncertain world of the theatre. Whether or not Honigmann is right, his suggestion that Shakespeare joined a group of household players who already knew something of his talents has a ring of truth. All that we know for certain is that by 1592 he was sufficiently well known to a London playwright to have earned the recognition of a studied insult.

The playwright was Robert Greene, and the notorious insult occurs in *A Groatsworth of Wit bought with a Million of Repentance*. The passage is quoted here, despite its lack of relevance to Stratford, because it marks the end of the long silence on Shakespeare's life: its London context will be more fully explored in subsequent chapters. The three addressees are, like Greene, graduates and playwrights:

Base minded men all three of you, if by my misery you be not warned: for unto none of you (like me) sought those burrs to cleave: those puppets (I mean) that spoke from our mouths, those antics garnished in our colours. Is it not strange, that I, to whom they all have been beholding; is it not like that you, to whom they all have been beholding, shall (were ye in that case as I am now) be both at once of them forsaken? Yes, trust them not: for there is an upstart crow, beautified with our feathers, that with his *Tiger's heart wrapped in a player's hide*, supposes he is as well able to bombast out a blank verse as the best of you; and, being an absolute *Johannes fac totum*, is in his own conceit the only Shake-scene in a country.

Greene was already dead when his confessional pamphlet was published in September 1592, dying when he wrote it. Not surprisingly, the unmistakable reference to Shakespeare has been exhaustively interrogated and Greene's authorship questioned by both literary critics and computer-handlers. Honigmann has even argued that Shake-scene's real offence is not authorship but moneylending.[39] The point that concerns us here is that Shakespeare at twenty-eight was familiar to Greene's London readers as both actor and playwright. His precise route to such notoriety remains matter for dispute. Almost certainly he had received encouragement and some financial reward from patrons. Lord Strange is one of the early contenders, preceding the Earl of Southampton to whom Shakespeare dedicated his first published works, *Venus and Adonis* (1593) and *The Rape of Lucrece* (1594). But these rich poems are not the work of an apprentice. At some time during the 'lost years', Shakespeare had not only written the plays that gave offence to Robert Greene, but also a great deal of poetry. Some of the sonnets, a famous minefield for biographical speculators, may date from the 1580s, as may the enigmatic *The Phoenix and the Turtle*.[40] Much more has been lost. There seems little reason to doubt that Shakespeare wrote with facility from an early age. He might otherwise have spent his days as a glover and whittawer in Henley Street and Stratford might have been docketed as a small town not very far from Bromsgrove.

If not safe, a Catholic Shakespeare would probably have been safer at home than in London in 1592. The bubbling discontents of England under the Elizabethan settlement burst during the 1580s. Puritan propaganda seized on the activities of Cardinal William Allen at the Catholic seminary of Douai. Allen had been conducting a remarkably effective campaign to sustain the Catholic faith in England since 1574, but what came with true hyperbole to be known as the 'Jesuit invasion' began in the summer of 1580, when Robert Parsons, Ralph Emerson and Edmund Campion landed in England on a mission of sustenance and conversion. The first Douai 'martyr', Cuthbert Mayne, had been hanged, drawn and quartered in Launceston in 1577, but it was the capture and execution of Campion in December 1581 that became the focus of the propaganda war. By the end of 1590, 103 seminary priests had been similarly humiliated and killed, thirty-one of them in the fraught Armada year of 1588. Since her excommunication in 1570, Elizabeth I had been under frequent threat from Catholic plots to supplant her. Edward Arden's execution in 1583 had been a backlash from one of them, although Arden was almost certainly innocent of any involvement. It was his crazed son-in-law, John Somerville, who implicated him under torture after boasting in a London tavern of his plans to kill the Queen. Somerville was infatuated with Mary, Queen of Scots, whose life Elizabeth I continued to protect despite the advice of her closest advisers. Only after the schoolboy excesses of the Babington Plot had been revealed in 1586 did the English Queen consent to the execution of her troublesome cousin. The reverberations of that death in 1587 brought closer the long-contemplated Spanish invasion, and as Philip II prepared his plans to destroy the

Church of England from outside, the Puritans grew shriller in their demands for reform from within. If Shakespeare was with Lord Strange's Men during the second half of the decade, he must certainly have felt the sting of a crisis that was at once political (as Mary Tudor's consort, Philip II claimed a right to the English throne) and religious, for the Stanley family was intimately involved. The Earl of Derby was President of the Court that tried Mary Queen of Scots, and both he and Lord Strange were active in the hunting down of Catholic recusants. Not active enough to satisfy the Puritan Edward Fleetwood, who accused the Earl of slackness, and in 1587 urged Lord Burghley to exclude him from the ecclesiastic commission.[41] In the same year, Lord Strange was singled out for commendation by the Privy Council for his anti-recusant diligence. The Stanleys needed to prove themselves good Protestants because the family was so thickly tarred with the brush of Catholicism. The Earl's estranged wife, his brother and his step-sister were all Catholics, as were the majority of his associates among the nobility and gentry of Lancashire. It was in the Catholic north of England that Nicholas Owen, supreme constructor of hiding-holes for seminary priests, was most in demand. Not everyone was convinced by the Protestant exertions of the Stanleys, and Lord Strange was kept under secret surveillance by government spies. In 1593, when he succeeded to his father's title, he became, willingly or unwillingly, the figurehead of a Jesuit plot. Urged, with the promise of Spanish support, to claim the throne on the Queen's death, he betrayed the plot – perhaps only because he learned in time that it had already been uncovered by the spies who were watching him.[42] Whitgift's energetic reformation of the Church of England (he was Archbishop of Canterbury from 1583 to 1604) was well advanced by then, and both Papists and Puritans had passed their Elizabethan prime, although the turbulent 1580s had ended on the high note of an all-too-rare Puritan smile from 'Martin Marprelate'. Ironically, the Marprelate tracts of 1588–9, the most brilliant of Puritan literature, may have helped to shift public affiliation towards the Whitgiftian accommodation by the very ebullience of their condemnation of the English bishops. The new mood, with the Spaniards for the moment defeated and the ageing Queen still heirless, was for peace at home.

There is no unambiguous manifesto among Shakespeare's works. The 'negative capability' admired by Keats leans towards positive anonymity. That is not to say that seekers after biographical inferences will find none. The anti-Catholic sentiment of the *Henry VI* plays and of *King John* is plain, but Shakespeare would not have been the only English Catholic to reject Rome's colonising greed, nor the only one to switch loyalties during the dangerous 1580s. Honigmann surmises that he became a Protestant during the Stratford years surrounding his marriage to Anne Hathaway. On the other hand, A. L. Rowse, for whom doubt is an unexplored country, baldly asserts that 'he was an orthodox, conforming member of the Church into which he had been baptised, was brought up and married, in which his children were reared and in whose arms he at length was buried'.[43] It is wholly reasonable to argue that the matter is of no significance since neither his plays nor his poems depend upon it. But we should be wary of accepting a Shakespeare immunised by his genius against the infections of his age. He was not a Stratford recluse but an exemplary Elizabethan venturer whose taste for social climbing is not particularly attractive when viewed unhistorically. His London success enabled him to accumulate property in his birthplace, and his social aspirations were enhanced by his privileged acquaintance with courtly contemporaries. The coat of arms, which John Shakespeare had first sought nearly thirty years earlier, was granted to the Shakespeare family in 1596. One historian has jovially compared the actions of the College of Heralds in providing coats of arms to the rising bourgeoisie of the sixteenth century with the similar 'civilising of new riches' by the nineteenth-century public schools,[44] but Sir William Dethick, the Garter King-of-Arms, was more interested in the incidental payment than in any grander scheme. Not everyone approved. Ralph Brooke, the quarrelsome York Herald, accused Dethick of carelessness and dishonesty in the elevation of unworthy candidates. The case of the Shakespeare coat of arms came fourth in a list of twenty-three which Brooke drew up in

2 The Shakespeare coat of arms: a gold shield, with a silver spear on a black band. There was also a crest with a falcon holding a spear.

1602.[45] The chosen motto, 'Non sanz droict' (Not without right) may have elicited from Ben Jonson a tartly allusive riposte. Sogliardo, in *Every Man out of his Humour* (1599), pays £30 for a coat of arms and is mortified by the suggestion that his motto should be 'Not without mustard'. It is just possible, of course, that Shakespeare played Sogliardo at the first per-formance, in which case the joke would have been quite different, but clearly his gentrification did not go unnoticed by his theatrical colleagues. His steady accumulation of property provides the best evidence of his continuing interest in Stratford. His only son died in August 1596, but he retained his concern to provide for his family despite the lack of male heirs. In 1597, for an unknown sum, he bought New Place, a substantial house of five gables and three storeys, the second largest in Stratford. The next year, with the poor of the town still suffering from malnutrition, Shakespeare was reported in the borough survey to be hoarding eighty bushels of malt, one of the more substantial stockpiles in the town. In 1601, on the death of his father, he inherited the double house in Henley Street, which can now be visited as 'The Birthplace'. His mother and married sister continued to live there, while Anne and their two daughters remained at New Place. Once in 1602 and again in 1608, he sued fellow-Stratfordians for debts jointly amounting to £10. Such cases were common and Shakespeare's litigation betrays nothing more than normal prudence. His greatest outlay came in 1605, with the purchase of a quantity of tithes in and around Stratford for £440. The likely annual income from these tithes was £60, so that the initial cost would not have been covered until he was fifty. He cannot have expected to enjoy the fruits for much longer, so that this particular transaction savours strongly of provision for the family. His only known London property was the Blackfriars gatehouse which he bought in 1613 and bequeathed to his favoured elder daughter, Susanna. The general view that he returned to live mainly in Stratford during his last years is strengthened by surviving documents from the year 1614. As a tithe-holder, Shakespeare was affected by the stubborn determination of William Combe to enclose common fields in the parish of Welcombe. It is not easy to determine whether he stood closer to Combe or to the people whose livelihood Combe threatened. The playwright Edward Bond has proposed his own interpretation in the splendidly con-tentious *Bingo* (1973), in which the retired and ailing Shake-speare is forced to reflect on his crimes (of omission) against the deprived, and the known facts allow but do not enforce Bond's conclusions. The £10 bequeathed to the poor of Stratford in Shakespeare's will represents a conventional, albeit not un-generous, gift. The outline is that of a rather ordered and ordinary life, something which has given offence to those who find ordinariness incompatible with genius. Francis Bacon must have written the plays, or the Earl of Oxford, not this small-town penny-pincher. However, those still concerned to deny Shakespeare's authorship amid the market forces of the twen-tieth century would do well to bear in mind Terry Eagleton's wry comment that 'it would be a brave man or woman who would try at this late date to close down Stratford'.[46]

It has been the aim of this brief survey to establish some local and national parameters for the professional career of an extraordinary writer. It is with that professional career that the rest of the book is concerned.

CHAPTER 2

Establishing a career: of patrons and provinces

A young man ambitious to earn his keep by his pen would, in Elizabethan England, have looked for patronage. There was no promising alternative, since there was such small return on the selling of manuscripts to a printer or publisher. For a pamphlet or a volume of poetry, a young author might receive £2, with a bottle of wine thrown in, or he might have to finance the publication himself. Since there was no system of royalty payments, such expenditure would be his attempt to inflate the bubble reputation and his only satisfaction might be the sight of copies of the title-page pinned up on posts around London to advertise the book. But patronage was not easy to come by, particularly for writers whose bent was literary rather than religious or historical. William Jaggard, the syphilitic printer responsible for the production of the famous First Folio of Shakespeare's plays in 1623, was more prepared than most of his fellow-stationers to venture into *belles-lettres*, but even so, such work accounts for less than a fifth of his known output. With few exceptions, courtly patrons preferred to support 'translations, handbooks, historical compilations, and works of piety and controversy'.[1] Drama, however, had a special place among courtiers keen to display their familiarity with the humanist tradition, and there would have been no disgrace in a glover's son's accepting service as one of a nobleman's company of players. We have insufficient evidence by which to determine whether Shakespeare was, from the start, a writer who found it necessary to act or an actor who discovered an ability to write. His subsequent career is the best demonstration of the falsity of any absolute distinction between actor and playwright in an evolving professional theatre.

The processes by which a mediaeval theatre of the people was transformed into our modern theatre of the self-selecting few have been variously analysed and accounted for. There is no doubt that Tudor legislation greatly accelerated those processes nor that the modern obsession with the literary products of the Elizabethan age has damagingly obscured what actually happened. It is not Shakespeare's fault that he has become the favourite icon of an elitist theatre, but the first significant steps towards such elitism were taken in his lifetime. By the end of the sixteenth century, it had become possible for the first time for people to think of 'drama' as something that took place in 'theatres'. Those who shared the Tudor mania sometimes to define, often to limit and always to control public enthusiasm would have been happy to outlaw drama altogether. The next best thing was to confine it to playhouses. Everyone in authority, from Privy Councillor to Stratford burgess, feared the unruliness of the mob, and it is this fear that lies behind the long sequence of parliamentary acts culminating in the closing of the London theatres in 1642. The seasonal explosions of carnival festivity could not, of course, be easily suppressed nor smoothly channelled into formal drama. The latent and sometimes actual subversiveness of the Elizabethan theatre, its readiness to confront Lenten authority with Carnival disorder, has been consistently underrated, and is only now undergoing a timely recognition. It is only recently, only since the installation of separate seats in a darkened auditorium, that the English theatre has become the decorous institution we take for granted. The Old Price Riots at Covent Garden in 1809 are only the best known of many nineteenth-century examples of the popular will expressing itself in theatrical disorder. In 1841, before his antics with the Light Brigade, when Lord Cardigan was the best-hated man in England, his attempts to attend the theatre were invariably met with such a cacophony of hisses and boos that the performance could not proceed.[2] If we are to understand the atmosphere of an Elizabethan playhouse, such precedents are more helpful than a visit to the West End or a local rep. Drama was not yet divorced from festival. It is possible to mine Shakespeare's plays for evidence of popular culture's muscular survival – a Lenten Malvolio confronted by the Carnival misrule of Sir Toby Belch; Lear as Carnival King tenuously replaced by Lenten severity[3] – and the effort is worthwhile, but, much as I would like to, I cannot wholeheartedly present a Shakespeare hostile to authority. Compared with many contemporary writers, his mistrust of the mob is tempered, but the dominant impression is of a man who recognised that individual discontent is a price paid for good order. The energies and urgencies expressed in the dramatic festivities of feudal England could not be easily dispersed in post-feudal society, but Tudor bureaucrats set about devising ways to contain them. There was always the recent example of Kett's Rebellion in Norfolk (1549) to act as a spur. Had that not begun during the performance of a play?[4]

The rudiments of the system that recommended itself to successive Privy Councils, and that was given definitive form in the 1572 'Act for the punishment of Vagabonds', already existed. Traditions of hospitality had combined with the demand for seasonal entertainment to persuade a few of the householders of feudal England to retain, periodically, groups of 'players of interludes' as well as minstrels, acrobats and dancers. Emulation spread the custom and refined it. We do not know who first employed players as permanent, rather than merely 'retained', members of his household, perhaps one of the great fifteenth-century northern families. Towards the end of the century, both Richard III and Henry VII employed troupes of actors, but the Wars of the Roses had seriously undermined the sovereign's rights of precedence. All that differentiated the King from his wealthiest companions – cousins, brothers, uncles – was their agreement to put their private armies at his disposal. If the King had players, they could have players too. By 1509, the Dukes of Buckingham, Northumberland and Oxford had presented their interluders at the King's Court. The element of competition grew stronger during the reign of the competitive Henry VIII. It mattered to an aristocratic patron that his troupe should excel that of the cattleman's son, Cardinal

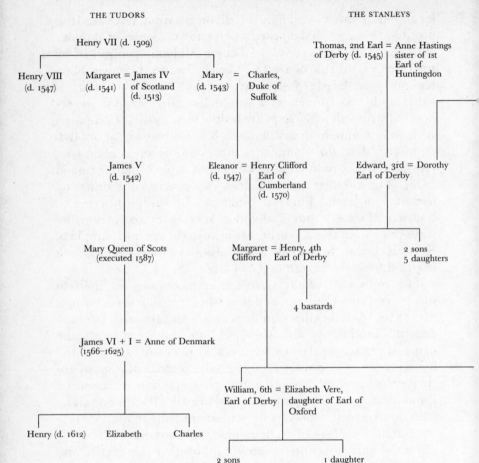

3 Family tree of the Stanleys (showing how the family interlocks with the Tudors, the Careys and the Howards)

Wolsey, for example, and it mattered to the Tudor dynasty that the dignity of such patrons should not be too far offended. Until the English Revolution, it was only through the power of the nobility that English monarchs could hope to survive, and only through the machinations of the nobility that they need fear to fall. The maintenance of a balance between aristocratic power and aristocratic dependence was Elizabeth I's supreme political achievement. Endlessly alert, she used even drama as an

THE HOWARDS (AND CAREYS)

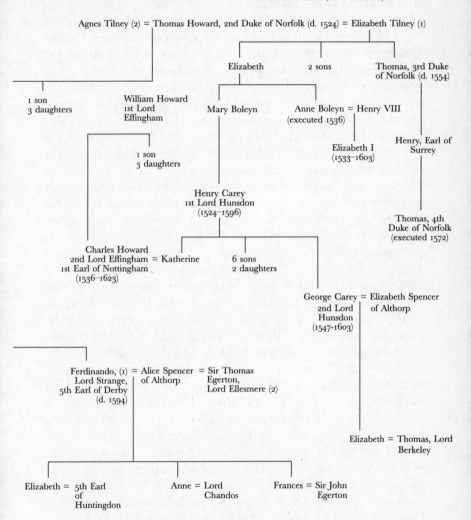

instrument of that policy. The royal command to perform at Court may have flattered the players, but it should not be forgotten that it flattered their patrons too. In absolute distinction from her successor, Elizabeth was parsimonious in the creation of peers and knights. A regulation of numbers went hand-in-hand with a regulation of power. I have already noted that England's last Duke, the Duke of Norfolk, was put to death in 1572. There would not be another one until King James created George Villiers Duke of Buckingham in 1623. During Elizabeth's reign, the number of true noblemen was restricted to about sixty. These were people who knew each other, met regularly at Court and in the House of Lords, entertained each other and strengthened bonds by arranging marriages. Several of them were patrons of players. The example of the Stanley family can stand as tolerably representative.[5] Historians of the Elizabethan theatre have been surprisingly reticent about the noblemen who gave much more than their names in order to validate and enable the new professionalism. This brief survey of a dynasty which contributed outstandingly to the rise of the theatre and therefore to the craft of the playwright provides no more than a temporary filling for a gaping hole. What has particularly intrigued me is the gloss it offers on Shakespeare's English history plays. Among the courtiers who watched these in performance would have been many descendants of the Knights and Earls who made up the *dramatis personae*. We know of the offence taken by Lord Cobham that necessitated the change of name from Oldcastle to Falstaff,[6] but what contortions of self-censorship are hidden? An investigation of the fortunes of the Stanleys will usefully expose the complex network of power and dependence, the jostling competition within and between 'great' families and their peculiarly contradictory awareness of permanence and insubstantiality, on all of which Shakespeare's dramatic plotting implicitly relies.

The first Stanley to come into prominence was the second son of a Cheshire landowner. Having been knighted as a result of military service to Edward III in about 1370, John Stanley was enriched by an astute marriage to the heiress of a Lancashire landowner and by awards of land from Richard II. Displaying a knack for choosing the winning side that was copied by many of his descendants, he opted to serve the usurping Henry IV, of whose household he was Steward from 1405 to 1412. By the time he died in 1414, Sir John Stanley was the owner of large estates in Lancashire, Cheshire and Staffordshire and of the whole of the Isle of Man. The unspectacular career of his son, also Sir

John Stanley, was marked by another advantageous marriage and the consolidation of the family's new estates. The second Sir John Stanley died in 1437 and was succeeded by the politic Sir Thomas. It was Sir Thomas Stanley's achievement, during the early stages of the dynastic struggles known familiarly as the Wars of the Roses, to be employed by both Lancastrian and Yorkist factions without gaining the full trust of either. His straddling was sufficiently agile to allow him purchase on new estates in the Welsh Marches and elevation to the peerage. As the first Lord Stanley, he was Chamberlain of the royal household during the crisis years from 1455 to 1457. When he died in 1459, the luck of the Stanleys was already proverbial. It was his son, the second Lord Stanley, who turned it into a byword. His policy at the Battle of Barnet in 1471 was essentially what it had been at the Battle of Blore Heath in 1459 – to sit with his considerable private army and wait to see who won. The victorious Edward IV was sufficiently deceived to appoint Lord Stanley Steward of the royal household for the duration of his reign. The family property was enlarged by the marriage of Lord Stanley's heir to Joan Lestrange, on the death of whose father he acquired land in Shropshire and the Welsh Marches and the title of Lord Strange, which was retained thereafter by all the Stanley heirs until they inherited the senior title. But the son's adroit marriage paled before his father's. Lord Stanley's first marriage to Eleanor Neville had made him brother-in-law to the Earl of Warwick, the 'Kingmaker'. His second marriage, to Margaret, Countess of Richmond, made him stepfather to the founder of the Tudor dynasty, England's future King Henry VII. While the Countess plotted on her son's behalf, Lord Stanley negotiated the awkward aftermath of Edward IV's death in 1483. Having survived imprisonment during the protectorate of the Duke of Gloucester, he was appointed Constable of England when Gloucester seized power as Richard III, and he assisted with uncharacteristic alacrity in the suppression of the Duke of Buckingham's rebellion. The King awarded his Constable a rich portion of Buckingham's estate in gratitude. But how was Stanley to react when his stepson brought his invasion force to Milford Haven in August 1485?

The story is partially told in Shakespeare's *Richard III*. There, Lord Stanley's active participation in the Battle of Bosworth is inhibited by Richard III's holding his son as a hostage:

> Sir Christopher, tell Richmond this from me:
> That in the sty of this most bloody boar
> My son George Stanley is frank'd up in hold:
> If I revolt, off goes young George's head;
> The fear of that holds off my present aid.   (iv.v.1–5)

But his loyalty to the cause of the future Henry VII is never in doubt in Shakespeare's version of the story:

> I, as I may – that which I would I cannot –
> With best advantage will deceive the time,
> And aid thee in this doubtful shock of arms:
> But on thy side I may not be too forward,
> Lest, being seen, thy brother, tender George,
> Be executed in his father's sight.   (v.iii.92–7)

The reality is that he reverted to his wait-and-see policy. The current historical view, less partial than Shakespeare's, is that Lord Stanley's army was kept out of the action until Richard III's defeat was inevitable and that the canny Constable of England may have arrived on Bosworth field just in time to place the crown on the head of his stepson, the victorious Henry Tudor. It was enough. In October 1485, Lord Stanley was created Earl of Derby.[7] He died in 1504, having outlived his son by a year.

The fifteenth-century fortunes of the Stanleys could be matched, with local variations, by many others of the great families of late mediaeval England: the Cliffords (Tudor Earls of Cumberland), the Talbots (Tudor Earls of Shrewsbury), the Hastings (Tudor Earls of Huntingdon). There is also a persuasive similarity in their vicissitudes under the Tudors. The years that divide Elizabeth I's accession in 1558 from the revolutionary disturbances of 1641–2 have become a battle-ground for historians of the aristocracy. The 'storm over the gentry', provoked by R. H. Tawney's 1941 proposal that the balance of wealth in England shifted, after 1540, from a peerage in decline to an advancing gentry, had not subsided by the time

Lawrence Stone published *The Crisis of the Aristocracy: 1558–1641* in 1965. Stone's controversial view that the great families experienced unprecedented financial hardships and decline under Elizabeth I can certainly be applied to the Stanleys, though the family's seventeenth-century recovery is in conflict with his thesis. Stone's second major contention, that the influence and power of the aristocracy was gradually eclipsed in the years preceding the Civil War, could have been exemplified by the story of the Stanleys. Against a background of the industrious officers of Tudor government from Thomas Cromwell to Walsingham and the Cecils, many of the Queen's great courtiers stand out like decorative but feeble butterflies. An exasperated sense of his own ineffectiveness contributed to the Earl of Essex's self-destructive rebellion in 1601, but exasperation was not unique to this most charismatic and neurotic of Elizabethan aristocrats. It is certainly discernible in the behaviour of the last three Tudor Earls of Derby. It was their fate, as it was the fate of other theatrical patrons like the Lord Chamberlain, the Lord High Admiral and the Earls of Leicester, Oxford and Worcester, to be fobbed off (or to *feel* fobbed off, which normally amounts to the same thing in politics) with immensely costly but ultimately insignificant duties. The merrymakings, which the young Henry VIII had encouraged out of his own high spirits, were increasingly demanded by his daughter as outward signs of lavish loyalty. To retain a company of players conferred status, certainly, and to assume a part in the engineered drama of the Accession Day Tournaments offered, somewhat less certainly, the rewards of courtly admiration. But intelligent players are always threatened by a perception of themselves as 'merely' players, and it was often the most intelligent of Elizabeth's courtiers who became the most disillusioned. To offer the protection of a family title to a company of players is one thing: *merely* to offer the protection of a family title to a company of players is another thing altogether, and that, as we shall see, is what the unfortunate sixth Earl of Derby was virtually reduced to.

Henry Stanley, fourth Earl of Derby, inherited his title in 1572, when he was already forty. Unlike his father, he was an enthusiastic Protestant, the result in part of sharing his early education with the future Edward VI. That was not his only royal connection. The first Earl, as we have seen, was stepfather to Henry VII. The fourth Earl had provided his own children with a place in the order of succession by marrying the grand-daughter of Henry VIII's sister, Mary. This marriage to Lady Margaret Clifford had taken place in 1555, when Henry Stanley was still Lord Strange, and had failed irretrievably by 1567, when the couple separated. Although Lady Margaret was a Catholic, there is no evidence that religion was a main cause of the breakdown. There was mutual recrimination, both before and after the separation, over her expensive tastes. Stanley was providing for her and their two sons as well as for his mistress and their four illegitimate children. By the time he inherited the Derby title, he was heavily in debt, and the debts continued to mount until his death in 1593, despite the revenue accruing from estates in at least seven counties as well as the Isle of Man, of which the Stanleys remained 'Kings'. His difficulties, and those of his two legitimate sons, offer lively insights into the conduct of the nobles in Shakespeare's tragedies and comedies as well as the history plays. The Gloucester of *King Lear* has also to balance the claims of legitimate and illegitimate offspring. A father's failure to do so in his lifetime informs the dangerous hatred of Don John for Don Pedro in *Much Ado about Nothing*. Oliver denies a rightful inheritance to Orlando in *As You Like It*, and there is no law to come to Orlando's aid. The loyalty of courtiers, as Prospero discovered too late in the pre-history of *The Tempest*, is a purchasable commodity. The usurping Antonio,

> Being once perfected how to grant suits,
> How to deny them, who t'advance, and who
> To trash for over-topping; new created
> The creatures that were mine... (*The Tempest*, I.ii.79–82)

And for one who has been 'trashed', like the unnamed Scottish Lord of Macbeth's court, the feared outcome is sleeplessness and hunger (*Macbeth*, III.vi.34). Shakespeare's sensitivity to these commonplaces of courtly tension may have been first awakened in the service of the Stanleys or in the observation of families whose history, resembled theirs.

If, despite debts and dissensions, the Earls of Derby felt it worthwhile to maintain a troupe of players, they must have been confident that there were real advantages. What can be said of them could apply, in various degrees, to all the other known patrons of the Elizabethan theatre. It will be convenient to summarise Henry Stanley's affairs under five headings:

I THE PATRONAGE OF PLAYERS

The Stanleys were immensely powerful regional overlords, with virtual control of justice in the Isle of Man, Cheshire and Lancashire. For such a family, it was not far short of a necessity to include in their extensive household a company of players. The troupe would have been expected to entertain visiting dignitaries, like the Lord President of the North, from whose jurisdiction the county of Lancashire was eccentrically exempt, or the local Lancastrian nobility. If the Queen had ever ventured north, there would have been a play to greet her, and the household players would have been sent to whichever of the many Stanley homes she elected to visit. The Earl's estates were so far-flung that it was impossible for him to keep in personal touch with them all. His players could serve an ambassadorial function whilst at the same time advertising the importance of their patron. The fourth Earl was evidently too interested by interludes to await his inheritance of the title before employing his own troupe, since a company known as Lord Strange's Men was active in the provinces between 1563 and 1571. The same impatience was exhibited by his son, Ferdinando, whose players are known to have performed in Exeter in 1576 and consistently thereafter. They seem to have outshone the fourth Earl's troupe, which toured contemporaneously, perhaps because Strange's Men excelled in spectacular acrobatics. They 'tumbled' at Court in January 1580, to be followed a month later by Derby's Men in a lost play. Over the next decade, Strange's Men established themselves as one of the finest companies of players in England. We do not know how far they owed their status to their charismatic patron. Ferdinando was one of the brilliant ornaments of Elizabeth I's Court and the actors he patronised were the beneficiaries of his brilliance. While they enjoyed their London reputation, Derby's Men continued to provide useful provincial service. The fourth Earl had in abundance the Stanley ability to reconcile opposites. As a radical Protestant, he might have been expected to view the public performance of plays as profanity and adultery as devilment, but he continued to make payments to Puritan preachers, liveried actors and his mistress, and he kept the peace in Lancashire by entertaining the predominantly Catholic gentry at Knowsley House. The favoured Elizabethan concept of *concordia discors* was given a diplomatic application by the Earl of Derby's resolute irresolution.

2 HOUSEHOLD SERVANTS

The Venetian ambassador who was impressed in 1554 by the amount of servants and the quantity of food consumed in the homes of the English nobility would have been even more wide-eyed in 1580. The consumption of meat was formidable, and the servants benefited from the appetite of their masters. The cost of food and drink varied from week to week. Payments to servants were constant. In 1561, the third Earl of Derby paid £153 to purchase liveries for his attendants, enough to cover the annual salary of fifteen schoolmasters in most Elizabethan towns. The fourth Earl's household is known to have amounted to 118 in 1587 and 145 in 1590. To run this private army was expensive, and surviving evidence suggests that the average aristocratic household of 100 in 1590 had been cut by more than a half by 1620. Liveried actors accounted for anything between four and twelve of the fourth Earl of Derby's permanent staff and musicians for an equal number.

3 USURERS AND THE ARISTOCRACY

To maintain the outward show of aristocratic splendour was extremely costly, but both convention and courtly competition demanded it. Food could be provided from the Earl's own estates, but the estate managers and agricultural workers had all to be paid. For a variety of reasons, the Earls of Derby overspent. One is of particular interest to anyone who has observed with surprise the amount Elizabethan actors were prepared to spend on their costumes. Clothes were a social and even a political issue at Elizabeth's Court. Those noblemen who came to Whitehall ready kitted in the expensive long cloaks that were the fashion in 1594 had to hide them in their wardrobes and return to their tailors when the Queen pronounced that her courtiers should wear short cloaks. The fourth Earl of Derby was dead by then, but, in the ten years from 1584 to 1593, he and his son Ferdinando had borrowed nearly £9,000 from prominent London merchants like Peter Vanlore and Michael Cornelius. Usury was a settled trade in the city and, indeed, in the country at large. John Shakespeare, and probably William too, went in for it on a small scale, whilst the theatrical entrepreneur Philip Henslowe was also a money-lender and pawnbroker who kept within the law by recording his transactions in the extraordinary document that has come to be called his *Diary*.[8] There was nothing unfamiliar to Londoners about Shylock's business. The usury now institutionalised by banks and building societies was then practised by wealthy individuals. Sir Nicholas Mosley, a London alderman, reaped the benefit of loans made to the Stanleys in 1595, when the sixth Earl sold him two manors near Manchester for a knock-down price. Both the fourth Earl and Ferdinando, Lord Strange seem to have repaid one money-lender by borrowing from another. The Earl's estranged wife continued to spend lavishly on clothes to her husband's cost, and among the £6,000 owed to London creditors by Ferdinando when he died in 1594, unpaid bills to tailors and shoemakers played a significant part.

4 INCOME FROM THE LAND

Despite the costliness of clothes in an age of display, it was the failure to maximise income from their estates that most consistently threatened to impoverish Elizabethan aristocrats.

That exemplary Puritan Henry Hastings, third Earl of Huntingdon, whom no one accused of extravagance, found himself
£5,000 in debt in 1594.[9] The chief difficulty was the chaotic
state of the land laws in what has often been seen as a period of
transition from feudalism towards capitalism. Opportunities for
litigation were limitless, but the law's costs as well as its delays
were a landowner's nightmare.[10] Even the legal status of
common land was undecided, a situation which encouraged the
fourth Earl of Derby to divide and enclose Toxteth Park and
William Combe, a landowner on a comparatively tiny scale, to
enclose the common fields of Welcombe, with or without the
support of William Shakespeare.

5   THE COSTS OF SERVING THE QUEEN

To be visited by the Queen once on a royal progress was an
expensive honour. To be visited regularly might well be
accounted a disaster. Elizabeth I saved her own money by
requiring her courtiers to spend theirs in her service. The costs
of an overseas army were borne by the Crown, but an army
fighting the Queen's wars at home was paid by its noble
generals. An Elizabethan audience watching Falstaff taking
bribes from his ragged army would have known that it was not
King Henry IV who was being cheated but one of his earls. It
was the costs he had to bear as Lord President of the Council of
the North that destroyed the Earl of Huntingdon's prosperity,
just as it was the outlay on his diplomatic missions in 1585 and
1588 that dealt the final blow to the Earl of Derby's. A
handbook of Renaissance diplomacy, Alberico Gentili's *De
Legationibus*, uses a theatrical analogy to clarify what would
have been expected from the Earl on his embassy to invest Henri
III of France with the Order of the Garter:

If we would hiss off the boards an actor who would, when playing the
role of a king, come on the stage with a shabby retinue, and in
anything but royal attire, what is to be done with the ambassador,
who is not merely taking part in a play for a few hours, but is actually
invested with the personality of his sovereign.[11]

Gentili was writing in the very year of Derby's first visit, which, he notes, 'displayed such splendour and pomp that France is said to be amazed at the magnificence of the embassy'.[12] There were seventy-nine people in the retinue, all to be suitably clothed and maintained at the Earl's expense during a stay of nearly two months in Paris. When James I wished to impress the Spanish Ambassador in 1604, he summoned the leading members of the King's Men, probably including Shakespeare, to attend the important visitor for a full eighteen days. If you are looking for people who can wear good clothes well, who better than an actor? It is not unlikely that the Earl of Derby included his players in his retinue. It is even possible that Shakespeare was one of them. Honigmann has argued that he was one of Lord Strange's Men from 1585 and, in the vacuum of the lost years, there is nothing to deter the further speculation that he transferred to the son's troupe after seizing the opportunity to visit France in the train of the father. It would mean that he was absent from Stratford when the twins were born, but other fathers before and since have put business before birth.

I turn now to consider the foreshortened life of the man who might well have been Shakespeare's most influential patron. Ferdinando, Lord Strange, was a flamboyantly gifted aristocrat with an eye for popularity of the kind later made infamous by the Earl of Essex. We see him as one of the Queen's champions, in company with the Earls of Essex and Cumberland, in George Peele's 'Polyhymnia', a verse celebration of the Accession Day tournament of 1590. Their successive entries to the tiltyard are striking examples of the theatrical splendour of these annual celebrations of the day that, so Elizabeth I's subjects were invited to believe, gave England a new and glorious beginning – 17 November 1558:

> The Earle of Darbies valiant sonne and heire,
> Brave Ferdinande Lord Straunge, straunglie embarkt,
> Under loves kinglie byrd, the golden Eagle,
> Stanleyes olde Crest and honourable badge,
> As veering fore the winde, in costlie ship,
> And armour white and watchet buckled fast,

4 Portrait of Ferdinando Stanley, Lord Strange.

Presentes himselfe, his horses and his men,
Suted in Satten to their Maisters collours,
Welneere twise twentie Squires that went him by
And having by his Trounch-man pardon crav'd,
Vailing his Eagle to his Soveraignes eies,
As who should say, stoope Eagle to this Sun,

5 William Segar's portrait of the Earl of Essex in sable armour (1590).

Dismountes him from his pageant, and at once,
Taking his choice of lustie Tilting horse,
Covered with sumptuous rich Caparisons,
He mountes him bravely for his friendlie foe,
And at the head he aimes, and in his aime
Happily thrives, and breakes his Azure staves.[13]

It is typical of the Earl of Essex that he should have capped Lord Strange's impressive display in white by making an even more sensational entrance in a black chariot pulled by black horses, with his retinue all dressed in black and himself in black armour and 'plume as blacke as is the Ravens wing'. It mattered desperately to Essex to come off best. Lord Strange, too, courted admiration. Richard Robinson of Alton paints in verse an idealised picture of him, seeming to invite a favourable comparison with his father, who had enclosed common land in Toxteth Park and elsewhere:

> Not markes and pounds, but hawkes and hounds,
> Is ever his desire:
> He layes not gether poores mens grounds,
> He is no countrey stroyer:
> He lives in love, of rich and poore,
> Sufficient he doth call his store:
> Full well knowes he, that men must dye,
> And therfore will not chaunge:
> But lives content, with auncient rent,
> Which argues to be Straunge.[14]

Born about five years before Shakespeare, Lord Strange was no more than seventeen when a company of his players performed in Exeter. He had talents of his own, either as a musician or actor, to judge from Spenser's reference to him in 'Colin Clout's come home again':

> Both did he other, which could pipe, maintaine,
> And eke could pipe himselfe with passing skill.   (442-3)

The lines rely on a reader's knowledge of his patronage of players. Spenser's poem is dedicated to Sir Walter Raleigh, with whom Ferdinando, Lord Strange, was popularly associated in the so-called 'school of night'. Ernst Honigmann was not the first to argue that this scholarly group of noblemen, whose debates on mathematics and astronomy were construed by contemporary scandalmongers as experiments in black magic, furnished the example on which Shakespeare based the King of Navarre's Court in Love's Labour's Lost. If that could be proved, it would greatly strengthen Honigmann's claim that Shakespeare was one of Lord Strange's Men during the years that brought them to the pinnacle of their national reputation in 1591–3. It was in the last of these years that the fourth Earl of Derby died, leaving his title and his debts to Ferdinando. Almost at once, the new Earl was visited by an agent from his Catholic cousin, Sir William Stanley, with a proposal that he lay claim to the throne. It is just possible that Ferdinando was a closet Catholic, and flimsy though his claims to succession may appear, they were sufficiently plausible to alarm Lord Burghley. When the fifth Earl of Derby died suddenly in 1594, after a short and excruciating illness, there were rival rumours; one, that he had been poisoned by Catholics in revenge for the death of the agent whose proposal he had betrayed, the other that he had been killed by witchcraft. Only a few thought it politic to broach the likelier possibility that he had been despatched on orders from Lord Burghley, whose whispering spies were the source of the alternative rumours. Sir George Carey, son of the Lord Chamberlain and future patron of Shakespeare's company, was among the providentially gullible. He wrote to his wife, sister of the Earl's widow, of 'the enchantment evident by the finding of his picture framed in wax with one of his own hairs pricked directly in the heart thereof'.[15]

The world of courtly intrigue was a small one. Ferdinando had died without male heirs, and the title of sixth Earl of Derby went to his cultivated brother, William. Lord Burghley had been looking for a suitable husband for his grand-daughter, whose father was another influential theatrical patron, Edward Vere, seventeenth Earl of Oxford. The first choice was the Earl of Southampton, Shakespeare's future patron, but the young Earl, if he was interested in women at all, was not interested by Lady Elizabeth Vere. The new Earl of Derby proved an amenable alternative. From Lord Burghley's point of view, the fifth Earl's death could not have been more timely. But he had reckoned without the widow. Ferdinando had married an heiress, the daughter of Sir John Spencer of Althorp in the county of Northampton. The Countess Dowager Alice was a formidable woman, and it was probably under her persuasion that, five days before his death, her husband had bequeathed his estates to his widow and, after her death, to his eldest daughter. With the land laws so confused, that was no more than a statement of intention, and litigation continued well into the next century, but the outcome was to leave the sixth Earl's status and finances in utter confusion. He had the authority of Lord Burghley and the Earl of Oxford on his side, but the Countess Dowager was not to be easily outfaced. Her comment to Burghley's famous son, Sir Robert Cecil, when she heard of her brother-in-law's proposed marriage, is characteristically forceful: 'I hear of a motion of marriage between the Earl, my brother, and my Lady Vere, your niece, but how true the news is, I know not, only I wish her a better husband.'[16] She chose as her legal adviser Sir Thomas Egerton, Attorney General of England. Soon after Ferdinando's death, Egerton was appointed Lord Chancellor, with the title of Lord Ellesmere, and soon after that, Ferdinando's widow committed him more strongly to the side of the heirs general in the dispute by marrying him. It was not until 1607 that the case was finally decided in the Earl's favour, long after an out-of-court settlement had enriched Dowager and daughters.

The sixth Earl of Derby was even more involved in the theatre than his brother had been. There is fairly wide agreement that *A Midsummer Night's Dream* was written, or adapted, for a wedding, and that of William Stanley to Elizabeth Vere on 26 January 1595 is one of three strong candidates: a romantic enough start, if so, to a decidedly unromantic story. After bearing three children in rapid succession, his wife, to the Earl's 'disenchantment', was granted a separation in July 1598. Elizabeth Vere is one of the remarkable Elizabethan women (Lady Alice Strange is another) who have been ignored by historians. Having schemed on her husband's behalf until their separation, she schemed on her own behalf thereafter, succeeding in making herself rich by, among other things, administering the Isle of Man between 1610 and 1627. She had been brought up in a cultured home. Her father was a playwright, first by right of social standing in Francis Meres's list of 'the best for Comedy amongst us'.[17] The reference has made Edward Vere one of the best backed of the Shakespeare claimants, among whom Lady Elizabeth's husband is also included. We know from a note by George Fenner, dated 30 June 1599, that the sixth Earl of Derby was at that time 'busye in penning comedyes for the common players'. His involvement was greater even than that. He was living unhappily in Lincoln's Inn, perhaps seeking consolation in drama for the failure of his marriage, and engaged in two significant theatrical enterprises. The first was the revival of one of the great boy companies, the Children of Paul's. We learn from a report of 13 November 1599 that 'My Lord Darby hath put up the playes of the children in Pawles to his great paines and charge'.[18] At much the same time, he was supporting Robert Browne and the rest of Derby's Men in their enterprise at the newly converted Boar's Head playhouse. His estranged wife was prepared to give him a helping hand in the hope that his current enthusiasm would keep him from costlier pastimes. Some time in 1599 or 1600, she wrote to her uncle, Robert Cecil:

Being importuned by my Lord to intreat your favor that his man Browne, with his companye, may not be bared from ther accoustomed plaing, in maintenance wherof they have consumde the better part of ther substance, if so vaine a matter shall not seame troublesum to you, I could desier that your furderance might be a meane to uphold them, for that my Lord taking delite in them, it will kepe him from moer prodigall courses.[19]

Derby's Men had a troubled time at the Boar's Head, and after 1602 are traceable only on provincial tours. Their patron can be further followed by devotees of lost causes in the writings of those who have made much of his initials 'W.S', even to the point of claiming that this unfortunate aristocrat who married late and lived long was the 'real' William Shakespeare. A fitter epitaph for the Tudor Stanleys is the advice given by the sixth Earl's son to his Lord Strange: 'Marriage is like a project in war, wherein a man can probably err but once.'[20]

Shakespeare's relations with his literary patron, the Earl of Southampton, have been subjected to scrutiny over the whole gamut from prurience to palaeography. His relations with his theatrical patrons have been comparatively neglected, but the picture that emerges, however shadowily, is of a playwright who, whilst having no absolute dependence on Lord Strange, the two Lords Hunsdon and even James I, was prepared to tailor his work to their measurements should occasion arise. His early theatrical experience was probably provincial, and some understanding of provincial practice is essential to a study of his professional career. It is apposite to begin with the wording of the 1572 Act for the Punishing of Vagabonds:

All and everye persone and persones beynge whole and mightye in Body and able to labour, havinge not Land or Maister, nor using any lawfull Marchaundise Crafte or Mysterye whereby hee or shee might get his or her Lyvinge, and can gyve no reckninge howe he or shee dothe lawfully get his or her Lyvinge; & all Fencers Bearewardes Comon Players in Enterludes & Minstrels, not belonging to any Baron of this Realme or towardes any other honorable Personage of greater Degree; all Juglers Pedlers Tynkers and Petye Chapmen; whiche seid Fencers Bearewardes Comon Players in Enterludes Mynstrels Juglers Pedlers Tynkers & Petye Chapmen, shall wander abroade and have not Lycense of two Justices of the Peace at the leaste, whereof one to be of the Quorum, when and in what Shier they shall happen to wander... shalbee taken adjudged and deemed Roges Vacaboundes and Sturdy Beggers.

There is here a manifest intention to suppress casual performances in town and country, and it is only historical hindsight that allows us to read the act as a charter for the establishment of a professional theatre in England. It is a typical Tudor imposition of order on the inchoate and, equally typically, it was disregarded quite as often as it was adhered to. Surviving records refer only to those cases in which local authorities enforced the regulations, and this fact denies us any adequate picture of actual practice. Even so, we must accept that those companies that fell within the letter of the law were, in general, beneficiaries of the 1572 Act.

Touring companies in Elizabethan England are of three distinct kinds. There are those whose activities were confined to the provinces, those who made their living by performing on the continent, particularly in the German states and in Poland,[21] and the London-based companies which toured, often without enthusiasm, during plague-affected summers. Our information about the first group will be greatly enhanced by the accumulation of volumes in the *Records of Early English Drama* series,[22] but it is already clear that, despite the stipulations of the 1572 Act, many landowners below the status of Barons maintained household companies of players. The size of such companies would have varied, as would their style and repertoire. Having evidently abandoned their metropolitan ambitions after their seasons at the Boar's Head, the Earl of Derby's Men numbered fourteen players when they performed at Chatsworth House in 1611 and thirteen at Londesborough the following year, when they entertained the Earl of Cumberland.[23] (If there was a breach between the Stanleys and the Cliffords after the separation of the fourth Earl of Derby and Lady Margaret Clifford in 1567, this visit was a sign that the breach was healed.) Most of the provincial companies, however, were smaller than that. Some fly-by-night troupes cheated gullible local authorities by claiming noble patronage when they had none or by the fraudulent copying of legitimate licences. The Lord Chamberlain saw fit, in 1617, to warn the Council of Norwich of two such miscreants who:

having separated themselves from their said company, have each taken forth a several exemplification or duplicate of his Majesty's letters patent granted to the whole company and by virtue thereof they severally in two companies with vagabonds and suchlike idle persons have and do use and exercise the quality of playing in diverse places of this realm to the great abuse and wrong of his Majesty's subjects.[24]

Similar tricks were certainly being played in the previous century. There was money to be made in the provinces for any actor prepared to take the rough with the smooth.

For English actors sufficiently bold, or sufficiently desperate, continental tours or residencies had become a possibility before the end of the sixteenth century. By the mid-seventeenth, English 'comedians' were well established in many parts of Europe, but such eminence did not come at once. An as-yet unidentified troupe performed in the courtyard of Elsinore's town hall in 1585, and the Earl of Leicester, during his ill-fated military campaign in the United Provinces in 1585–7, was able to present entertainments by some of his players in Elsinore and as far south as Dresden. The Danish King, Frederick II, maintained a company of English actors at his Court for some months in 1586 and seems to have passed them on for a longer period to the Elector of Saxony. Nor was this a group of English rejects. Among the names listed are three of Shakespeare's future colleagues in the Lord Chamberlain's Men: Thomas Pope, George Bryan and the finest Clown of his generation, William Kempe. One of the most successful and persistent of the English visitors, the namesake of the Robert Browne who later led the sixth Earl of Derby's Men, made his first tour in 1590. It was the custom of continental strollers, as of their stay-at-home counterparts, to seek out the major fairs as their performance venues. Many surviving records emphasise the extraordinary popularity of the English players, who seem to have impressed above all by the fineness of their costumes, by their agility and by the unfamiliar bawdiness of their clowning. Richard Jones, for example, already a leading London actor by 1592, knew the importance of good costume when he joined Browne's company on the continent. His letter to his former and future associate Edward Alleyn is a clear declaration of Elizabethan theatrical priorities:

I am to go over beyond the seas wt Mr Browne and the company ... now, good Sir, as you have ever byne my worthie frend, so helpe me nowe. I have a sute of clothe and a cloke at pane [pawn] for three pound, and if it shall pleas you to lend me so much to release them, I shall be bound to pray for you so longe as I leve; for if I go over, and have no clothes, I shall not be esteemed of.[25]

It was not long before the splendour of the English actors became proverbial in Germany. John Sommer, for example, deploring the growing German taste for self-flaunting, complains that 'such a display of finery is indulged in, that they strut along like the English comedians in the theatre'.[26] It is clear from the introductory chapter to Jerzy Limon's invaluable *Gentlemen of a Company* (1985) that the performance of plays was enlivened, perhaps sometimes replaced, by the acrobatic 'feates of activitie' for which English actors were famous. It will be recalled that Lord Strange's Men made their first appearance at Queen Elizabeth's Court as 'tumblers', and it is a pleasing possibility that England's greatest playwright gained access to his profession on the strength of a back-flip or a cartwheel. We can learn something of the special qualities of English clowning through foreign eyes

> For, know that those who paid their fee
> To witness a bright comedy,
> Or hear the tunes of fine musicians
> Were more entranced by the additions
> Of bawdy jests and comic strokes,
> Of antics and salacious jokes,
> And what, with his tight-fitting hose
> The well-bred tumbler did disclose.[27]

This translation from a German poem, printed in Frankfurt in 1597, calls attention to dress and behaviour that the writer has found remarkable. If English commentators were less inclined to note that 'His hose they fitted him so tight, / His codpiece was a lovely sight', it may be because they took such display for granted. Not all the Puritan objections to the English theatre were unfounded.

Shakespeare could have visited the European mainland with a company of players, but there is no documentary evidence that he did. It is, despite a similar absence of documentary evidence, almost certain that he toured the English provinces with the Chamberlain's Men, the King's Men or, perhaps, Lord Strange's Men. Once they had established themselves in London, the major companies went on the road only if there were obvious advantages to be gained – a request to perform at a noble marriage-feast or as featured embellishments to a royal progress – or when plague deaths in London reached above thirty or forty in a week.[28] Bubonic plague was endemic in London until it was burned out in the Great Fire of 1666. Major outbreaks, causing the banning of performances in playhouses and bear-pits, occurred in 1563, 1574, 1577, 1578, 1581, 1593, 1603, 1625 and 1636, and the stutter of a secondary outbreak often led to a restraint on plays in the years immediately following major epidemics, as in 1580, 1583, 1586 'in respect of the heat of the year now drawing on', 1587, 1594 and each year from 1604 to 1610.[29] On such occasions, the London companies had either to take to the road or find other ways of making good their loss of income. The threatened diminution of audiences at the height of summer, when wealthier citizens fled to the comparative safety of the country, might have been sufficient incentive for a well-designed summer tour, even if the plague had not reached a peak of virulence. We know too little about the patterns of professional forward planning to rest comfortably on generalisations. It was on 6 February 1599 – neither summer nor plague-time – that Henslowe noted in his *Diary*: 'Lent unto the company the 6 of February for to buy a drum when to go into the country 11s 6d.'[30] The two trumpets bought the following day by the actor Robert Shaw were for the same purpose. Wherever and whenever they went, the touring players announced their presence with drums and trumpets.

We have not as yet any reliable record of the whole detailed itinerary of a London company on tour, nor of their means of transport. They were surely too grand to match Dekker's description of players who 'travel upon the hard hoofe from village to village for chees & buttermilke'.[31] Horseback seems more likely, and they would have stuck to main roads where possible, seeking protection on stretches that were notoriously the resort of highwaymen, like Falstaff's Gadshill or the Coventry road through Dunchurch. When they reached a proposed performance venue, protocol demanded a preliminary visit to the mayor or bailiff. They might be refused, particularly during the last decade of the sixteenth century when radical Protestant prejudice had become more respectable. There is documentation in parish records up and down the country of occasions when visiting players were sent packing, sometimes with the blow tactfully softened by payments 'not to play'. If permission was granted, it was probably customary for the first performance in a designated town to be financed by the Corporation for an invited audience.[32] At subsequent performances, the company would have to rely on the takings for cash in hand. They travelled with their Lord's licence as a passport, as they were bound to do by the 1572 Act. It was in the wake of that Act that the first of the great companies, the Earl of Leicester's Men, wrote to their patron, humblie desiring your honor that (as you have bene alwayes our good Lord and Master) you will now vouchsaffe to reteyne us at this present as your houshold Servaunts and daylie wayters, not that we meane to crave any further stipend or benefite at your Lordshippes hands but our lyveries as we have had, and also your honors License to certifye that we are your houshold Servaunts when we shall have occasion to travayle amongst our frendes as we do usuallye once a yere, and as other noble-mens Players do and have done in tyme past, Wherebie we maye enjoye our facultie in your Lordshippes name as we have done hertofore.

Fifteen years later, Leicester's Men performed in Canterbury, Dover, Southampton, Marlborough, Oxford, Bath, Exeter, Gloucester, Stratford (where, according to Fripp and others, Shakespeare made his break from home by joining them), Coventry, Leicester and at the Lathom House home of the Stanleys (where, if we follow Honigmann, Shakespeare might have got to know them).[33] Travelling amongst friends, such a well-connected company would hope to find free accommodation and board, but success could be fleeting. Within a year of Leicester's Men's 1587 grand tour, their patron was dead and the company dispersed. We do not know whether there was a *normal* duration for a provincial tour, though surviving letters between Edward Alleyn and his immediate family, when he was travelling with Lord Strange's Men in 1593, indicate a six-month absence from home on that occasion. But 1593 was a fierce plague year in London, and the tour may have been extended for that reason. It was probably during a shorter tour the previous summer that Strange's Men petitioned the Privy Council to permit the early opening of the Rose after its refurbishment, because,

oure Companie is greate, and thearbie our chardge intolerable, in travellinge the Countrie, and the Contynuaunce thereof wilbe a meane to bringe us to division and separacion, whearebie wee shall not onelie be undone, but alsoe unreadie to serve her maiestie when it shall please her highenes to commaund us.

The sting in the tail would have been appreciated by the Privy Council, since it reflected their own tactic of appeasing the generally disapproving officers of the city of London by

reminding them that the public performances in London
playhouses were not really public performances at all: they were
rehearsals to keep the companies in readiness to gratify the
Queen. This fiction, a collusion between courtiers and players
against hostile authority, sustained companies on the road as
well as in London. Everything, from a first run in Barnstaple to
a revival in the Rose on the Bankside, was at root for Elizabeth
I.

Shakespeare was not with Strange's Men on their 1593 tour.
He can be variously accounted for, seeing *Venus and Adonis*
through the press, writing plays in preparation for a plague-free
theatre, sheltering with the Earl of Southampton at Titchfield,
even holidaying in Italy or ensnared by the Dark Lady of the
Sonnets. There is a flimsy argument that he was with the Earl
of Pembroke's Men, about whose disastrous provincial tour of
1593 Philip Henslowe informs his son-in-law, Edward Alleyn:

as for my lord a Pembroke's which you desire to know where they be
they are all at home and have been this five or six weeks for they
cannot save their charges with travel as I hear and were fain to pawn
their apparel for their charge.

Henslowe knew all about the ruined company's costumes: it
was to him that they had been pawned. It is obvious that not all
actors enjoyed touring in 1593. Not all actors enjoy it in the
1990s, when transport is infinitely more comfortable and Equity
rules afford some protection against exploitation. Because the
senior actors or sharers put themselves at financial risk by
touring, they may, sometimes or always, have reduced the
salary of their hired men.[34] It is even possible that the hired men
were required, as a pre-condition, to purchase a short-term
share in the company for the duration of the tour.[35] If the
company was reduced in size, the playscripts would have to be
adjusted. That is the kind of task which we would expect
Shakespeare to have undertaken, though attempts to prove that
he did are fraught with textual problems. Whether at home in
London or away on tour, Elizabethan companies had to be
adaptable. A play written for performance in the Rose for a
company of twelve might be commanded at Court (with

additional music) or staged in the Great Halls of Colleges and Inns of Court, in a provincial Guild Hall, schoolroom, innyard or Moot Hall (with a company of eight). Only in Bristol is there contemporary evidence of a purpose-built provincial playhouse,[36] and playing there would still have required physical adjustments to the *mise en scène*. We are exasperatingly without hard evidence on which to base textual conclusions. We do know that some companies toured with extensive repertoires,[37] but we know nothing of re-rehearsal and can only guess about the adaptation of texts to suit local circumstances. In 1593, when Lord Strange's Men were in Bath, Edward Alleyn was too ill to perform. Henslowe found out indirectly, and wrote to say that 'we heard that you were very sick at Bath and that one of your fellows were fain to play your part for you ...'. Alleyn is most unlikely to have been acting in a minor role. Was there a system of understudying? Who played the part, and how? Such unsung heroes are part of the hidden history of the Elizabethan theatre.

For all Honigmann's exertions, Shakespeare's 'lost years' remain an enigma. Greene's 1592 reference is to a playwright who, whilst comparatively new to London, has had time to establish himself there. Let us say that he first settled in the capital in 1590. I have assumed, though certainly not proved, that he went there with the experience of patronage and probably some provincial touring behind him. What, then, was the condition of the professional theatre in London in 1590?

CHAPTER 3

Establishing a career: London 1590

Whenever and however it was that Shakespeare arrived in London, he would have found a theatrical establishment without parallel elsewhere in the country. As early as 1567, John Brayne, a grocer from Bucklersbury, paid for the construction of a playhouse in and around the courtyard of 'the messuage or farme house called and knowen by the name of the Sygne of the Redd Lyon'.[1] The discovery in 1983 of new documents about this Whitechapel enterprise has necessitated some historical re-assessment. The Red Lion was not, as had been supposed, an inn, serviceable to actors, like many other inns, with no more than minor structural modifications. It was a farmhouse, and what Brayne was proposing was the erection of a more ambitious and more specialised structure than modern scholars had realised. The information is contained in records of a lawsuit conducted in the Court of the King's Bench in 1569, when Brayne brought an action against John Reynolds, the carpenter he had engaged to carry out work at the Red Lion. The details of the case need not concern us. Like so many Elizabethan lawsuits, it may not have ended but petered out without bringing financial satisfaction to anyone but the lawyers. What is of great importance is the architectural information that is revealed. Brayne had asked Reynolds to construct a 'Skaffolde or stage for enterludes or playes'. Its dimensions are clearly stated in court: 'in height from the grounde fyve foote ... in lengthe Northe and South fortye [a word has been scored out here] foote ... and in bredthe East and West thyrty foot'. It is the only precise reference we have to the height of an Elizabethan stage, which makes it precious, and the

length and breadth are satisfyingly comparable with those of
the Fortune (43 ft × *c*.27 ft), built over thirty years later – in
1600. If Brayne was working from common sense rather than
from precedent, he seems to have anticipated the staging
demands of the emergent professional theatre with notable
accuracy. Grocer Brayne has not yet been accorded his rightful
place in the history of the English theatre. We do not, of course,
know that he designed the Red Lion theatre, but it was evidently
he who would determine the appropriate positioning of a trap-
door – there was to be 'a certayne space or voyde parte of the
same stage left unborded in such convenyent place of the same
stage as the said John Braynes [sic] shall thynk convenyent' –
which implies that he was, at the very least, the architectural
adviser. One other feature of the Red Lion demands attention.
John Reynolds was contracted to build 'one convenyent turrett
of Tymber and boords'. This turret, or tower, was quite
separate from the galleries surrounding the courtyard. It was to
be thirty feet high (from ground level) and 'sett upon plates',
presumably to stabilise it. There is room for confusion here,
since the document also states that the frame of the turret was
'sett up uppon the sayde skaffolde', but no builder would erect
a thirty-foot tower on the flimsy base of a five-foot scaffold-
stage. What the phrase tells us is that the turret was secured to
the stage, to which it presumably formed a backing unit. There
is a further statement that, 'within the same turrett seaven foote
under the toppe', there should be built and braced a floor 'of
Tymber and boords'. What for? Seen from in front, the stage-
tower would have risen eighteen feet above stage level (the five
feet below the stage would be invisible) to a first-floor enclosure
with ample seven-foot headroom to accommodate a tall man in
a tall hat. *But* if spectators sat there, they would not have felt (or
been) safe. And why go to the trouble of erecting a thirty-foot
tower of which only the top seven feet were to be used? There
was, of course, need at ground or stage level for entrance and
dressing space for the actors, but no one needs eighteen-foot
ceilings to change a costume under. If the purpose of the tower,
as on the face of it must have been the case, was to provide the
actors with a 'tiring house' and privileged spectators with the

chance of seeing and being seen, Brayne would have been well-advised to add a lower floor-level, some eight or nine feet above the stage. It would have stabilised the structure, accommodated more spectators or a musicians' gallery with greater security and still, by the simple hanging of drapes, have concealed the actors while they changed or prepared for their entrances. The documentation of the Red Lion, like that of all London's Elizabethan theatres, combines informative detail with frustrating riddles.

John Brayne was not a fantastical speculator with a theatrical bee in his bonnet. If he was prepared to invest in building a playhouse in 1567, five years before the 1572 Act for the Punishment of Vagabonds gave its implicit endorsement to the great acting companies, he must have been confident that there was a call for so specialised a structure and an audience for the performances it would house. London was certainly undergoing a population explosion. Having stood at approximately 60,000 in 1520, the population had risen to 100,000 by 1560 and to 220,000 at Queen Elizabeth's death in 1603. By 1700 it would have climbed to 575,000.[2] Many of the immigrants, driven from the land by harvest-failures, enclosures and the blight of dispossession, would have been too poor to attend plays. They lived squalidly in crowded tenements or in the very suburbs that housed the open-air theatres. Playhouses were built outside the city walls for a single and significant reason; to escape the immediate jurisdiction of the Lord Mayor and Corporation. John Brayne was already alert to that in 1567. Within the walled city, the Lord Mayor wielded immense power, taking precedence even over Earls. During the reign of Elizabeth, it became almost a knee-jerk reaction for each successive Mayor to address the Privy Council with a request for a restraint on the playhouses, which, though not strictly under his control, were recognisably part of the London scene. Almost as inevitably, the Privy Council accepted the justice of the Mayor's complaint – and did nothing about it. The players, after all, needed somewhere to practise if they were to perform for the Queen. Brayne could not have been confident of the Privy Council's interest as early as 1567, however. His reliance was on the

evident willingness of Londoners to attend the sporadic performances within the city. Very little, beyond the fact that they
happened, is known of these early public performances. Certain
of London's largest inns, among them the Bell, the Bull, the Bel
Savage, the Boar's Head and the Cross Keys, accommodated
players at various times during the sixteenth century. In the
plague year of 1563–4, it was thought necessary to prohibit 'all
interludes & playes during the Infection', a prohibition wholeheartedly endorsed by the pious Edmund Grindal, then Bishop
of London:

> ther is no one thinge off late is more lyke to have renewed this
> contagion, then the practise off an idle sorte off people, which have
> ben infamouse in all goode common weales: I meane these Histriones,
> common playours; who now daylye, but speciallye on holydayes, sett
> up bylles, wherunto the youthe resorteth excessively, & ther taketh
> infection.[3]

Grindal specifically includes in his indictment 'the owners off
the howses, wher they playe theyr lewde enterludes', and if
Brayne was to be undeterred by such powerful opposition, it
must have been because he anticipated powerful support. Was
he, perhaps, already in correspondence with the Earl of
Leicester's Men, one of whose leading players was his brother-
in-law, James Burbage? There is no mention of Burbage in the
Red Lion documents, but Leicester's Men were certainly
interested in London venues. If Brayne hoped to attract them to
Whitechapel, he seems to have hoped in vain. On their London
visit in 1571, Leicester's Men were exceptionally licensed by the
Court of Aldermen 'to playe within this Citie such matters as
are alowed of to be played, at convenient howers & tymes, so
that it be not in tyme of devyne service'. There is no evidence
that they, or anyone else for that matter, ever played at the Red
Lion. John Brayne's great project may have been a total failure.

London's second public playhouse has an altogether more
distinguished history. Known simply as the Theatre, it was a
joint speculation by Brayne and James Burbage, and a very
costly one by Elizabethan standards. The eventual outlay was
in the region of £700, more than twice as much as Shakespeare

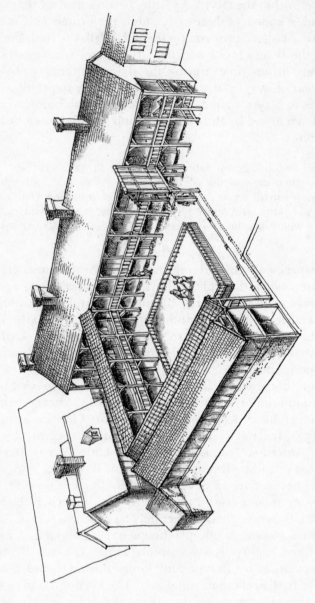

6 An imaginative reconstruction by C. Walter Hodges of a simple stage set up centrally in the enclosed yard (one side is not fully drawn in) of the Boar's Head. Spectators can watch from the yard or from the galleries.

would pay for 100 acres of arable land in 1602; and it should be noted that Brayne and Burbage were not buying the land on which the Theatre stood, but leasing it for twenty-one years. That kind of expenditure betokens confidence. The lessons of the Red Lion had evidently been learned by 1576, when the Theatre was erected in Shoreditch, about half a mile north of the Bishop's Gate, and therefore under the jurisdiction of the County of Middlesex rather than of the City of London. The new playhouse had three galleries surrounding an open yard, in which stood the scaffold stage with its attached 'turret'. Both stage and turret could, if wished, be dismantled, leaving the yard free for spectacles other than plays – fencing, acrobatics, even animal-baiting. It seems to me improbable that, as early as 1576, Brayne and Burbage would have invested all their hopes and most of their money in drama alone. The national repertoire of plays was still very small, and it was common sense to keep their options open. Thirty-seven years later, Philip Henslowe, the most persistent of theatrical profiteers, stipulated that the new Hope should have a 'fitt and convenient Tyre house and a stage to be carryed or taken awaie, and to stande upon tressells', and this is much less likely to have been an innovation than a return to earlier practice. There was no elaborate machinery in the Theatre; probably nothing more than two access doors giving onto the stage from the tiring-house facade, or even a simple concealing curtain after the fashion of the booth stages, and a trap-door in the stage itself. Brayne and Burbage spent their money on the good oak out of which the Theatre was built and on providing the kind of comfort that might attract wealthier patrons. Theatres are not built because plays cannot survive without them, but because audiences can be made to pay to come into them. Their managerial centre is not the stage, but the box-office. It was probably the custom at the Theatre, as it was in later Elizabethan playhouses, for the owners of the building to be given an agreed share of the gallery-takings. As an ex-actor, James Burbage would not have neglected his stage, but his greater interest was in the galleries.

The Theatre proved to be a much more successful speculation

than the Red Lion. Its building made 1576, in Muriel
Bradbrook's view, 'the most significant date in the history of
English drama'.[4] From the fact that another playhouse, known
as the Curtain and situated close by, was in operation in 1577,
we can assume that the Theatre proved its appeal quickly. It
was for such an unadorned, open stage that the first plays with
which Shakespeare is confidently associated were written. The
three parts of *Henry VI*, much admired in their own day, fell into
fashionable disrepute during the centuries that witnessed the
triumph of the proscenium arch. That is not surprising. The
plays depend on the spectacular occupation by actors of an
empty stage. We do not know how, why, or even exactly when
Shakespeare became involved in their composition. E. K.
Chambers argues that it was his 'first dramatic job', but revised
his initial idea that the job belonged to the spring of 1592 to the
earlier and more approximate 1590–1.[5] There was a highly
acclaimed staging of *Henry VI*, probably of the whole trilogy in
or out of sequence, at the Rose during the spring and early
summer of 1592. The company in residence at that time was
Lord Strange's, reinforced by the powerful presence of Edward
Alleyn. It was more to Alleyn, if it was he who played Talbot in
the first part of *Henry VI*, than to Shakespeare that Thomas
Nashe was alluding in *Pierce Penilesse* that summer:

How would it have joyed brave *Talbot* (the terror of the French) to
thinke that after he had lyne two hundred yeares in his Tombe, hee
should triumphe againe on the Stage, and have his bones newe
embalmed with the teares of ten thousand spectators at least (at
severall times), who, in the Tragedian that represents his person,
imagine they behold him fresh bleeding.[6]

How, too, it might have 'joyed' Gilbert Talbot, who had not
long inherited the title of Earl of Shrewsbury in 1592. It would
be surprising if he missed the play, which contains a scene that
might have been inserted with him in mind. In April 1592, the
Queen conferred on Gilbert Talbot the Order of the Garter.
Novice as he was, Shakespeare knew how to flatter an aristocrat.
It is at least a possibility that the scene in which Talbot strips the
Garter from the leg of the cowardly Sir John Fastolfe was

intended to greet the occasion or to delight both Earl and
Queen at a command performance. Talbot's exposition of the
Order's history would certainly be more purposeful in such a
context:

> When first this order was ordain'd, my lords,
> Knights of the garter were of noble birth;
> Valiant and virtuous, full of haughty courage,
> Such as were grown to credit by the wars;
> Not fearing death, nor shrinking from distress,
> But always resolute in most extremes. (*I Henry VI*, IV.i.33–8)

Nashe's tribute to the power of an actor has been purloined
by Shakespearean commentators because it counts, alongside
Greene's better known 'upstart crow', as one of the earliest
references to Shakespeare's work. Greene, too, alludes to *Henry
VI* in his studied misquotation of Shakespeare's 'tiger's heart
wrapp'd in a woman's hide' (*3 Henry VI*, I.iv. 137). The 1592
performances of the trilogy were sufficiently the talk of the town
to give two writers who specialised in being up to the minute the
confidence to rely on their readers' immediate recognition. If
the play was then the possession of Lord Strange's Men, there is
no reason to assume that they had come by it dishonestly, and
if Shakespeare wrote it for them, Honigmann's argument that
he belonged to the company is strengthened. Were Henslowe
reliable enough to be an acceptable single source, we could take
his claim that *Henry VI* was 'new' when it opened at the Rose on
3 March 1592 as an indication of its date of composition. But
that would be to beg many questions: did the 'newness' of a
play refer to its writing or its licensing? would Henslowe
distinguish between what was new to a playhouse or a company
of players and what was newly written? to which part of *Henry
VI* is he referring on 3 March 1592? and does Henslowe's cryptic
'ne' mean 'new' in the first place? There is even the possibility
that the *Henry VI* plays had reached Lord Strange's Men after
passing through the hands of another company. On the
available evidence, 1592 is too late to be a likely date of
composition and Honigmann's dating of Part One in 1588,
Part Two in 1589 and Part Three in 1590 unproven.

This dating of Honigmann's is part of an extended argument that Shakespeare began writing his known plays earlier than has been allowed by the post-Chambers orthodoxy; that, in fact, the 'lost years' were seasons of dramatic apprenticeship whose other surviving products are *Titus Andronicus* (1586), *The Two Gentlemen of Verona* (1587), *The Taming of the Shrew* (1588), *The Comedy of Errors* (1589), *Richard III* (1590), *King John* and *Romeo and Juliet* (both 1591). Not unexpectedly, Honigmann's revised dating has been widely resisted, not least in a disputatious essay by Sidney Thomas.[7] Thomas makes two points strongly. For the first, he calls up Greene's 'upstart crow':

That Greene could have used this contemptuous language, with its clear implication that its object is a Johnny-come-lately trying to imitate his betters, in reference to an established playwright with eleven plays[8] to his credit, including the enormously popular *Romeo and Juliet*, beggars belief.

But then, Honigmann might argue, Greene quite often beggared belief as well as beggaring himself. The second point is harder to refute, although it depends on our accepting Meres's list of Shakespeare's work in *Palladis Tamia* (1598) as essentially complete up to the time of Meres's writing. Given this:

We are faced with the conclusion, if we follow Honigmann, that whereas Shakespeare wrote eleven plays in the five years between 1586 and 1591, he wrote only five plays in the seven years between 1591 and 1598, when his creative powers were at their peak.[9] Even if we accept the possibility that Shakespeare wrote little or nothing for the theatre during the great plague years 1592–94, it is difficult to credit this disparity.

Despite the minor distortions which make Thomas's case against Honigmann seem more irrefutable than it is, it has to be said that Honigmann's 'solution' of the vexed problem of Shakespeare's apprenticeship is some way short of being its resolution. I must stress, however, that *Henry VI* is not the crude monstrosity that critics of the proscenium age supposed it to be. It is a masterpiece of an epic theatre that flourished briefly in the wake of Marlowe's astonishing (and astonishingly popular) *Tamburlaine the Great* (1587), to which the actor Edward Alleyn

7 Edward Alleyn as Tamburlaine.

mightily contributed. It may, indeed, have been Alleyn's temporary retirement from the stage in 1597, rather than a shift in dramatic taste, that turned Elizabethan playwrights decisively away from the rhetorical display and rapid expansiveness of the epic style. If his work on the *Henry VI* plays was, as Chambers argues, Shakespeare's first dramatic job, its fulfilment demonstrates an intimate acquaintance with theatrical practice and a sophisticated application of lessons learned somewhere or other. Even if we accept the reasonable assertion that Greene's attack on Shakespeare was an attack on a 'Johnny-come-lately' to the world of writing, it is hard to believe that he was also new to the world of the theatre. It can no longer be seriously doubted that some, at least, of the 'lost years' were spent in a company of players.

At the beginning of the year 1590 Shakespeare was twenty-five and unknown. If he was already an actor, he was probably an undistinguished one. Some time before 1610, John Davies of Hereford wrote an epigram 'To our English Terence: Mr Will: Shake-speare' which refers to Shakespeare's playing 'some Kingly parts in sport', but that could as well allude to a shared memory of participation in mock-king ceremonies as to the type-casting in his own and others' plays that some Shakespearean commentators have chosen to deduce from it. The London theatre had, of course, moved on since 1576. The practice of daily playing, excluding Sundays and periods of prohibition, had become established, bringing with it a demand for a rapid increase in the number of performable plays. With the backing of the Privy Council and despite the protests of the Corporation, the social status of licensed players in London had risen to new heights. E.K. Chambers, from his painstaking examination of relevant documents, notes that acting was described by the Privy Council as a 'trade' in 1581 and as a 'profession' in 1582. By 1592, the Council would refer to it as a 'qualitie'.[10] The long dispute with the Corporation was effectively resolved in March 1582, when Sir Edmund Tilney, Master of the Revels, was summoned to Court and asked 'To choose out a companie of players for her maiestie'. For the five years of Richard Tarlton's membership, the Queen's Men were the leaders of their profession, whether touring the provinces or playing in London inns or at the extramural Theatre. But Tarlton died in 1588, 'a fellow of infinite jest, of most excellent fancy', and the company dwindled into comparative incon-spicuousness, outshone by Lord Strange's Men and those of Charles Howard, Lord High Admiral. The increasing authority of the Master of the Revels during the 1580s was double-edged. He served as an official guarantor of royal interest in the practice of playing and as a buffer between actors and the Corporation, but he exacted regular fees for the licensing of plays and playhouses and could, though he did so only rarely, prevent the performance of controversial plays or demand the emendation or excision of passages that offended him. Every new playhouse brought him an increase of income, in addition to that he derived from the licensing of occasional venues. The Theatre and Curtain were still open in Shoreditch, with Burbage continuing in control of the former and associated, in ways that are not yet clear, with the management of the latter. His partnership with John Brayne had dissolved in disputes – a cause or a result might have been Brayne's ill-fated plans to convert the George Inn in Whitechapel into a playhouse. This scheme foundered in or around 1580, but the disputes continued, even after Brayne's death in 1586. That matters came to a head in 1590 we know from a lawsuit, which brings into the foreground for the first time the actor who was destined to replace Alleyn as the leader of the London stage, James Burbage's younger son, Richard. Exasperated by Burbage's characteristic refusal to answer complaints, Brayne's widow marched on the Theatre with three bodyguards. In the skirmish that followed, Richard Burbage beat one of them with a broom-handle and threatened to do the same to another whilst 'scornfully and disdainfully' pulling him by the nose. Richard Burbage was about twenty at the time, sturdily built and evidently frightened of nobody. The physical 'attack' that distinguished his acting – a contrast to the rhetorical flow of Alleyn – can plausibly be discerned in this early confrontation.

Two other playhouses were active in 1590. About the older, near the butts set up for archery practice in Newington, very little is known. About the second, the Rose, we know far more than about any other theatre of the period. The Newington theatre could be reached by continuing south along Southwark High Street. It was not popular with the major companies, as is made clear in a petition from Strange's Men to the Privy Council, dating probably from the summer of 1592. The answering warrant from the Privy Council throws shafts of light over the working practices of London's daily life:

Whereas not longe since upon some Consideracions we did restraine the Lord Straunge his servauntes from playinge at the Rose on the banckside, and enioyned them to plaie three daies at Newington Butts, Now forasmuch as wee are satisfied that by reason of the tediousnes of the waie and that of longe tyme plaies have not there been used on working daies, And for that a nomber of poore watermen are therby releeved, Youe shall permitt and suffer them or any other there to exercise them selves in suche sorte as they have don heretofore, And that the Rose maie be at libertie without any restrainte solonge as yt shalbe free from infection of sicknes, Any Comaundement from us heretofore to the Contrye notwithstandinge.

And so, by reason of the tediousness of the way, the Newington playhouse fell increasingly into disuse. No reference to it after 1595 has been found. The new Rose had stolen its thunder.

The Rose was probably completed in 1587 for an initial outlay of £360, only half as much as Burbage and Brayne had expended on the Theatre. But we should not be deceived into thinking that the Rose *looked* cheap. London's playhouses were designed to be eye-catching, outside as well as in. When Jack Wilton, the narrator of Thomas Nashe's picaresque novel *The Unfortunate Traveller* (1594), is trying to give his English readers an impression of the splendour of a Roman banqueting house, he begins, 'It was builte round of greene marble, like a Theater with-out.'[11] The book was published before the building of the Swan, which the Dutch visitor Johannes de Witt considered the finest of the four amphitheatres he saw in 1596. A little earlier in his notes is the comparative judgement that 'the two more magnificent of these are situated to the southward beyond the Thames, and from the signs suspended before them are called the Rose and the Swan'. Almost certainly, then, it is of the Rose that Nashe is thinking. De Witt tells us that the wooden stage-pillars of the Swan were 'painted in such excellent imitation of marble that it is able to deceive even the most cunning'. Nashe's observation invites the conclusion that the mock-marble motif was applied to the outer walls of the Rose.

The first thing to notice about the Rose is its location. It was

within the old borough of Southwark on a part of the Bankside
that belonged to the liberty of the Clink prison. In its specialised
sense when referring to land, a 'liberty', like a 'manor', was an
area previously or currently belonging to a Lord, and therefore
outside the jurisdiction of the local authorities. In 1590, this
independence, although being disputed, had not yet been
overturned. There was a further advantage to the site. There
was, in both Southwark and the County of Surrey, an ingrained
resistance to the encroachments of the city of London. London
had taken formal possession of the borough of Southwark on 9
May 1550, when the Lord Mayor rode round its precincts,
stopping at five points to allow the common crier to read a
proclamation. The charter made it clear that Southwark should
henceforth be deemed the twenty-sixth ward of the city of
London. The incorporation of its transpontine neighbour
mattered to the Lord Mayor most of all because an independent
and surly Southwark offered dangerously easy access to invaders
from the south. The 1550 charter should have signalled the end
of rivalry, but, as so often in Tudor England, the letter of the law
was inconsistently followed in practice. In the view of a modern
historian, there were economic reasons for this: 'The failure to
establish a good source of revenue for the support of its
jurisdiction in Southwark left the City with little inducement to
endeavour to preserve its rights there.'[12] The long-established
tradition of unruliness died hard. Southwark had, for centuries,
been known as the resort of criminals and prostitutes. The
brothels or 'stews', so called because of the vapour baths
through which clients tried to steam themselves free of venereal
disease, had been officially suppressed in 1546, but they had
soon re-established themselves in the liberties and manors of the
Bankside. When Philip Henslowe, the prime mover in the
playhouse project, took out his lease on the Rose, it was a
brothel. The likelihood is that he left the brothel standing as a
useful and profitable adjunct to the theatre, which was built in
the brothel yard.[13] 'Rose' was a street euphemism for a
prostitute, and the sign of the Rose was one of many colourful
Bankside icons, many of them equally allusive. (One of the most
fashionable of Southwark's brothels, the Cardinal's Hat, owes

its name to the colour of the tip of the penis. Edward Alleyn sometimes took his business dinners there.) Henslowe and Alleyn had a financial interest in brothels other than the Rose, and Alleyn's wife (Henslowe's step-daughter) may have been a partner. In 1593, when her husband was on tour with Strange's Men, she suffered the punishment of captured prostitutes when she was drawn through the streets of Southwark in an open cart. It may, of course, have been a case of mistaken identity, but Henslowe seems to have taken no action against the zealous Constable, and it is certainly possible that Joan Alleyn was a brothel Madam. Bigger fish than the Alleyns made money through prostitution. The whores of Southwark were sometimes called 'Winchester geese', because the land on which many of the brothels stood was leased from successive Bishops of Winchester, all of whom received a good financial return on their property, and Lord Hunsdon, Elizabeth I's Lord Chamberlain and patron of Shakespeare's company, was similarly enriched by the brothels in the manor of Paris Garden, which the Queen had granted to him. The most notorious of Jacobean and Caroline brothels, Holland's Leaguer, moated and semi-fortified like a military camp or lager/leaguer, was originally the manor house of Lord Hunsdon's Paris Garden. All of this would have been known to Shakespeare, whose familiarity with the Bankside brothels is displayed through Doll Tearsheet and Mistress Quickly and in the misfortunes of the dim-witted Constable Elbow in *Measure for Measure*. The County of Surrey had surrendered jurisdiction over Southwark with ill grace in 1550, but had maintained the limited permissible authority over the liberty of the Clink and the Paris Garden manor. Its stand against the London authorities was altogether firmer than that of Middlesex,[14] and known to be so. For John Donne, the lawlessness of Southwark was proverbial. His first elegy takes the part of a prince's subjects who have fled abroad to escape his tyranny:

> There we will scorne his household policies,
> His seely plots, and pensionary spies,
> As the inhabitants of Thames right side
> Do Londons Mayor: or Germans the Popes pride.

It was, then, a politic decision of Henslowe's to build his playhouse on the south bank of the Thames, close to his own home. With its inns and taverns and the meals available in its brothels, Southwark was a centre of the catering industry. Now, with a theatre as well as a bear-baiting house and the annual attraction of its famous September Fair, it could claim to be a centre of the entertainment industry as well. The watermen were delighted by the new development. In 1592, they joined Henslowe in a petition for the re-opening of the Rose, on the grounds that 'wee your saide poore watermen have had muche helpe and reliefe for us oure poore wives and Children by meanes of the resorte of suche people as come unto the said playe howse'.

The second notable thing about the Rose, then, is its proximity to the Thames. It would be hard to overstate the importance of the river in the daily life of Tudor London. In the port, shipping was still brisk under Elizabeth I, buoyant against the rivalry of the busy Hollanders who would contribute to its decline under the Stuarts. It was only on the river that there was any regular public transport: up to 2,000 rowing boats (or wherries) available for hire. One of the outstanding features of the contemporary maps and views of London, from the fragments of the Copperplate Map (*c.* 1557) to Hollar's Long View (etched in 1647), is the variety of vessels depicted. Tall ships are moored downstream of London Bridge, with wherries and barges plying between them and the shore. Upstream the wherries dominate, carrying passengers and manoeuvring among loaded barges, herring busses, the occasional pleasure-boat, eel ships at anchor and the royal barge speeding downstream under twenty-four oars-power. It has taken the sinking of the pleasure-boat *Marchioness* in 1989, with the loss of over fifty lives, to remind Londoners how dangerous a thoroughfare the tidal Thames can be. Few of the population could swim. They were sensibly wary of the turbulence created by the nineteen piers of London Bridge, with their protective 'starlings'. Barges delivering goods from the west off-loaded at landing-docks upstream of the bridge, and wise passengers would disembark to by-pass it on foot. For the watermen, as we have seen, the Rose was a godsend and London Bridge an eyesore. To deal with the river trade, the playhouse needed a wharf of its own or an agreement to hire moorings along the waterfront. Henslowe recorded a payment of eight shillings for 'wharfyng' in 1592–3 and the very considerable expense of seventy shillings for a barge that same year.[15] He would not have neglected the opportunity to decorate the playhouse barge with the sign of the rose or to use its river-passages as a means of advertising. I have suggested elsewhere that Shakespeare's company would have been missing an opportunity if they did not display 'the barge she sat in' on the Thames as an advertisement for *Antony and Cleopatra*.[16] By that time they had long followed Henslowe's lead to the Bankside and the sturdy shelter of Southwark and Surrey.

The financial management and custodial oversight of the Rose remained with Henslowe throughout the playhouse's active life. It can be followed, not without occasional stumblings, through the pages of the unique record that is usually called Henslowe's *Diary*. The interpretation of that disorderly document is greatly aided by recent commentaries,[17] and some understanding of Henslowe's practice is valuable to anyone who wishes to appreciate the conditions of a career in the Elizabethan theatre. Shakespeare's managerial engagement in the Globe would, however it may have varied in detail, have had its points of contact with Henslowe's in the Rose. In the first place, then, Henslowe's 'diary' is an assemblage of various theatre records, three sets of pawn accounts, details of personal affairs including money-lending and an optimistic list of cures for physical ailments. Associated papers include the deed of partnership between John Cholmley and Henslowe for the building of the Rose, the contract for the building of the Fortune and a wardrobe inventory in Edward Alleyn's handwriting. It is no longer fashionable to portray Henslowe as the miserly scourge of an infant profession. Carol Rutter presents him as 'only so ambiguous a figure as modern bank managers who willingly underwrite hope but insist on cold cash back and who, though intimidating, gain nothing from forfeited debts'.[18] He had begun his business life as apprentice to a dyer called

Woodward and consolidated it by marrying the dyer's widow. (There is nothing abnormally sharp about this practice: such marriages were a consolation often sought by bereaved wives.) By 1590, Henslowe was about forty and had financial interests in mining, real estate, brothels, the manufacture of starch and in pawnbroking, usury and the Rose playhouse. So long as the Rose remained a 'free' house – a theatre without a single company in semi-permanent residence – Henslowe's income from the building he owned would have come from his agreed share of the gallery takings. Even when the Admiral's Men, led by Henslowe's son-in-law Edward Alleyn,[19] took up residence in 1594, he remained a landlord rather than a company manager; albeit with a proprietary interest greater than is normal in landlords. It was he who made the statutory payments to the Master of the Revels, he who paid for the extensive alterations to the Rose in 1592, he who posted the £100 bond ensuring the maintenance of law and order in the playhouse and he who increasingly eased the cash-flow problems of the company by making payments on their behalf – at interest, to be sure, but knowing the risks of non-repayment. If Carol Rutter is right that his average income from the Rose in a moderately successful year was £250 and that it might have risen as high as £400, it is no surprise that he stayed in the theatre business for so long.[20] Recurrences of plague made some years very unsuccessful, of course, but even so, the return on an initial investment of about £200 must have been gratifying. It was sufficient, even without his other interests, to make Henslowe wealthier than most people in England. We have seen that schoolmasters were lucky to receive as much as £20 per annum. A London artisan would earn from six to eight shillings for a seventy-hour week (about £17 per annum if his health held). Outside the costly city, it was just possible to survive on £2 per annum. Only a tiny number of Elizabethans earned as much as £1,000. Judges were among them: and a competent barrister in this litigious age would make £600 in an average year.[21] As James Burbage had already proved, there was money to be made in playhouse ownership.

We cannot leave the Rose without considering some of the

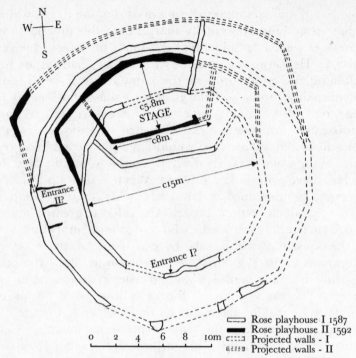

8 Plan of the Rose Playhouse (1587 and 1592), based on
archaeological findings in 1989.

discoveries made about its physical proportions during the 1989
excavations. This is how the Museum of London information
pamphlet describes the findings:

The theatre was small – the diameter of the inner *yard* or *pit* and stage
area was perhaps no more than 13 metres. [Subsequent work suggests
that this is an underestimate. 15 metres is closer.] Its inner and outer
walls were 3.5 metres apart, giving us the width of the galleries. An
extensive organic layer may represent the remains of roof thatch, and
the demolition debris shows that the theatre, presumably timber-
framed, had lath and plaster walls. The superstructure rested on a
trench-built foundation of brick and chalk and in the first phase was
given extra stability, in the wet clayey subsoil, by a series of closely-
spaced chalk-built piles. A weathered strip discovered around the edge
of the yard was the result of rain water dripping from the eaves of the
overhanging thatched roof above. The yard appears to have been

floored with a layer of mortar on which spectators could stand: the southern half of this floor was level, but the northern half sloped down towards the stage. The stage seems to have been between 5 and 6 metres from front to back, and perhaps 11 to 13 metres wide.

At some point – perhaps at the time of the 1592 alterations – the design of the theatre was changed, perhaps to accommodate a larger audience. The yard's area was increased and refloored with a layer of cinder and hazelnut shells. The stage, while maintaining its size, was pushed to the north by some 3 metres and backed by the construction of a new internal wall.[22]

This measured statement conceals the excitement of the discovery of unique physical evidence about the construction and basic dimensions of an Elizabethan playhouse. The remains have encouraged the archaeologists to make one further suggestion; that 'the parallel inner and outer walls formed a polygon with perhaps 12 or 14 sides'. This is the first issue to be addressed.

The Rose was a polygon

There are innumerable references to the roundness of London's early public playhouses, but it has been increasingly accepted that they were more likely to be polygons partially disguised as circles by the way in which the plaster of the outer walls was applied. The basis for such a view is, of course, practical carpentry. As a general rule, the more sides there are to such a polygon, the easier will be its construction and the more readily will it be disguised as a circle. The matter has been explored in great detail by John Orrell,[23] whose preference, for the Globe at least, is for twenty-four sides, but he considers the possibility of both twelve and fourteen. If the Rose excavations support the polygon argument, we need not assume that all of London's playhouses had the same number of sides.

The Rose was small

Smallness is comparative. The Rose excavations reveal an inner diameter for the whole building of twenty metres or about sixty-six feet, which is the length of a cricket pitch from wicket to wicket. Even with the additional thickness of the outer walls, the whole building cannot have been more than seventy-four feet across, and the diameter of its inner yard was little more than fifteen metres, about forty-nine feet. This needs to be set against John Orrell's proposals that the first Globe had a diameter of about 100 feet, with an inner yard seventy feet in diameter.[24] (Even as I write, excavation of the Globe site is in progress.) It should be said that Orrell's strenuous attempts to prove that the Globe was significantly bigger than had previously been thought have not been unanimously accepted, and both the Rose findings and the initial post-excavation surmise that the Globe had a diameter of eighty feet threaten his suggestion that 'there may have been a standard Elizabethan public theatre frame design, some 100 feet or so across';[25] but the Globe may well have been altogether grander than the Rose, which was, after all, abandoned by Henslowe soon after the Globe opened in 1599. It is very likely that Henslowe's decision to build his new playhouse, the Fortune (1600), north of the river was an acknowledgement that the Bankside competition was too much for him. He had survived the rivalry of the ill-managed Swan, but the new Globe was a different matter. Even so, the only concrete evidence we yet have of the dimensions of an Elizabethan playhouse are more likely to lead to the conclusion that Orrell's Globe is too big than to confirm that the Rose was too small.

The Rose stage was moved backward and a
new internal wall constructed

Does this mean that, by 1592, the old Red Lion-style 'turret' had had its day? On the evidence so far, it seems possible that Henslowe had the old-fashioned tower removed and reconstructed the tiring house within the structure of the existing galleries. One of the puzzles of the Swan sketch, after De Witt, is the apparent lack of alignment between the galleries and the tiring-house facade. Perhaps Francis Langley, when he had the Swan built in 1595, was still relying on the sort of stage turret that Henslowe had abandoned three years earlier at the Rose. The main aims of the alterations seem to have been to provide

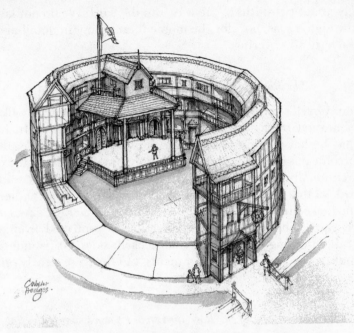

9 Reconstruction of the Rose by C. Walter Hodges. Hodges has
based it on the archaeological discoveries.

the stage with pillars supporting a roof (or 'heavens') capable of
housing machinery and to enlarge the capacity of the playhouse.
The reconstruction I am suggesting would certainly have
achieved the second of these.

The shape and dimensions of the Rose stage remained unaltered

There are some surprises here. Firstly, the stage area defined by
its sub-structure tapered towards the front, so that a width of
some thirty-eight feet along the tiring-house facade may well
have been reduced to about twenty-five feet at the front edge.
Secondly, the depth of at most eighteen feet means that, unlike
the Fortune stage which reached 'to the middle of the yarde'
and unlike that of the Globe which the Fortune stage was to be
'Contrvyed and fashioned like unto',[26] the Rose stage jutted

only about two-fifths of the way into the yard. We do not know how high it was, nor, for the moment, anything in detail about its overhead covering.

The Rose stage is built at the north end of the yard

John Orrell's industry and ingenuity in determining the likely orientation of the Globe have been monumental.[27] Much of what he has written remains incomprehensible to me, but its outcome has been a confident assertion that the Globe stage was intentionally built at the south end (veering south west) of the yard, so that it was not the actors but portions of the audience who looked into whatever summer sun shone over the eaves into the yard. The stage, that is to say, was protected from the erratic lighting-effects of cloud-flecked skies. It is not my concern to refute Orrell's arguments, but the Rose clearly offers contrary evidence.

The northern half of the Rose yard sloped down towards the stage

This is a bombshell. There is no reference to any gradient in the Fortune contract, and yet it seems highly unlikely that, once one playhouse had included such an amenity, any of its successors could have afforded to do without it, unless their design was avowedly multi-purpose. The 1613 Hope, it will be remembered, had 'a stage to be carryed or taken awaie', but this was not the case with the Fortune, nor with the Globe on which the Fortune was modelled. Our only information about the Swan is provided by De Witt's jottings and the copy of his drawing made by his Dutch friend Arend Van Buchell. On that sketch, the yard is defined as 'planities sive arena', the neutral word 'planities' meaning nothing more than 'flatness'. 'Arena' is a much more specific word. De Witt parades his classical learning by using it, implying a comparison with the Roman arena, which accommodated the most acrobatic and violent of imperial entertainments. If the 1595 Swan disregarded the sloping floor of the earlier Rose, that may be an indication that its owner intended it to be used for more than plays. But if the

1599 Globe and the 1600 Fortune disregarded it, there are questions to be asked. It would be extraordinary if the Rose's raked floor was unpopular with spectators. Those standing in the back half of the yard must have benefited from the rake. Indeed, such concern for the sightlines of the groundlings is exemplary. I find three possible explanations for the silence of the Fortune contract on this feature of the Rose. The first is that the Fortune, like the Globe, pitched its social ambition higher than the Rose and was comparatively careless of the groundlings. The second is that such a gradient was well enough established to be taken for granted and is therefore included under the covering clause:

And the said howse and other thinges beforemencoed to be made & doen To be in all other Contrivitions Conveyances fashions thinge and thinges effected finished and doen according to the manner and fashion of the said howse Called the Globe.

The third is that the rake caused severe drainage problems in an open-air theatre. It would seem that the 1592 renovations saw a reduction in the angle of the rake. It is at least possible that later playhouses abandoned it altogether in order to prevent the waterlogging of the area around their stages. Although the suggestion is probably mischievous, the sloping front half of the Rose yard may even contain an answer to the unsolved problem of where the musicians were accommodated in the Elizabethan theatre. Is this the first intimation of an orchestra pit?

Before the unexpected discovery of its foundations, the Rose was comparatively neglected by Shakespearean scholars. Shakespeare's own direct involvement with it seems to have been slight, although, in the absence of records, we cannot say what plays were performed there before 1592. But it was into the small Rose that Nashe's roughly calculated 'ten thousand spectators at least' crowded to see Alleyn in the first part of *Henry VI*. It was a proud playhouse in 1590, standing alone on the south bank of the Thames and with a lease that had nine years longer to run than Burbage's at the Theatre. Shakespeare's arrival in London coincided with an unprecedented demand for new plays. Nothing is clearer from Henslowe's

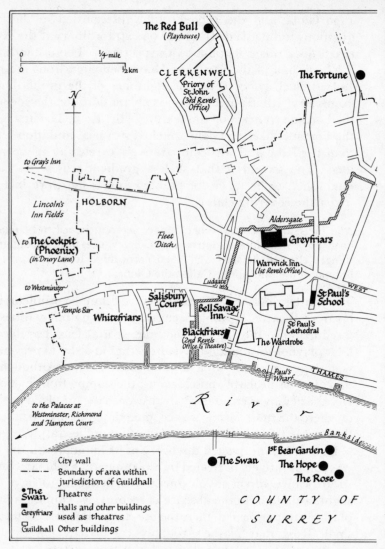

10 Names and approximate sites of London's playhouses have
been imposed on the Braun and Hogenberg map of 1572.

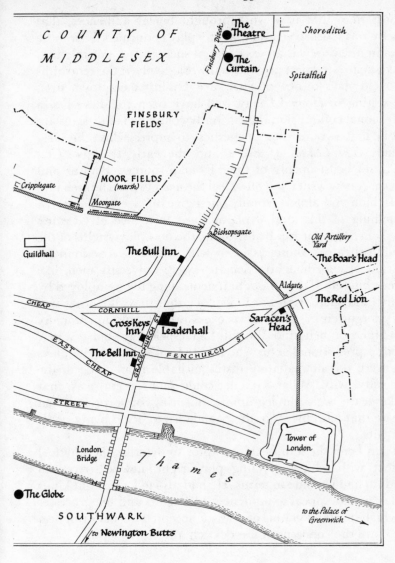

COUNTY OF
MIDDLESEX

Finsbury Ditch

The
Theatre

The
Curtain

Shoreditch

Spitalfield

FINSBURY
FIELDS

Cripplegate

MOOR FIELDS
(marsh)

Moorgate

Bishopsgate

Guildhall

The Bull Inn

Old Artillery
Yard

The Boar's Head

CHEAP

CORNHILL

Aldgate

The Red Lion

Cross Keys
Inn

Leadenhall

Saracen's
Head

EAST

The Bell Inn

FENCHURCH ST

GRACECHURCH ST

CHEAP

STREET

London
Bridge

Thames

Tower of
London

The Globe

SOUTHWARK

to the Palace of
Greenwich

to Newington Butts

records than that new work brought bigger audiences, that
novelty was short-lived and that any play performed six or more
times in a season was an exceptional success. It is possible that
Shakespeare's earliest professional work involved the refurbish-
ing of old plays for new performance. His initial employment in
the writing of *Henry VI* may well have been collaborative, a
professional commission industriously completed. The signs are
that he had a young man's eagerness to impress. Both the early
comedy *The Comedy of Errors* and the early tragedy *Titus
Andronicus* boast openly of their Roman sources, Plautus and
Seneca. A new writer will often feel the need to push himself into
the fashion and almost equally often give offence by his efforts.
Something of this kind explains the vehemence of Greene's
attack on Shakespeare. Before 1590, the new playwrights of the
London theatre – those, at least, with whom Greene found it
pleasant or expedient to associate – were university men, like
Greene himself. If they thought it demeaning to be employed by
actors (and there is no hard evidence that they did), that was
easily forgotten in convivial or excessive drinking in company
with others of their kind. But this Shakespeare was one of a new
breed: a professional actor who had the audacity to write plays
that were not immediately distinguishable from those of the
university wits. What Greene could not accept was that
Shakespeare was the legitimate offspring of a professional
theatre that had, by 1590, the confidence to begin living on its
own wits.

It has been the aim of this chapter to describe the physical
context with which a young playwright, newly arrived in
London, had to come to terms. He had also to learn what kinds
of play would appeal to audiences and actors and the processes
by which he could get his own work accepted for performance.
These are the concerns of the next chapter.

CHAPTER 4

A playtext and its context

It was during the decade of the 1590s that the variable pragmatism of the professional theatre was replaced by systematic practices. That is not to say that each new play followed precisely the same route from conception to performance, but it is to say that there was a 'normal' procedure against which each individual case could be measured. It was a procedure that took account of three distinct but closely related groups – playwrights, actors and audiences.

The playwright's part

To be successful, a professional playwright needed to observe fashion. Only the outstandingly successful or outrageously arrogant, like Marlowe or Jonson, would presume to challenge or lead that fashion. It was to the journeyman-writer that 'normal practices' applied. Such a journeyman would begin his campaign for performance by proposing a story to a company of players or to a single leading member of such a company. If the story seemed promising, he might be asked to furnish the company with a plot. It is presumably to this practice that Meres refers in *Palladis Tamia* when he calls Anthony Munday 'our best plotter'. There is, of course, a genuine skill in the effective division of a story into appropriately dramatisable episodes, however short of high art that skill may be. Armed with his 'plot', the playwright could then return to the players for further discussion. He would be carrying something not unlike the prose 'argument' with which Shakespeare prefaced

The Rape of Lucrece in 1594. If the decision then taken is that the plot merits expansion into a play, detailed plans for its writing can be undertaken, perhaps with the sweetener of £2 as a down-payment. With new plays at such a premium, speed of completion is a recommendation for future employment, and joint-authorship is a useful aid to rapidity of composition. Richard Dutton has alertly compared the playwrights' syndicates of the Elizabethan theatre to Hollywood's 'writing factories' of the 1930s and 1940s.[1] Our modern squeamishness about collaboration is anachronistic. Shakespeare's evident reluctance to collaborate might just as well be used as proof that he was unusually unpopular among fellow-writers as in support of his greater artistic integrity. The more important point is that he was uniquely secure among late Elizabethan playwrights in his status as a member of the 'board of directors' of London's most successful theatre company. Sole composition has many advantages over collaboration, but speed is not one of them. For a man like Thomas Dekker, dependent on his income from writing to support an inclination to spend money prodigally, collaboration was a necessity. Carol Rutter emphasises the point with a nice contrast of two playwrights at work for Henslowe in the summer of 1598:

Chapman at thirty-eight years of age was something of a donkey, content to plod along, solitary, while the young veteran Thomas Dekker (only twenty-six) was the stable's sociable farmyard cock, perpetually scratching around for more work. The same month Chapman was working on a single play, and finding it difficult to produce even a title for it, Dekker was involved in six plays, all of them collaborations.[2]

But this suggests too readily, perhaps, that such frenzy was a source of delight to Dekker. The stresses of professional writing were, in fact, considerable, and Dekker was quite as much the victim as the beneficiary of market forces.

Let us, for convenience, assume that the task of filling out an accepted plot has been divided five ways, with each of five writers undertaking to combine a sequence of episodes into a single Act. The syndicate must, presumably, meet at least once during composition in order to avoid damaging repetitions, resurrections from the dead or other inconsistencies, and once at the end to read over the finished product and make the necessary emendations. The manuscript, written in five different hands and dotted with corrections, is then delivered to the players, who demonstrate their satisfaction by paying a further £4 or £5 for appropriate division among the authors. The manuscript is now the possession of the acting company. If they are lucky, each author will have written in a legible hand and the manuscript will not be too defaced by late corrections, but such good luck is hard to credit. The players must anyway deliver the precious pages to a scribe, paying him to make a fair copy. In doing so, the scribe may correct some errors in the original whilst, almost inevitably, making new ones of his own. I have not tried to work out how long it would take to complete a fair hand-written copy of *Hamlet*, but the task would not have been a light one. And, of course, one copy is not enough. What, after all, is the fate of the fair copy? It has to be chopped up so that it can reach each of the actors in the form of a complete 'part'. This part, pasted together and presented to him in the form of a scroll, is then adorned with the minimum necessary cues and stage directions. Before this can happen, then, a second fair copy will need to be made, presumably using the first as a master with reference made to the authors' original manuscript only rarely, if at all. Again, more errors are bound to creep in, more unintentional emendations to be made. Now, with all the necessary payments made, the company possesses three copies: the first is the 'foul papers' of the original conglomerate manuscript, the second has been chopped into pieces and turned into a collection of various-sized scrolls, and the third can be marked up as the promptbook. If we follow the career of the second copy, we get close to the heart of playhouse pragmatism. To 'possess' a part in the Elizabethan theatre could mean, literally, to possess the scroll on which that part was written. To lose a part – by dropping it in the street or leaving it in a tavern – might threaten a whole performance. The storing of parts, once memorised by the actor, may have been an important playhouse task. How else, without frequent additional payments to a scribe, could new actors replace old ones? and how else could the danger of an actor's defection to a rival company, with all his parts in his possession, be avoided? We have nothing but surmise on which to base an assessment of exactly how many fair copies of a play were held by the company which owned it, but one 'part' survives. It was Alleyn's in Robert Greene's *Orlando Furioso* (1591). Opened out, the part is about seventeen feet long (it was, Alleyn being Alleyn, much the biggest in the play). No scene divisions are marked and the cues are minimal, three words, two words, sometimes only one. There are scattered stage directions, the short ones in Latin and a few longer ones in English. The text also carries alterations in Alleyn's hand. There is no reason to assume that Greene had colluded in these alterations. There were, I have no doubt, occasions of hurt pride when the parts in a new play were first distributed. Everyone could tell the size of the part by the size of the scroll. Shakespeare exploits the humour of these occasions in *A Midsummer Night's Dream*, when Peter Quince gives out parts to the mechanicals; substantial scrolls for Bottom and Flute, smaller ones for Starveling and Snout, none at all for Snug, who 'may do it extempore, for it is nothing but roaring' (i.ii.71–2). Later, during the interrupted rehearsal, Flute excites the laughter of the *cognoscenti* in the audience by his inability to cope with the conventional lay-out of a part on the scroll. Quince is a little impatient: 'you must not speak that yet; that you answer to Pyramus: you speak all your part at once, cues and all' (iii.i. 103–6). Incidentally, either the compositor or the playhouse scribe seems to have omitted something from Shakespeare's original text. The Flute of the received version has no cues to speak. Such are the hazards of the transmission of a script from Elizabethan playwright to Jacobean printer.

A deal of archaising sentimentality has entered into the assumptions of literary scholars about the beauty of the original performances of Shakespeare's plays. The antics of Quince's company, though risibly exaggerated, represent something closer to reality. At the point where his individual creativity entered the public domain of playhouse practice, an Elizabethan dramatist had to accept the fact that, whilst each actor might (or might not) know his part, he was in no position to *know the play*. For those neo-Stanislavskians whose practice dominates the twentieth-century English stage, those for whom a text, however accomplished, serves primarily as the pretext for a histrionic revelation of the subtext, Elizabethan precedent sounds a salutary warning. Carol Rutter offers as exemplary of the pressure under which the Admiral's Men worked at the Rose a ten-week period in 1595 when they gave fifty-seven performances of twenty different plays, four of them new.[3] For an actor like Snug, 'slow of study', such demands would be unsatisfiable, and even the most able must have had difficulty in avoiding the confusion of today's words with those they spoke yesterday and the entirely different ones they would have to speak tomorrow. That is not the particular dilemma of the eight boys who bustle out for the Induction to Marston's *Antonio and Mellida* (1599/1600), each carrying his part. 'Faith, we can say our parts', says the boy who is to play the important role of Piero, 'but we are ignorant in what mold we must cast our actors.' For adult players, it may have been easier to fashion a character out of memorised words than it was for these boys, but Marston is clearly indicating how an Elizabethan playwright's hopes could be disappointed in performance. The concept of 'character', developed in the nineteenth century, would not have been understood by the Elizabethan actor or his audience. If we are to believe that Shakespeare grasped it intuitively, before there was any available linguistic formulation, we must also recognise that his intuitions would not often have been realised in the playhouse. The primary task of an Elizabethan actor was to deliver a story and to retain the attention of the audience by delivering it effectively. It was less often the playwright whose name attracted audiences (playbills seem not to have mentioned it), than the reputation of the actors, who had bought the plays as commodities and laboured to turn them into profitable merchandise. If the actors failed, the playwright would retain his initial payment but lose the bonus of the takings from a 'benefit' performance, granted to the author at the play's second or third presentation.

For a playwright like Ben Jonson, it was probably galling to see his play transformed into a number of various-sized scrolls, and the fair copy (as well, probably, as the foul papers) in the possession of the company that had bought the play. There was nothing to stop him 'cheating' by paying a scribe to make a copy for his own keeping, though the actors would not have been pleased. There was almost certainly a clause against it in any signed agreement. But Jonson was able to provide the printers with good copy for the production of the unprecedented folio edition of his *Works* in 1616. The volume was met with admiration by some and with sneers by others. One epigram, addressed 'To Mr Ben Jonson demanding the reason why he called his plays works', enquired:

> Pray tell me, Ben, where doth the mystery lurk,
> What others call a play, you call a work?

Four years earlier, the bibliophile Sir Thomas Bodley had grouped plays with almanacs and proclamations among 'idle books and riff-raffs'. Reproaching the keeper of his library for cataloguing them, Bodley conceded that 'Haply some plays may be worth the keeping: but hardly one in forty.'[4] Jonson's handsome volume contributed to the gradual rise in the respect for plays as literature, but it should be remembered that Bodley's love of books was exceptional in the England of Elizabeth I and James I. The inventory of Sir Henry Unton's house at Wadley draws attention to the 'many books of divers sorts' in his study, but the actual number given is only 220.[5] Unton was a cultured diplomat whose library was of sufficient size to draw comment: we do not know whether it included any plays. There is, in fact, no way of determining who bought the plays that the London printers and provincial chapmen sold. New books were customarily brought out during the legal terms, when London was buzzing with lawyers and their litigious clients. Such people would certainly have figured among the playhouse audiences, and there was no shortage of unscrupulous printers eager to cash in on theatrical popularity. Plays sold best when the acting companies would least have wished them to be available, at the height of their on-stage success. The provenance of the copy from which some of these hastily printed quarto editions were printed was highly suspect. Like Shakespeare, Thomas Heywood was drawn into publication chiefly by the urge to provide accurate alternatives to stolen and butchered texts of his plays, as he is at pains to explain in the prologue to *If You Know Not Me, You Know Nobody* (1605):

> ... some by Stenography drew
> The plot: put it to print: (scarce one word trew:)
> And in that lamenesse it hath limp't so long,
> The Author now to vindicate that wrong
> Hath tooke the paines, upright upon its feete
> To teache it walke ...

But, again like Shakespeare, Heywood was an active member of a company of players and was, therefore, professionally reluctant to publish his plays. He knew that other playwrights were less scrupulous and protested, in an address to the reader prefacing the published text of *The Rape of Lucrece* (1608), against what he considers the dishonest practice of those who sell their labours twice, 'first to the stage, and after to the press'. In this respect, Heywood and Shakespeare exhibit a purism that many other playwrights could not afford and a few, Ben Jonson among them, might have taken issue with. The relationship of plays to books was still far from clear. After all, nobody chopped books into pieces to stick them higgledy-piggledy together again.

The last indignity for a sensitive playwright with high poetic ideals might have been to see his play, which had begun as a plot, reduced to a plot again at its first performance. The allusion here is to a straightforward playhouse custom. As an *aide mémoire* to busy actors, the company's book-keeper would write out a synopsis or 'plot' of the play and hang it on a wall backstage in the tiring-house. A surviving example is written on foolscap, divided into two columns, with marginal notes on properties and sound-effects. The names of the actors and the characters they are to impersonate are then listed against the episodes in which they are to be involved. The precaution is

The Tragedy of Hamlet

And so by continuance, and weakenesse of the braine
Into this frensie, which now possesseth him:
And if this be not true, take this from this.

   King Thinke you t'is so?

   Cor. How? so my Lord, I would very faine know
That thing that I haue saide t'is so, positiuely,
And it hath fallen out otherwise.
Nay, if circumstances leade me on,
Ile finde it out, if it were hid
As deepe as the centre of the earth.

   King. how should wee trie this same?

   Cor. Mary my good lord thus,
The Princes walke is here in the galery,
There let *Ofelia*, walke vntill hee comes:
Your selfe and I will stand close in the study,
There shall you heare the effect of all his hart,
And if it proue any otherwise then loue,
Then let my censure faile another time.

   King. see where hee comes poring vppon a booke.

      Enter Hamlet.

   Cor. Madame, will it please your grace
To leaue vs here?

   Que. With all my hart.   *exit.*

   Cor. And here *Ofelia*, reade you on this booke,
And walke aloofe, the King shal be vnseene.

   Ham. To be, or not to be, I there's the point,
To Die, to sleepe, is that all? I all:
No, to sleepe, to dreame, I mary there it goes,
For in that dreame of death, when wee awake,
And borne before an euerlasting Iudge,
From whence no passenger euer retur'nd,
The vndiscouered country, at whose sight
The happy smile, and the accursed damn'd.
But for this, the ioyfull hope of this,
Whol'd beare the scornes and flattery of the world,
Scorned by the right rich, the rich cursied of the poore?

                      The

11 Pages from the 'bad' Quarto of *Hamlet* (1603). The text may be a pointer to the limitations of stenography.

sensible enough. It is recorded of the eighteenth-century actor, John Palmer, on the occasion of his being entrusted with the title role in William Hayley's new tragedy, *Lord Russel* (1784), that he

had done with Lord Russel, as he did with many other characters, that is, totally neglected to study the words of the part; and in this dilemma he bethought himself of an expedient, which answered astonishingly, and, indeed, by the audience was never suspected. As much of Lord Russel was unlearned on the night of its performance, he thought it was better to speak from some character that he did know, than one that he did not; whenever, therefore, he felt himself at a loss, he dexterously introduced some passages from the Earl of Essex, which he contrived to fit into the cues received by Lord Russel; and thus, really giving some parts, and masking others, he gained another day to perfect himself in the character. It will be remembered that to his audience this play was completely new; while the dialogue was in progress, and not seemingly irrelevant, there were no means of detection.[6]

Whilst the anecdote smacks of familiar theatrical exaggeration, it contains a germ of truth. Palmer was a competent actor, sometimes required by circumstance to take on more than he could handle. What is here recorded as intentional confusion of the audience might have begun with the accidental confusion of the actor. Such disorientation would have been all too possible among Elizabethan actors, whose task was to keep separate in their heads the lines and actions of one play from the broadly similar ones of another. Lord Letoy, in Brome's *The Antipodes* (1636), speaks fondly but realistically of his household players:

> ... Well sir, my actors
> Are all in readiness, and, I think, all perfect
> But one, that never will be perfect in a thing
> He studies: yet he makes such shifts extempore,
> (Knowing the purpose what he is to speak to)
> That he moves mirth in me 'bove all the rest.
> For I am none of those poetic furies,
> That threats the actor's life, in a whole play,
> That adds a syllable or takes away.
> If he can fribble through, and move delight
> In others, I am pleas'd.   (II.i. 14–24)

Not all authors were as complacent as Letoy, but they would have needed to accustom themselves to the 'fribbling' of actors. Letoy's favourite may not know his part, but he knows 'the purpose what he is to speak to' and will not, therefore, disrupt the flow of the story. He can check his entrance on the hanging 'plot' and will know to leave the stage when his 'purpose' is fulfilled. His on-stage conduct is no longer within the control of the playwright.

The actor's part

We know nothing of rehearsal practices in the Elizabethan theatre. With so many plays in the repertoire, available time was clearly restricted. On playing days, only the mornings would have been open to the company, and rehearsal was only one of the many activities that would need to be carried out then, the memorising of parts among them. Neil Carson suggests that the normal preparation time for a new play, involving annotation, transcription and the cutting and pasting of parts, was two weeks. Only then could rehearsals begin, unless, as seems sometimes to have happened, they began before the preparation of the play was finished; but Carson has also found examples of plays rushed into rehearsal after nine, six and three days of preparation.[7] The schedule for *Civil Wars: Part One* is instructive. Dekker and Michael Drayton delivered the manuscript to the Admiral's Men on 29 September 1598, and the play was staged five weeks later, on 4 November. Five weeks from page to stage is not implausible in a theatre untrammelled by the demands of directors and designers. But we cannot simply divide this period into two weeks of text-preparation and three of rehearsal. Why not? Because another new play, *Pierce of Winchester*, received its first performance on 21 October, and we must surely assume that *it* was given priority in the week before it opened. That would mean a maximum of two weeks – say, twelve mornings, to take account of Sunday observance – to complete the learning, making, costuming and rehearsing of *Civil Wars*. Some of the work was wisely started earlier. On 11 October, Henslowe recorded a loan of £4 to the actor Thomas Dowton, 'to bye divers thinges for the play called the first syvell

wares of france', the same actor having borrowed £6 for equally
unspecified purposes three days earlier. This play was evidently
Dowton's responsibility. Perhaps he had recommended its
purchase. By 3 November, Dekker and Drayton had completed
the second part of the play, which opened on 9 December. The
authors received £6 between them for each part and a further
£6 for a third part, completed by 30 December. To rehearse a
five-act play in something like twenty-four hours requires both
high efficiency and low expectations. My own view is that most
scenes would not have been rehearsed at all. Those involving
courtly formality might have been ignored, or briefly 'blocked'
according to an established formula, whilst those centred on
low-life clowning would have been left to the improvisatory
inspiration of the favoured actors. Only the few technically
demanding scenes would have been selected for genuine
rehearsal. For the rest, the actors needed time to learn and space
to practise by themselves.

Next to his part, an actor's most precious possession was his
costume. The better established actors owned their own and
called on the playhouse wardrobe for special requirements only.
Shakespeare's colleague Augustine Phillips, for example, bequeathed to his 'late apprentice' Samuel Gilburne 'my mouse
colloured velvit hose, and a white teffety dublet, a black taffety
sute, my purple cloke, sword and dagger'.[8] Such a gift would
have been of immense value to young Gilburne as he embarked
on his career as an adult actor. The wardrobe inventories of the
Admiral's Men describe a surprisingly small stock. That of
March 1598 lists thirteen doublets, ten suits, four jerkins, eight
gowns, five coats, eight pairs of hose, thirteen cloaks and six
venetians (breeches cut according to Venetian patterns) for
primary characters and, for 'Clownes, Hermetes and divers
other sewtes', twenty gowns, twenty-five capes, twenty-three
coats, twenty suits, six trousers, five jerkins, two doublets and
eight pairs of hose. That is to say that the tireman made and
maintained many more costumes for minor characters than for
the major ones. The supply of female garments listed is
astonishingly small: three bodices, four farthingales, six head
tiers and four rebatoes (stiff collars).[9] The implication here must

be that the women's clothes were kept where the boy apprentices lived, in the homes of leading actors who instructed them and from whose womenfolk extra items might always be borrowed. The period was notable for the extravagance of male as well as female dress. Even in old age, the Lord Admiral paid detailed attention to his clothes. 'He was in fact a bit of a peacock; he paid close attention to the cut of his doublet and the angle of the plume, to the fullness of the cape and the fit of the hose.'[10] Such a man would not wish his household players to be badly turned out. But he need not have worried: self-display through costume was part of an actor's stock-in-trade. A character's status, his place in the hierarchy of any play, was signified by his clothes. The assumption that the Elizabethan stage was drab because it lacked elaborate scenery cannot be sustained. On the empty platform, costumes were individual splashes of colour and the composite picture was always vivid and could be splendid. The texts are rich in references to their characters' dress, and the prominence of disguise as a mechanism of plotting is easily accounted for once the audience's almost-obsessive interest in clothes is appreciated. Two examples, selected from many in Henslowe's papers, will serve to illustrate the priorities of a typical professional company. Having bought *Civil Wars* for £6 on 29 September 1598, the Admiral's Men borrowed £19 from Henslowe on 4 October to purchase 'a Riche clocke of mr langley'.[11] As a commodity, then, a cloak was worth more than three times as much as a play, a comparative valuation reinforced by the terms of the agreement between the actor Robert Dawes and Henslowe in 1614. Dawes was required to accept certain specified fines for lateness, drunkenness etc., committed to 'attend all such rehearsall which shall the night before the rehearsall be given publickly out' and to accept the fixed penalty for absenteeism. The agreed fine for removing a costume from the playhouse was forty times greater than that for missing a performance.[12]

Although we know very little about the terms of apprenticeship for fledgling actors, we can tell from such bequests as that of Augustine Phillips that some system, presumably modelled on the practices of the trade guilds, was in operation.

12 Daniel Mytens' portrait of the Lord Admiral, still dressed in finery
in his old age as Earl of Nottingham.

Vocal training, under the broad heading of rhetoric, was reasonably well-established, but the idea that styles of performance might be adapted to suit the particular character portrayed was in its infancy. Edward Alleyn was a rhetorician, not an actor of characters, and the gradually growing interest in 'personation' may suggest a greater subtlety in the style of his natural successor, Richard Burbage. It is tempting to suppose that the kind of historical shift in acting styles brought about in the early twentieth century by the coincidence of Chekhov's plays and Stanislavsky's concern for performance standards was prefigured in the collaboration between Shakespeare and Burbage, but there is only the evidence of the text's demands to support such a belief. The skills most needed by an Elizabethan actor were, in modern parlance, 'external'. He would wish to dance, to fence, to tumble, perhaps to sing. In addition, he would develop his instrumental skills, sharing the contemporary assumption that music and drama were not distinct arts, but allied. We have seen that Augustine Phillips left his costumes to his former apprentice, Samuel Gilburne, but omitted to mention the further gift of 'my base viall'. To James Sands, Phillips's apprentice at the time of his death in 1605, the bequest included 'a citterne, a bandore, and a lute, to be paid and delivered unto him at the expiration of his terme of yeres in his indenture of apprenticehood'. Elizabethan Englishmen boasted of the nation's musical leadership. William Byrd (1543–1623), John Dowland (1563–1626) and Thomas Campion (1567–1620) were acknowledged masters, whose reputation was high on the continent as well as at home. Provincial cities employed small orchestras or 'waits' from early in the fifteenth century, and the growing interest of family groups and associations of friends in banding together to make music was reflected in the development of the 'broken consort'. Thomas Morley's acclaimed *Consort Lessons* (1599) were designed for these chamber orchestras, consisting variously of lute, pandora, cithern, bass viol, treble viol and flute. It was, almost certainly, to such broken consorts that the playhouses turned for incidental music or entr'acte entertainment. An inventory of 'books of musicke in ye Chamber where ye musicyons playe' in the home of the wealthy merchant, Sir Thomas Kitson, is indicative of domestic taste in the last year of Elizabeth I's reign:

> vi bookes covered with parchment, cont vi setts in a book, with songes of iiii, v, vi, vii, and viii partes.
>
> v bookes, covered with parchment, with pavines, galliardes, measures and cuntry dances.
>
> v bookes of leavultoes and corrantoes.
>
> v bookes covered with parchment, with pavines and galliards for the consert.
>
> one great booke which came from Cadis, covered with redd lether and gylt.
>
> v bookes contg one sett of Italyan fa-laes.[13]

The music-loving second Lord Hunsdon, patron of Shakespeare's company, would have called for a consort from his actors when they performed at his house in the Blackfriars, as well as for displays of the acrobatic 'feates of activitye' which were part and parcel of a professional troupe's repertoire. The assumed connection between music and drama, so significant for theatrical apprentices in Elizabethan and Jacobean England, is well exemplified by the licence granted to the Norwich city waits in 1576, empowering them to perform tragedies, comedies and interludes within the city.[14] Even Oxford University, skilled in the making of distinctions, found it natural to call on Matthew Gwynne, a lecturer in music, to arrange the staging of the plays for the Queen's visit in 1592. In the next century, he would present a play of his own to James I.[15]

If Shakespeare underwent anything approaching an apprenticeship as an actor, it belongs to the 'lost years' which Professor Honigmann has worked so hard to recover. At no known point was the profession closed to people who had not served as apprentices. Available evidence suggests that those who succeeded as actors were less improvident, more solid citizens than most of the successful playwrights. On occasions, the latent tension between actor-employers and playwright-employees broke the surface of fellowship. Greene's scorn for the upstart crow, who, as a jack-of-all-theatrical-trades, disputes the distinctness of the playwright's craft, is an early expression of the tension. Shakespeare's Hamlet, in offering advice to the players, stands firmly with the playwright in protest at contaminating practices. John Webster, in addressing the reader of the 1612 edition of *The White Devil*, lays the blame for the play's failure in performance on those who staged it 'in so dull a time of winter … in so open and black a theatre', though he carries his anger into yet more dangerous territory by attacking also the 'ignorant asses' in the Red Bull audience. As so often, the most extreme Elizabethan case is Ben Jonson's. We do not know the precise cause of his quarrel with Gabriel Spencer, one of the leading members of the Admiral's Men at the Rose, but it is not impossible that Spencer had seen fit to denigrate Jonson's current success, *Every Man in His Humour*. The duel they fought on 22 September 1598 ended when Jonson thrust his three-shilling rapier six inches into Spencer's right side. Henslowe's biased account of the fatal incident grants Jonson a status neither as actor nor playwright but only as a 'bricklayer'. The intention is almost certainly contemptuous – Jonson had deserted Henslowe's stable and sold his new play to the Chamberlain's Men – although one could kindly argue that Henslowe bestows on Jonson the credit of the trade for which he had served an apprenticeship rather than either of the trades (actor and playwright) for which he had served none. Jonson was sensitive about his own achievements and Spencer probably paid for underrating that sensitivity with his life. Jonson was also sensitive about his poverty and probably resented the conspicuous prosperity which Spencer enjoyed – or imitated (he owed Henslowe money when he died). Leading actors had a style of living, perhaps beyond their means, of which we catch a glimpse in an anonymous letter of complaint sent to Sir Francis Walsingham on 25 January 1587:

Yt is a wofull sight to see two hundred proude players jett in their silkes, wheare five hundred pore people sterve in the Streetes … The lord of hostes will surely forsake to dwelle amongst the tentes of Israell yf the synnes of the people do still provoke hym.

The eminently practical response of the professional companies to such righteous indignation was to contribute to poor relief in the parishes where their playhouses were sited – one more item of expenditure to be set against income from the box office.

Balancing the books was, of course, a major preoccupation, and it would be foolish to suppose that all actors could afford to 'jett in their silkes'. Formally engaged apprentices would receive no more than pocket money, board and lodging from the actor under whom they served. In the best organised companies, it was probably from among apprentices that the female roles were cast. We do not know the precise size of the whole establishment of any professional company, nor how often it was reduced or augmented. Players were occasionally brought in for particular roles, sometimes hired for a season, and it seems to have been normal practice for these hired men to receive a weekly wage (recorded amounts range from five to ten shillings per week). When the theatres were closed, such casual labourers lost their livelihood. It would have been difficult to perform Shakespeare's plays with less than twelve actors, and that can stand as a minimum number for the Chamberlain's/ King's Men during the years of their supremacy. Calculations on the basis of available figures suggest that sixteen was a maximum, except on special occasions. The immediate employers of the hired men were the sharers. When Shakespeare joined the Chamberlain's Men in 1594, he joined as one of six or seven sharers. Theirs was the overall control of income and expenditure. They would divide among themselves whatever remained after they had paid the wages of the hired players and musicians, the scribes, money-gatherers, tiremen, book-keepers and stage-hands, after they had covered the costs of each individual production and after they had handed over to their theatrical landlord his agreed share of the takings. It was only the last of these costs that the Chamberlain's Men shed when they moved to the Globe in 1599. There was no precedent for this move. Actors had never owned their own building before and never would again on the same principles of 'commonwealth'. The example followed in later centuries was that of Shakespeare's contemporary and some-time fellow-actor, Christopher Beeston, whose later career marks him out as the first commanding actor-manager in England. The risk taken by the

Chamberlain's Men in 1598–9 paid off, but it was a mighty one, and no other company had the nerve or the means to follow their lead. It may have brought Shakespeare an average of £150 per year over the twelve years of his active involvement, in addition to separate payments for his plays; quite sufficient, were he so inclined, to allow him to jet in his silk.

The audience's part

Three books on Elizabethan audiences, spanning nearly fifty years, offer importantly contrasting basic arguments. Alfred Harbage's *Shakespeare's Audience* (1941) presupposes a homogeneity among the paying customers of the various public theatres, with all classes represented and their position in the playhouse determined by their willingness or unwillingness to pay more than the minimum admission price. But Harbage, whose Shakespeare is determinedly a 'popular' playwright, finds the dominant presence that of the artisan. His view that the more privileged sections of London society preferred the atmosphere of the private theatres and boy companies is amplified in *Shakespeare and the Rival Traditions* (1952). Against this, Ann Jennalie Cook, in *The Privileged Playgoers of Shakespeare's London* (1981), argues that the public theatres, too, were dominated by people who stood 'firmly apart from the mass of society':

Most people ate, dressed, worked, and lived as best they could. The fortunate wrote music and poetry. They made the laws. They ruled the government and the church. They monopolised education. They led armies. They claimed estates and controlled companies. They elevated dining and dress and decor to an art. And they were avid playgoers, men and women alike.[16]

Cook strengthens her argument by finding privilege under every stone she lifts. Andrew Gurr, in *Playgoing in Shakespeare's London* (1987), is carefully critical of both Harbage and Cook. He takes account of historical developments in drawing distinctions, not only between 'private' and 'public' audiences, but also between the adherents of the different playhouses

within each category. Gurr's systematic survey of the possibilities opens new roads to an understanding of the mutual
relations of playwright, actor and audience during a period of
high excitement in the English theatre. Even to find the right
term to describe the paying customers is difficult.[17] 'Assembly',
'throng', 'multitude', 'congregation', 'quality' and 'company' all occur. Ironically, it was not until after the Restoration,
when poetic drama had lost its grip, that 'audience' became
more frequent than 'spectators'. For Ben Jonson, who generally
used 'audience', the term 'spectators' barely concealed his
contempt. He would have preferred the one, but had to suffer
the other. But Jonson always held extreme views. It is
impossible, with hindsight, not to admire the alertness of
Elizabethan playgoers. Certainly they could be unruly. The
early history of professional theatre is peppered with stories of
riots (often involving apprentices), with confrontations between
members of the audience or between individual spectators and
actors, with the recorded activities of cut-purses and prostitutes.
But, given the eagerness of theatre-haters to discover evidence of
the corruption inherent in playhouses, it is the comparative
scarcity of such evidence that impresses. In public theatres,
where the wearing of sight-obstructing hats went unchallenged,
where there were no privies (Gurr supposes that buckets were
provided[18]), where the custom of tobacco-smoking prevailed
and where actors shared their playing-space with audiences
(not until that innovation of the proscenium arch did actors
have a 'room' of their own), playwrights saw fit to present poetic
tragedies whose allusiveness continues to exercise modern
scholars. There is no doubt that Elizabethan playhouses were
noisy: a delight in noise-making is common to nearly all
popular festivities. The mystery of Elizabethan performance is
its evident capacity to charm silence out of commotion.

Shakespeare wrote for an audience that may not always have
been discriminating, but which he clearly deemed capable of
discrimination. His plays do not become suddenly more elevated
after 1608, when the Blackfriars, with its more privileged
audience, became a home for the King's Men. It is an obvious
cause for wonder that the company continued at the open-air

Globe to perform plays which were first staged at the indoor Blackfriars, and *vice versa*. A particularly striking point here is that, whilst the penny-paying groundlings stood closest to the actors at the Globe, it was the costliest seats that abutted the Blackfriars stage (not to mention the on-stage stools where fashionable young men delighted to display themselves). If this caused difficulties of adjustment for the actors, we hear nothing of them. I have already stated my belief that the primary purpose of an Elizabethan actor was to deliver his part of a story, but it cannot be doubted that all sections of the audience, however variously, were excitable by the particular words used as a means of conveyance. Gurr has usefully recorded evidence of the theatrical inclination of the four social classes of Elizabethan England: nobles and gentlemen, citizens and burgesses, yeomen, artisans and labourers. It is his view that the dominant presence in the public playhouses was that of the citizens and burgesses.[19] We need, however, to remind ourselves that the adoption of appropriate class behaviour was not expected in the sixteenth century as it is in the twentieth. Aristocrats did not find it necessary to assert their superiority by eschewing manifestations of popular culture, whether in the playhouse or outside it, and the anxiety of the merchant classes to imitate their betters and shun their inferiors had not yet established its rigidities of conduct. That is to say that, if the citizen class dominated, its domination was not such as to exclude, or even to colonise, others. If Shakespeare and his fellow-leaders of the Chamberlain's Men could reconcile their contradictory roles as bourgeois entrepreneurs and feudal retainers, similar reconciliations were within the capacity of the audience. It was not land, as in rural England, but cash that dominated social interplay in London, and the citizen playgoer was as much at ease with cash as the nobleman. We should not, then, too readily believe that social tensions operated as a major threat to playhouse harmony in late Tudor and early Stuart London. There were, of course, times when such tensions declared themselves, but Shakespeare's preparedness to stigmatise particular sections of society would have been foolishly provocative in a more volatile auditorium.

Before turning to a consideration of Shakespeare's own adaptation to the London theatre, I should draw attention to one more of Gurr's important observations on playhouse audiences. In 1590, when we left him, Shakespeare was not clearly identified with a single playhouse. When we next meet him in 1594, he will be a member of the Lord Chamberlain's Men and his association will be with James Burbage's Theatre. Gurr argues for a cultural shift that brought to the playhouses north of the river a rougher, less discerning audience than to those on the Bankside. The implication is that the move from the Theatre to the Globe was not only a change of location, but also a change of clientele. The soft pornography of Will Kempe's jigs, then, would have been welcomed at the Theatre but less favoured at the Globe, and Kempe's sudden departure from Shakespeare's company in 1599 can be seen as the first step in his planned return to a more congenial home north of the Thames. The taste of the northern playgoers was more conservative, whereas, in the bold world of Southwark, free thinking and the new philosophy found its theatrical adherents. The Globe was more attractive to this group than the Rose, where, Gurr speculates, 'the whole Henslowe repertoire was mainly inspired by its citizen and conservative allegiance'.[20] Outgunned by the Chamberlain's Men, Henslowe and the Admiral's Men abandoned the Rose and moved north of the river to build the Fortune in Clerkenwell, leaving their rivals to cultivate an audience whose tastes were less conservative, more open to political debate, less committed to the Tudor Settlement:

Shakespeare's plays already had a particular appeal for law students and gallants in the 1590s. In the new century the Globe company's allegiance to the specific tastes of the London citizenry drained away.[21]

We may go further than this. I have argued above for comparative social harmony within the playhouse walls; but this is not an argument, as it would have been in Victorian England, that each section of society was publicly submissive. The very inclusiveness of the audiences at the public theatres embodied a significant restraint on the too-wilful exercise of the royal prerogative. Where the people cannot be easily divided, a wise ruler treads with caution. Martin Butler has recently argued that that implicit restraint was transformed to explicit threat in the years immediately preceding the Civil War, but his eloquent conclusion applies no less convincingly to the original audiences of Shakespeare's English history plays, of his *Julius Caesar* and *Measure for Measure* and of the political tragedies:

If the court stage was excessively exclusive, performing before a tiny political elite, the outdoor houses compensated by being inclusive, addressing a tumultuous multitude, not only the gentry and professions but men of the middle and lower ranks – those shopkeepers, craftsmen, apprentices, applewives, chimney boys, rogues and rabble who were normally excluded from political life but for whom one penny bought an entry to participation in political fantasies in the playhouse yards.[22]

The peculiar ease with which Shakespeare made his way into and in the London theatre was understandably resented by Robert Greene. The 'upstart crow' grasped intuitively the richness of the new world that Greene and others had laboured, however sporadically, to chart. In order to succeed in the theatre of any age or place, a playwright must know its rules. In order to succeed greatly, a playwright must break them. Shakespeare was thirty when he joined the Lord Chamberlain's Men and accepted the 'rules' that this chapter has outlined. We can assume his experience as a member of the audience, know (frustratingly little) about his acting, and can reconstruct, however tentatively, a checklist of the plays he brought with him for the use of his new colleagues. Had he, like Oscar Wilde, declared his genius, no one would have believed him; but there was good cause to be confident in his talent as a playmaker. Some, at least, of the company would have acted in his plays and recognised, perhaps, the unusual scope his work gave to the inventive actor. The national drama had, by 1594, assembled a variety of serviceable roles, of stage 'types' whose conduct could be relied on to carry a story through to its necessary end. Such are the *dramatis personae* whom Shakespeare deployed with precocious dexterity in *The Two Gentlemen of Verona*. By the time

Shakespeare left the theatre, the national drama had assimilated a method of recording human behaviour that gave due recognition to its complexity. Shakespeare was both the major inspirer of this shift and its supreme exemplar, but it would be a mistake to underrate the contribution made, wittingly or unwittingly, by his companions in the Lord Chamberlain's Men.

The Elizabethan perception of the world as a theatre may have been a commonplace, but there is nothing commonplace about the ability to see the significance of what is taken for granted. It is all very well to acknowledge that 'all the men and women' are 'merely players', but what does it mean? Is 'playing' their aspiration or their fate? If the King is an actor, what is a king? And what is an actor? Is he a two-hour king? He has the kingly power to stand above an assembly and command its attention. Shakespeare's response to the disquieting trope of king and player was so intense as to challenge the accepted discourses of both government and theatre. The challenge is central to all the plays on English history from *Richard III* to *Henry VIII*, to the great tragedies and, with new resonances, to the late romances. More, perhaps, than any other single insight, it raised Shakespeare's aspirations above those of the 'mere' professional. That is not to assert that the decision was a conscious one, which Shakespeare could have stamped with its appropriate time, date and place; but the play that seems to me most irresistibly to have shaped his future is *Richard III*, and I shall endeavour to explain why.

There is nothing but presumptive evidence to say that Shakespeare ever saw Richard Tarlton perform, but this greatest of Elizabethan clowns remained an overpowering theatrical 'presence' even after his death in 1588. It was in the body of Tarlton that the mediaeval Vice, servant of the devil, merged with the stage clown, a popular troublemaker whose *rapport* with the audience gave him the power to subvert not only the good order of the play he was in, but also good order. Tarlton's Clown, like the Vice of the Morality Plays, was ambiguous even when he was most endearing. His *Jests* were intended to put people down and the clown *persona* (uncertainly

13 Drawing of Richard Tarlton, showing the squint, squashed nose and face and a hint of a hunchback. It is taken from an illuminated manuscript in which Tarlton represents the letter T.

distinguishable from Tarlton's own) worked to produce discomfort among fellow-actors and audiences alike. The labour was lightened by his extraordinary ugliness. Small and hunchbacked, with a squint and a button-nose squashed into his face, he invited pity from the spectators and threw power back at them. Whether entertaining in a theatre or tavern or at a banquet, Tarlton was no safer than Lenny Bruce, and he was all the more dangerous because he was popular. And this is the figure who strides onto the platform at the opening of *Richard III*, no subtle Machiavel but a self-declared Vice, confined in a pitiable body:

> I, that am curtail'd of fair proportion,
> Cheated of feature by dissembling nature,
> Deform'd, unfinish'd, sent before my time
> Into this breathing world, scarce half made up,
> And that so lamely and unfashionable
> That dogs bark at me, as I halt by them;
> Why, I, in this weak piping time of peace
> Have no delight to pass away the time,
> Unless to see my shadow in the sun
> And descant on mine own deformity:
> And therefore, since I cannot prove a lover,
> To entertain these fair well-spoken days,
> I am determined to prove a villain ...   (i.i. 18–30)

Whatever the precise provenance of this bold opening scene, Shakespeare must have recognised it in performance as a trope of Richard III as Tarlton, King as Vice/Clown. The image is reinforced in the next scene. There, the hunchback who has claimed our pity because he 'cannot prove a lover', confronts the bereaved Lady Anne across the dead body of Henry VI. She reviles him, even spits at him, but is finally overpowered by his demonic pursuit. There is a telling parallel with one of Tarlton's best-known outfacing *Jests*. When a lady offers to 'cuff' him, he agrees provided that she reverses the spelling.

We do not know who first played Richard III, but we do know that, after 1594, the part became identified with Richard Burbage. It was the first substantial collaboration between playwright and leading actor. They would remain collaborators for twenty years. Against the sustained rhetoric that Marlowe provided for Alleyn, the tonal variety of Shakespeare's writing for Burbage stands out vividly. We cannot say whether Shakespeare exploited or created in the energetic young actor the ability to make the vocal shifts from the colloquial ('Pray you, undo this button') to the operatic ('Blow winds and crack your cheeks'), but we can say that the whole course of the Elizabethan drama was affected by it. In stressing the signifi-

cance of *Richard III*, I am saying neither more nor less than that
Shakespeare empowered his actors as no English playwright
had done before him. It was through working with the company
that he developed a confidence in the lyrical voice as well as in
the rhetorical and the curt. *Romeo and Juliet* and *A Midsummer
Night's Dream* express his certainty that, with the actors at his
disposal, he could play the solo instruments of the lyric against
the groundswell of the narrative without encountering abuse
from the Theatre's audiences. It was out of this certainty that
the Shakespearean 'character' was born. Shakespeare invented
character by building on role. If, without knowing an actor, you
watch him in a role, you cannot readily distinguish actor and
role. Quite possibly, Tarlton was, for Shakespeare, identical
with his role. But to watch Burbage playing Tarlton playing
Richard III is something else altogether. This, for an Elizabethan in the 1590s, was 'personation' – the making concrete of
something so intangible as an invented personality. It is in
behaviour inconsistent with personal impulse that the idea of
character is contained. Shakespeare observed his fellow-actors/
histriones at work and created characters for them through his
perception of the histrionic temperament in action. At the end
of that road lay Hamlet, but Mercutio and Juliet's Nurse,
Bottom and Quince are heading that way. Bottom, though no
less a victim of a savage practical joke, is no longer Christopher
Sly because he lives through his indignity. It is not mere
bardolatry, though bardolatry has tainted it, that has made
Shakespeare's characters part of our cultural heritage. It is the
directness with which, through the art of the actor, Shakespeare
came to apprehend both the duplicity and the human honesty
of language under pressure from events.

CHAPTER 5

Servant to the Lord Chamberlain: 1594–1603

Between the publication of Greene's attack on Shakespeare in September 1592 and the summer of 1594, London's professional companies were driven out of their theatres by plague. We have already seen Lord Strange's Men on tour and Pembroke's Men plunged into bankruptcy by provincial failure. It cannot be positively proved that Shakespeare was with neither of these companies, but it seems unlikely. His major involvement was with poetry. *Venus and Adonis* was announced for publication in April 1593 and *The Rape of Lucrece* in May 1594. Both were dedicated to the Earl of Southampton, an ambitious and highly strung young nobleman whom legend has claimed as Shakespeare's lover during this period. Speculation on the issue is arid. Loving friendships between men were openly celebrated, but homosexuality was not acceptable in Elizabethan England, where it invoked, almost inevitably, images of Sodom and Gomorrah,[1] and, by an Act of 1533, convicted sodomites were liable to the death penalty. We should give no particular credit to the many attempts made to blacken by association the reputation of all professional players. Philip Stubbes is characteristically vehement in his anatomy of the corrupting effect of plays:

... these goodly pageants being ended, every mate sorts to his mate, everyone brings another homeward of their way very friendly, and in their secret conclaves covertly they play the Sodomites or worse.[2]

How could he possibly know? And how can we? Whatever may be read into the sonnets or in the discernible increase of warmth in the second dedication to the Earl of Southampton it remains unproven that Shakespeare was ever actively homosexual. What is more relevant is that the two Ovidian narrative poems were his claim for recognition as a poet among the leaders of refined society. He may, of course, have had a callow hope that the writing of poetry would be sufficient to earn him a living, but that is unlikely. Richard Field, the fellow-Stratfordian who printed *Venus and Adonis* so well, would surely have put him straight on that. Generous financial patronage might, in 1593–4, have reshaped Shakespeare's subsequent career, turning him from playwright and occasional poet into poet and occasional playwright, but such generosity was extremely uncommon. There is a legend that the Earl of Southampton rewarded him with £1,000; but Nicholas Rowe, the eighteenth-century editor to whom we owe its transmission, betrays his own scepticism through an analogy: 'A Bounty very great, and very rare at any time, and almost equal to that profuse Generosity the present Age has shown to *French* Dancers and *Italian* Eunuchs'.[3] Southampton had financial troubles of his own in 1594, and beneficence on almost any scale is out of the question. A likelier gift from a caring patron would have been a household office, but there is no evidence that Shakespeare was offered one, either by the Earl of Southampton or by another of his patrons, Alice Spencer, wife and imminently widow of Lord Strange. Whatever he did and thought during the plague-scarred year of 1593, Shakespeare was ready, in 1594, to commit himself, temporarily at least, to a career in the professional theatre.

Because we know that Shakespeare was one of the Lord Chamberlain's Men when they played at Court over the Christmas of 1594, and because he was then prominent enough to be one of three joint-payees mentioned in the Treasury accounts, we can be fairly confident that he joined the company at its re-formation in May or June of 1594, just when Richard Field was printing *The Rape of Lucrece*. No one could have known what an extraordinary moment this was. Lord Hunsdon, the Lord Chamberlain, had patronised companies of players before, the first recorded as early as 1564, but this was a new group, and a remarkable one. The detail demands careful recording. Lord

TO THE RIGHT
HONOVRABLE, HENRY
VVriothefley, Earle of Southhampton,
and Baron of Titchfield.

HE loue I dedicate to your
Lordfhip is without end:wher-
of this Pamphlet without beginning is but a fuperfluous
Moity. The warrant I haue of
your Honourable difpofition,
not the worth of my vntutord
Lines makes it affured of acceptance. VVhat I haue
done is yours, what I haue to doe is yours, being
part in all I haue, deuoted yours. VVere my worth
greater, my duety would fhew greater, meane time,
as it is, it is bound to your Lordfhip; To whom I wifh
long life ftill lengthned with all happineffe.

Your Lordfhips in all duety.

William Shakefpeare.

A 2

14 The dedication to the Earl of Southampton in the 1594 edition of
The Rape of Lucrece.

Strange's Men had completed their provincial tour by the beginning of November 1593 and were not, perhaps to their chagrin, called to Court that Christmas. Instead of benefiting from their brilliant patron's elevation to the Earldom of Derby, they were sidelined by his involvement in the Catholic succession plot. Matters were made even worse by his mysterious and untimely death in April 1594. Well-established actors like Augustine Phillips, Thomas Pope and George Bryan were threatened with vagabondage, and the whole profession, after its long London lay-off, was in tatters. Crippled companies had been forced to contradict custom by selling plays to printers. There were twenty published in 1594, against an annual average for the rest of the decade of about six. The possession of a playscript was among the primary assets of an active company and strenuous efforts were normally made to keep them from publication. In March 1599, for example, Henslowe records a payment of £2 made to a printer 'to staye the printinge of patient gresell'.[4] The position in early 1594 was desperate. There is something frantic about the stop-start seasons at the Rose and at Newington in the spring. Sussex's Men, the Queen's and the Lord Admiral's follow each other in untidy succession as restraints on playing are lifted and re-enforced. Then, briefly, in June 1594, comes a significant collaboration. For ten days at the unfashionable Newington playhouse, the amalgamated companies of the Lord Admiral and the Lord Chamberlain performed to disappointingly small audiences. The collaboration lasted no longer than that. By mid-June, Alleyn and the Admiral's Men were back at the Rose and Richard Burbage had presumably led the novice Chamberlain's Men north of the river to his father's Theatre. The story of the London playhouses over the next decade features a jostling for supremacy between the Admiral's Men at the Rose and then the Fortune and the Chamberlain's Men at the Theatre and then the Globe. The usual winners were the Chamberlain's Men. Very rarely in theatrical history have rival companies admired each other's work and I have found no evidence that these rivals did. Their patrons, both Privy Councillors, were related by marriage, Charles Howard, Lord Admiral and nominal victor over the Spanish Armada, having married Lord Hunsdon's daughter, and relations between these two elderly men were cordial. But that would have had small bearing on the attitudes of their liveried players. Carol Rutter endorses Andrew Gurr's suggestion that the two companies were aligned on opposite sides of a political gulf, with the Chamberlain's Men associating themselves with the Earl of Essex and the Admiral's Men with Robert Cecil and the conservative establishment.[5] In 1594, though, both troupes were bent on survival. The death of Marlowe in the fallow year of 1593 was a blow to the Admiral's Men, who owned his plays, and their chief attraction in 1594 was the majestic Edward Alleyn. Against that, the Chamberlain's Men could set the up-and-coming Richard Burbage, the popular clown William Kempe and the thirty-year-old William Shakespeare.

Shakespeare was not, at this stage, the greatest of these attractions. Audiences were more interested in plays and in players than in playwrights, whose names did not even figure on the advertising bills. Even so, his new colleagues had reason to be hopeful about Shakespeare's future contribution, and perhaps about his influential friends, too. Little is known of the reception of *The Two Gentlemen of Verona*, but the other early plays had all been theatrical successes. Attempts to establish a strict chronology are always hazardous, but it is reasonable to assume that Shakespeare, by the time he joined the Chamberlain's Men, had added *The Taming of the Shrew* and *Richard III* to the *Henry VI* plays, *The Comedy of Errors*, *Titus Andronicus* and *The Two Gentlemen of Verona*. My own view is that *Love's Labour's Lost* also belongs to the early years of the 1590s. Even when playing stopped at the public theatres, it continued in private houses, and *Love's Labour's Lost* has all the appearance of having been written for a coterie. Honigmann's argument that the coterie included Ferdinando, Lord Strange, deserves to be taken seriously.[6] Scholars have often mounted arguments that particular plays were designed for particular occasions and been met by down-to-earth resistance from other scholars, who reasonably insist that Shakespeare was too much a professional to allow himself to be so circumscribed. My basic sympathy is with the second party, but the manifest allusiveness of *Love's Labour's Lost* swings me towards the first in this instance. The received text shows signs of doctoring and, unless and until further evidence is discovered, it is for individuals to decide whether that reveals an initially public text made private or an initially enclosed text opened out for public consumption. The view that *Love's Labour's Lost* belongs to 1593 is not an argument against Shakespeare's professionalism: it is an argument that, in that year, his professional instinct and ambition led him towards the nobility. By 1594, he had shifted his ground. If even the sensational popularity of *Venus and Adonis* could not ensure him a literary living, he had better stick with the theatre.

The company he now joined would prove remarkably durable. They had, during the early years at the Theatre, to deal with the intractable James Burbage, presumably through the mediation of his sons, Cuthbert and Richard. Cuthbert was not evidently an actor but an entrepreneur. Richard, if he was not already the possessor of leading parts, quickly became so. William Kempe was a specialist clown, distinct in style from his opposite number in the Admiral's Men, John Singer.[7] Clowns had a playhouse status that would have been immediately recognisable in the responses of their audience and was fully acknowledged in the post-play jigs, of which they were often the authors and always the central performers. The popularity of Kempe's jigs was an important factor in the early success of the Chamberlain's Men. Their impact is astutely reconstructed by David Wiles in his *Shakespeare's Clown* (1987), where they are linked back to the world of Tudor festival and, in particular, to the seasonal servitude to lords of misrule. Thomas Pope was a clown, too, but of the boisterous Singer style, in contrast to the stolidly passive Kempe. Augustine Phillips was probably the most versatile member of the group, musician as well as actor, and author of at least one jig 'of the slyppers', which was entered for publication in the Stationers' Register on 26 May 1595. George Bryan was the first of the original sharers to leave the company, probably in 1596. The appearance of his name in a list of Grooms of the Chamber in the next century suggests that the Lord Chamberlain was prepared to provide a haven for

Kemps nine daies vvonder.

Performed in a daunce from
London to Norwich.

Containing the pleasure, paines and kinde entertainment
of *William Kemp* betweene *London* and that Citty
in his late Morrice.

Wherein is somewhat set downe worth note; to reprooue
the slaunders spred of him: many things merry,
nothing hurtfull.

Written by himselfe to satisfie his friends.

LONDON
Printed by *E. A.* for *Nicholas Ling,* and are to be
solde at his shop at the west doore of Saint
Paules Church, 1600.

15 Will Kempe on his nine-day morris dance from London to Norwich.
This is the title page of his celebratory pamphlet he wrote in 1600.

his favoured household players after their retirement from the
stage. Other members of the company may have included John
Heminges and Henry Condell, who would jointly edit the Folio
edition of Shakespeare's plays in 1623, the thin man John

Sincler (Sincklo or Sinklo) and the versatile Richard Cowley. There are various views of what constituted the full complement of a professional company. William Ringler has argued for sixteen, made up of twelve adults and four boy-apprentices,[8] but the evidence of cast-lists can be differently interpreted. Richard Mansfield, for example, in a careful study of doubling, finds that 'the vast majority of Shakespeare's own plays were probably performed by a company of twelve players'.[9] Mansfield argues on aesthetic and numerological as well as economic grounds, and makes a lively case for an Elizabethan delight in doubling that was intentionally conspicuous rather than disguised. We know from the surviving plot of *The Seven Deadly Sins* (*c*. 1592) that an actor might play as many as six parts in a single play, and Mansfield's thesis is a useful warning to those who have too readily accepted Ringler's calculations. On the other hand, it is sound, practical sense to use sixteen actors if you can afford them, just as it is sound, practical sense to use twelve if the saving involved will turn loss to profit.

No records of the Chamberlain's Men's first summer season survive. The popular *Richard III* would certainly have been among the plays performed, together with revivals of some of Shakespeare's early comedies. From the fact that the students of Gray's Inn booked a performance of *The Comedy of Errors* for their Christmas revels, we can be fairly certain that it was part of the repertoire. But Shakespeare would surely have been expected to sing for his supper by providing something new. *Richard II* and *King John*, successors to the popular series of plays on English history, are likely candidates. Shakespeare was never a mass-producer of plays in the way that Henslowe's man, Thomas Dekker, was; but Dekker had not Shakespeare's earnings as actor and shareholder to fall back on. Many of the Elizabethan playwrights were improvident, but that is not to say that they were underpaid. In general, they earned more from writing than other literary men of the period. If they 'belonged' to a company, they were probably paid a retainer to ensure their loyalty. In addition, they received £6 or more when they sold a play to the actors, and were given an agreed proportion of the takings at the second or third performance.

The author's 'benefit' remained customary in the English theatre well into the nineteenth century. We do not know when, or even whether, Shakespeare was formally appointed house playwright ('ordinary poet' was a contemporary description of the post) to the Chamberlain's Men. His contract, if he had one, would not have differed greatly from that signed by Richard Brome in 1635.[10] Its stipulations were:

1   That Brome should write exclusively for the company.
2   That he should produce three plays a year. (Two is likelier in Shakespeare's case.)
3   That he should write prologues and epilogues as required.
4   That he should write new scenes for old plays.
5   That he should add songs as required.
6   That he should write inductions (prefatory scenes, normally detailing the performance context) as required.
7   That he should not allow the publication of his plays.

In return, Brome was assured a weekly salary of fifteen shillings and a benefit for each performed play. We have no record of Shakespeare's tinkering with other people's texts, other than the much debated 'Ill May-Day' scene from *Sir Thomas More*, but exclusivity, unwillingness to publish and an annual productivity of two plays characterise his working life with the Chamberlain's Men. It would be very odd if he did not take on the smaller jobs assigned to Brome, as well, but since he was so fully a member of the company, it may be that a spoken contract was sufficient to bind him.

   It would not be surprising if the first season was an uneasy one. Many of the company were old associates from the days of Lord Strange's Men, but the circumstances were new, and James Burbage was not an easy man to deal with. In October 1594, the Chamberlain's Men prevailed on their patron to write on their behalf to the Lord Mayor. His letter gives important insights into established theatrical practices:

After my hartie comendacions. Where my nowe companie of Players haue byn accustomed for the better exercise of their qualitie, & for the seruice of her Maiestie if need soe requier, to plaie this winter time within the Citye at the Crosse kayes in Gracious street. These are to requier & praye your Lo. (the time beinge such as, thankes be to god, there is nowe no danger of the sicknes) to permitt & suffer them soe to doe; The which I praie you the rather to doe for that they haue undertaken to me that, where heretofore they began not their Plaies till towards fower a clock, they will now begin at two, & haue don betwene fower and fiue, and will not use anie Drumes or trumpettes att all for the callinge of peopell together, and shalbe contributories to the poore of the parishe where they plaie accordinge to their habilities. And soe not dowting of your willingnes to yeeld hereunto, uppon theise resonable condicions, I comitt yow to the Almightie.

Few richer documents survive. We learn of a change in performance times, the anticipated duration of the afternoon's entertainment, the custom of drumming up an audience (to be avoided inside the city) and the expectation that the players will make their proper contribution to the poor of the parish; and we also learn, or can deduce, something about the relationship of the Lord Chamberlain to the city authorities. Lord Hunsdon is not pleading. He comes as close to insisting as he politely can: 'These are to requier & praye...'; '... not dowting of your willingness to...'. The tone is almost threatening. It would require a brave and defiant Lord Mayor to turn down this request from a Privy Councillor. And there is yet another challenging point in the letter. It has often been assumed that references to playing in Tudor inns are to outdoor performances in the courtyards. Why, then, move from the open-air theatre 'this winter time'? The implication, surely, is that the actors wished to move to the Cross Keys because they could play indoors there.[11] Their case would be strengthened by the Lord Chamberlain's support. As the officer responsible for Court entertainment, he would be able to imply, without needing to state, that the conditions in the great chamber of the Cross Keys would more closely approximate those in the Queen's palace. It seems unlikely that Lord Hunsdon would have supported his players so strongly if their real wish was only to escape from James Burbage to the Cross Keys courtyard.

The Chamberlain's Men performed twice at Court and once at Gray's Inn that first Christmas of their new association. The Admiral's Men performed three times at Court. No other company was called, but the balance was slightly in favour of Alleyn and his colleagues. It would no longer be so by the end of 1595. This year marked a turning-point for the Chamberlain's Men. Shakespeare probably contributed *Romeo and Juliet* and *A Midsummer Night's Dream*, two plays that confirmed his unique range and popular touch. His capacity to please audiences was no longer in doubt, and the company could face competition with confidence. The ambiguous status of professional actors becomes more manifest now: they are servants of a noble lord whilst also being fully engaged in trade on their own terms. And the competition is hotting up. In June, Henslowe added to the technical attractions of the Rose by installing a throne in the 'heavens'.[12] Later in the year, Francis Langley, probably the most cut-throat of London's theatrical speculators, began the building of the Swan, the most luxurious of the city's playhouses to date. Situated not far from the Rose, in the manor of Paris Garden, the Swan alarmed the Admiral's Men more than it did the Chamberlain's. The spread of interest in plays certainly alarmed the Lord Mayor and Aldermen. Their September petition to the Privy Council asserts that the 'profane fables' on display at 'the Theator & Bankside' are the chief cause of the 'disorders & lewd demeanors which appeer of late in young people of all degrees, as of the late stirr & mutinous attempt of those fiew apprentices and other servantes, who wee doubt not driew their infection from these & like places'. This is a wilful evasion of the economic realities of the time. The abnormally wet summer of 1594, whilst helping to restrict the spread of plague in London, inaugurated nationally a sequence of bad harvests. There was a huge increase in the price of foodstuffs during the 1590s, and no compensating increase in labourers' wages. Sunk into penury, agricultural workers took to the road, many of them arriving in London to swell the numbers of masterless men in the city. At the same time, aristocratic families were reducing their households, thereby consigning former servants to the streets. Vagrancy, already a major problem in Elizabethan England, provided ever more vivid evidence of a scandalous failure of government. The people had been stripped of their resource, the land, and all that authority did was to devise ways of punishing or restraining them. The wars against Spain provided occupation for some of the dispossessed, but tossed the weak or wounded back to the mercy of the streets; 'Elizabethan London', ventures A. L. Beier, 'sounds a great deal like twentieth-century Calcutta.'[13] The playhouses, because they continued to prosper, became convenient scapegoats for beleaguered authority, but the Privy Council took no action against them. That Christmas of 1595, the Chamberlain's Men were called to Court four times against the Admiral's twice. Since it was ultimately the Chamberlain's task to select the plays for the Queen's entertainment, we cannot discount the possibility of bias, but, old and favoured as he was, Lord Hunsdon would still not have risked incurring Elizabeth I's displeasure. By the end of 1595, his company was riding high.

The February of 1596 was freakishly sunny. It was the month appointed for the wedding of the Lord Chamberlain's granddaughter to the heir of the ancient but impoverished Berkeley family. The occasion may have been embellished by a private performance of *A Midsummer Night's Dream*. Such invitations were perks to professional players, and it would be surprising if patrons refrained from issuing them. The bride's father, heir to the Hunsdon title, had a house in the Blackfriars precinct. David Wiles goes so far as to suggest that this performance may have taken place in the former Blackfriars theatre, home of a company of boy players over the years from 1576 to 1589.[14] There is no confirmation that Shakespeare's wedding play was performed then or there, though Wiles finds ample and ingenious proof in the text itself. New work from Shakespeare for the 1596 season probably included *The Merchant of Venice* and the beginning, at least, of the first part of *Henry IV*. Antonio's marine misadventures in Venice had a significance in Elizabethan England that cannot easily be recaptured. It was an age that dignified piracy under the title of legitimate conquest in the continuing wars and skirmishes with Spain. In April, the Spaniards captured Calais, to the shame of the Lord Admiral and the Earl of Essex. In June, that failure was partially redeemed by the taking of Cadiz. There were some who saw these military escapades as useful distractions from domestic gloom, some who saw them as meretricious aids to dangerous delays in the solving of pressing problems in England. Against the interests of the powerful radical Protestant faction, of which the Earl of Essex was the flamboyant figurehead, Robert Cecil, son of the aged Lord Burghley, was appointed Principal Secretary to the Queen and Council in July, when the citizens of London were mustering against the threat of Spanish invasion. That same month, the Chamberlain's Men were dealt a blow by the death of their patron. His successor as Chamberlain, Lord Cobham, was not noted for his sympathy towards players. Furthermore, he was a descendant of the Sir John Oldcastle whom Shakespeare had vilified in *Henry IV*. We do not know the detail of demand and diplomacy that lay behind the changing of Sir John Oldcastle into Sir John Falstaff, but this was clearly a testing time for Shakespeare and his company. They were in no position to stand on principle, since they had none that would pass historical examination. Furthermore, the play was far too popular to be sacrificed to a detail of nomenclature. The real danger, in the aftermath of Lord Hunsdon's death, was that the new Lord Chamberlain would make common cause with the Lord Mayor and Corporation against the playhouses. A surviving letter from Thomas Nashe, bemoaning the 1596 threat to the 'harvest I expected by writing for the stage', refers to the actors' plight: 'howeuer in there old Lords tyme they thought there state setled, it is now so uncertayne they cannot build upon it'. Such uncertainties were common in the Elizabethan theatre, and the Chamberlain's Men – now, briefly, Lord Hunsdon's Men under the patronage of the old man's middle-aged son – met the present one with professional fortitude. Shakespeare had a more personal sadness to cope with. In August 1596, his only son Hamnet died in Stratford at the age of eleven. No recorded sense of loss remains for a biographer to quote, but it is impossible to believe that the author of the first seventeen sonnets was unaffected by the loss of his heir. The confirmation of the family coat of arms in

October is, in this context, a bitter irony. Shakespeare was probably with his wife and family that autumn, when there was a fracas over a proposed Blackfriars playhouse. James Burbage had purchased a lease on the Parliament Chamber of the dissolved monastery in February 1596, and his sons were preparing to establish it as an indoor theatre for the company. The inhabitants of the privileged precinct had organised a petition against the contamination of their enclave by common players and, worse still, rowdy audiences, and the petition was upheld. For London's adult companies, the dream of regular indoor performances in London remained unrealised for a further twelve years. It was a company of boy players who would soon take advantage of James Burbage's conversion work.

It is not until 1597 that we have our first record of Shakespeare's London accommodation, though his inclusion among rateable residents of the Bishopsgate ward refers back to the previous October. With the Chamberlain's Men at the Theatre, his residence within easy walking distance of his place of work is no surprise. The worst fears of 1596 had been swiftly allayed. If Lord Cobham bore a grudge against his predecessor's company of players, he concealed it. All four of the calls to Court during the Christmas festivities of 1596–7 were for Lord Hunsdon's Men, and they were still in favour at Shrovetide, when again they were the only company to perform for the Queen. The precise dating of the *Henry IV* plays is uncertain, but early 1597 seems an appropriate time for the completion and performance of the second part. Although historically set 200 years in the past, the events of the play have a bearing on the late and lamented Lord Hunsdon. If Henry IV had had his rebellious northern earls, Queen Elizabeth I had had hers; and Lord Hunsdon had been her victorious general in the decisive battle of 1569. It would not have been difficult for the shrewd businessmen of the company to introduce their new play as homage to their dead Lord. Lord Cobham died in March, and the Oldcastle crisis may have died with him. He was succeeded as Lord Chamberlain by the second Lord Hunsdon, so that Shakespeare's troupe recovered their old title under a new patron. Many scholars now believe that one of Lord Hunsdon's earliest decisions, with the dignity of his new office about to be enhanced by the conferral of the Order of the Garter, was to commission from Shakespeare a new play about Falstaff. The Easter investitures and the processions that preceded them became increasingly extravagant in the last years of Elizabeth's reign, as the fading Queen pasted over the cracks of Court faction with loyal pageantry, and the Garter ceremonies were second in splendour only to the Accession Day tilts. By the 1590s, as Roy Strong has amply demonstrated, 'this old Catholic order was made to represent something quite different, a band of fiercely Protestant knights bound in union to defeat the dragon of St George, now re-identified as the pope, the Beast of the Apocalypse'.[15] St George's Day, 23 April, was celebrated in towns and cities throughout England, but at Windsor it had become a chivalric cavalcade. For his installation, Lord Hunsdon rode with a train of 300, all dressed in the orange taffeta of his livery. He was accompanied by Sir Henry Lee, former grand master of the Accession Day tilts, with 200 attendants in blue, by Lord Mountjoy, whose livery was blue and purple and by Lord Howard, cousin of the Lord Admiral, whose train was also dressed in blue, though faced with 'sad sea colour green'.[16] A fit-up performance of *The Merry Wives of Windsor* may seem an incongruous complement to such grandeur, but the Elizabethans had none of the purism of the modern cultural elite. Like the theatre they patronised, Elizabethan noblemen were still participants in popular festivities and seasonal pageantry alongside chamber concerts and decorous masques. If *The Merry Wives* was first seen in closed Court on St George's Day 1597, it would soon have found its way onto the stage of the Theatre, in popular association with the two parts of *Henry IV*. While the death-rate soared nationally, the London playhouses were thriving through the early summer. In May, Shakespeare's sense of a secure future found expression in the purchase of New Place, in Stratford. The thunderbolt, when it came, took everyone by surprise.

It emanated from the Swan, so recently visited by De Witt,

and now occupied by a newly constituted company of the Earl of Pembroke's Men. After his uncertainty in the autumn of 1596, Thomas Nashe had sold to this accident-prone company a plot for a play to be called *The Isle of Dogs*. Having sold the plot, he may not have completed the play. One of Pembroke's actors, Ben Jonson, certainly took a hand in the completion. It was Jonson's first known dramatic work. He had only recently broken free of his apprenticeship to a bricklayer, initially by enlisting as a soldier in the anti-Spanish campaign in the Netherlands and then by turning player. At thirty, Nashe was five years older than Jonson and more practised in controversy. The performed version of *The Isle of Dogs* gave offence to the Privy Council and, perhaps, to the Queen herself, who can have heard about it only by report. So effective was the subsequent action to suppress the play that we have no account of its contents. It can be reasonably surmised that it contained a veiled attack on a person or persons in high authority; or, at least, that it was believed to contain such an attack. This was an age that took a sometimes malicious delight in decoding literature and painting. The Queen was herself a mistress of these cryptic games. Lord Burghley recognised and sometimes exploited her facility: 'I think never a lady besides her, nor a decipherer in the court, would have dissolved the figure to have found the sense as her Majesty hath done', he wrote in a private letter.[17] Nashe was well aware of the tendency to nose out secret meanings. He had written in *Christs Teares* (1594): 'Let one but name breade, they will interpret it to be the town of Bredan in the lowe countreyes.'[18] But forewarned was not, on this occasion, forearmed. The Privy Council's response to *The Isle of Dogs* was a threat to the whole future of the professional theatre in London:[19]

Her Maiestie being informed that there are verie great disorders committed in the common playhouses both by lewd matters that are handled on the stages and by resorte and confluence of bad people, hathe given direction that not onlie no plaies shalbe used within London or about the citty or in any publique place during this tyme of sommer, but that also those playhouses that are erected and built only for suche purposes shalbe plucked downe.

This order appears in a letter to the Justices of Middlesex and Surrey, dated 28 July 1597, and prompt, if inconsistent, action was taken. Three of Pembroke's Men were imprisoned in the Marshalsea, and probably tortured. They included Ben Jonson and Gabriel Spencer, which allows the whimsical speculation that Jonson was, for two months, a cell-mate of the man he would kill the next year. Nashe escaped the city and was given refuge in the defiant town of Yarmouth. The remnant of Pembroke's Men undertook a desperate tour of the provinces. The Chamberlain's Men, planning more deliberately, took to the road in September. They would have taken comfort from a manifestly inconsistent sentence in the Privy Council letter, ordering that 'there be no more plaies used in any publique place within three myles of the citty untill Alhalloutide next'. No one would have chosen to tour the provinces in the starvation year of 1597, but the Chamberlain's Men had reason to hope that they would be back in action in London by 1 November, Allhallows Day, despite the Privy Council's thundering threats.

In one crucial instance, the Council's orders were utterly disregarded. The Justices of Middlesex and Surrey had been instructed to 'send for the owners of the Curtayne Theatre or anie other common playhouse and injoyne them by vertue hereof forthwith to plucke downe quite the stages, gallories and roomes that are made for people to stand in, and so to deface the same as they maie not be ymploied agayne to suche use'. Nothing of the sort happened. Either the Justices did not summon the owners or the owners, perhaps in collusion with the noble patrons of the players, ignored the Justices. There were other things to occupy the attention of the city that autumn. The gossipy John Chamberlain reported to Dudley Carleton on 20 October: 'The Lord Chief Justice hath played rex of late among whores and bawds, and persecutes poor pretty wenches out of all pity and mercy.'[20] This prototype for Angelo in *Measure for Measure* was Sir John Popham, and his attempted suppression of prostitution would have deflected the County Justices from the supererogatory task of inhibiting performances at already empty playhouses. News filtering back from the Earl of Essex's disastrous expedition to the Azores would have been a further distraction. When Ben Jonson was released from the Marshalsea in early October, he found the nearby Rose and Swan still standing, and the Rose about to re-open for business, three weeks ahead of the Privy Council's Allhallows stipulation. Historians, including those whose special subject is the theatre, have often to puzzle over ways of reconciling the vigour of the Privy Council's Orders with the repeated failure to enforce them. Throughout the August of 1597, Henslowe continued to conduct theatrical business, unabashed by the threat to the Rose's very existence, and the Admiral's Men, augmented by members of the dispersed *Isle of Dogs* company, were back at the Rose after 11 October. For Cuthbert Burbage, who had inherited the Theatre when his father died in January 1597, there were different problems. His lease was up, and his landlord, Giles Allen, was obstructing its easy renewal. The Chamberlain's Men may have been forced to perform in the Curtain when they returned to London, but the troubled year came to a satisfactory end when they were called three times to Court at Christmas. The Admiral's Men were called once.

Since Christmas 1594, the honour of being commanded to perform at Court had been shared by the Chamberlain's and the Admiral's Men. No other company had been called, and this evident elevation of the two troupes over all their rivals was given clearer definition in early 1598, when the Privy Council issued licences exclusively to them. The licences themselves have disappeared, but they are referred to in a Council letter to the Master of the Revels and the County Justices, dated 19 February 1598. A third company, perhaps under the patronage of the Earl of Worcester, was performing somewhere around London, and the Council wished its displeasure to be made public:

Wee have therefore thought good to require you uppon receipt heereof to take order that the aforesaid third company may be suppressed and none suffered heereafter to plaie but those two formerlie named belonging to us, the Lord Admyrall and Lord Chamberlaine.

The two patrons are sticking their necks out in this proprietary document in a way that must have gratified and restored the two senior companies of players, but the attempt to establish a monopoly was no more successful than other restraints on theatrical activity. In the early part of 1598, for example, Oliver Woodliffe was supervising the conversion into a playhouse of the courtyard of the Boar's Head Inn in Whitechapel High Street, just outside the Aldgate. He may have been hoping to attract the Chamberlain's Men, whose tenure of the Theatre remained under threat, but his is equally likely to have been an independent enterprise. We can only guess what the Chamberlain's Men were thinking.

Shakespeare's reputation as a playwright was by now secure. The publication of good quarto editions of *Richard II* (significantly shorn of the deposition scene) and *Richard III* in 1597 may signal financial anxiety on the company's part during the enforced interruption of performances that summer. It was not until the second quartos were published in 1598 that the title-pages bore Shakespeare's name. By then, that name had also appeared in Francis Meres's idiosyncratic anthology, *Palladis Tamia*. As the first known assessment of Shakespeare's quality, Meres's uncritical enthusiasm has been endlessly quoted:

As *Plautus* and *Seneca* are accounted the best for Comedy and Tragedy among the Latines: so Shakespeare among the English is the most excellent in both kinds for the stage.

All that can be usefully said about Meres's encomium is that he supposed that he could get away with it and must, therefore, be recording an acceptable view of Shakespeare's professional status. His amateur status is celebrated, too, in *Palladis Tamia*:

As the soule of *Euphorbus* was thought to live in *Pythagoras*: so the sweet wittie soule of Ovid lives in mellifluous & hony-tongued Shakespeare, witnes his *Venus* and *Adonis*, his *Lucrece*, his sugred Sonnets among his private friends, &c.

Just who these 'private friends' were, and how Meres gained access to the sonnets, we cannot know, but it is reasonable to suppose that they included the Earl of Southampton and, perhaps through the young Earl, his greater mentor, the Earl of

Essex himself. I am confident that Shakespeare admired the Earl of Essex, though not that that admiration led to uncritical support of his actions. After the fiasco in the Azores, Essex's behaviour at Court stood out as frantic, even against a frantic background. One biographer has seen it as the possible reaction to syphilis, now entering its tertiary stage.[21] In time, the Chamberlain's Men would become openly embroiled. If they were already of Essex's faction in 1598, they would have needed to exercise their customarily cautious pragmatism. The elevation of the Lord Admiral to the Earldom of Nottingham in October 1597 had given him formal precedence over the Earl of Essex, who, despite the Queen's attempts to mollify him, read this as a deliberate snub. The two men's cordial dislike for each other dated at least from the 1596 campaigns against Spain, when the Lord Admiral took umbrage at Essex's deliberate signing of a joint report to the Queen so high that Howard could not insert his own signature above it. It is quite possible that 1598 saw the hardening of the theatrical rivalry between the Chamberlain's Men and the Admiral's (now, properly, Nottingham's) Men into clear political division. Something of the sort seems implicit in the decision taken the following year by Nottingham's Men to commission from a team of writers a play called *The true and honourable historie, of the life of Sir John Oldcastle, the good Lord Cobham*. The performance by a second company of a deliberate counter – Brecht would have called it a *Gegenstück* – to plays performed by a first company has, in its context, a political edge. It was, perhaps, after consultation with his colleagues that Shakespeare undertook the writing of *Henry V*, an overtly patriotic piece trumpeting the achievements of the King whose brief reign had been slyly incorporated in the Tudor myth. The Chamberlain's Men felt the need to affirm their loyalty to the Queen, who had angrily cuffed the Earl of Essex on the ear in July 1598. On that occasion, the infuriated Earl seemed about to draw his sword and it was the Lord Admiral who stepped between him and the Queen. However indistinct their association with the Earl of Essex may have been, the Chamberlain's Men would have found *Henry V* a tactically sound contribution to their 1598 season. Shakespeare's second play for the year was probably *Much Ado about Nothing*, with Kempe in good fooling as Dogberry.

By the end of 1598, Elizabeth I's confident authority was being slenderly maintained. An account by the German Paul Hentzner of a reception in the Presence Chamber at the summer palace in Greenwich dates from that year. Its ambiguous impression is of splendour sustained at some cost:

next came the Queen, in the 65th year of her age (as we were told), very majestic; her face oblong, fair but wrinkled; her eyes small, yet black and pleasant; her nose a little hooked, her lips narrow, and her teeth black, (a defect the English seem subject to, from their too great use of sugar); she had in her ears two pearls with very rich drops; her hair was of an auburn colour, but false; upon her head she had a small crown, reported to be made of some of the gold of the celebrated Luneburg table; her bosom was uncovered, as all the English ladies have it till they marry; and she had on a necklace of exceeding fine jewels; her hands were slender, her fingers rather long, and her stature neither tall nor low; her air was stately, her manner of speaking mild and obliging. That day she was dressed in white silk, bordered with pearls of the size of beans, and over it a mantle of black silk shot with silver threads; her train was very long, the end of it born by a marchioness ...[22]

In August 1598, Lord Burghley died, the last of the great councillors of the high Elizabethan age. His ability to *seem* to stand outside or above faction was not shared by his equally industrious son. Indeed, in the fraught atmosphere of late Elizabethan government, Robert Cecil could not have hoped to keep clear of factional disputes. The threat of Spanish invasion, perhaps through Ireland, was a continuing concern, even after the death of Philip II of Spain in September 1598. The theatres had a sensational death of their own that month. On 22 September, Ben Jonson and Gabriel Spencer fought their duel in Hoxton Fields, close to the Theatre and the Curtain. Accused of manslaughter, Jonson escaped hanging by claiming benefit of clergy,[23] but his goods were confiscated and he was branded on the base of the left thumb to ensure that he would not repeat his plea in the future. Henslowe's report to Edward Alleyn is a further illustration of the relative status of actor and playwright in the still-youthful professional theatre of the 1590s:

... sence you weare with me I have loste one of my company which hurteth me greatley that is gabrell for he is slayen in hoges den fylldes by the hands of bengemen Jonson bricklayer.

Spencer was a better actor than Jonson and, therefore, more valuable to a business manager. To be sure, 'bricklayer' Jonson was emerging as a substantial playwright, but plays were basic commodities, more easily replaced than players. To some extent, Henslowe's priorities were already old-fashioned. Shakespeare's dramatic skills were more highly prized by the Chamberlain's Men than were any individual playwright's since Marlowe by Henslowe. Even so, it was as an actor that he maintained his place in a company of players.

In the freezing winter of 1598, the Chamberlain's Men found themselves at a crisis. Giles Allen's terms for renewing the lease of the Theatre were unacceptable. The Curtain was no more than a temporary alternative, perhaps for no other reason than that its audience-capacity was too limited. A clause in James Burbage's original lease offered a possible way out. It was there specified that Burbage could 'take down and Carrie awaie ... all such buildinges and other thinges as should be builded erected or sett upp'. Such an operation was obviously hazardous, not least because, with the lease over a year expired, its legality was dubious. That it was undertaken successfully speaks volumes for the commitment of the company. At some time between their Court performance on 26 December and their reappearance there on 1 January 1599, the Theatre was dismantled, timber by timber, and carried across the frozen Thames to a plot of land on the Bankside, in the liberty of the Clink. Some, or all, of these timbers would be incorporated in the building of the Globe in the early months of 1599.

The Globe enterprise was a landmark in the history of the professional theatre. It may be that Cuthbert Burbage had to buy the participation of the actors in the dangerous scheme to transport the Theatre's timbers, or it may be that the relationship of the actor-tenants to their new landlord was one of confirmed friendship. Whatever the precise reasons, the Globe became the first playhouse to be part-owned by the actors who would perform in it. In an agreement formally

16 This section from the Visscher panorama shows the view from the top of the Globe or Bear Garden across the Thames to the towered and towering old St Paul's.

signed on 21 February 1599, the owner of the land assigned half the lease to Cuthbert and Richard Burbage and the other half to five of the Chamberlain's Men: Pope, Phillips, Heminges, Kempe and Shakespeare. It may well be that the leading actors had purchased a share in the profits of the company while it was at the Theatre, but now they were full shareholders in the whole project. The significance of the move south of the river was quickly recognised by the Admiral's Men. The Rose struggled to meet competition from the new Globe, whose repertoire included, as well as Shakespeare's plays, such runaway successes as Jonson's *Every Man in His Humour* and the anonymous *Mucedorus*. Through the second half of 1599, Henslowe was looking for building land at a safe distance from the Globe. Shakespeare's first Globe play may have been a still-auspicious one, *As You Like It*, but by September the Swiss visitor Thomas Platter was watching *Julius Caesar* there:

After dinner on the 21st of September, at about two o'clock, I went with my companions over the water, and in the strewn roof-house saw the tragedy of the first Emperor Julius with at least fifteen characters very well acted. At the end of the comedy they danced according to their custom, with extreme elegance. Two in men's clothes and two in women's gave this performance, in wonderful combination with each other.

Platter's reference to fifteen is not a reliable guide to the number of actors in the company, but the prominence he gives to the post-play jig is certainly informative. Particularly through the genius of Tarlton, the jig had developed from festival song-and-dance into a sophisticated, though frequently ribald, afterpiece. For many spectators, it was the main attraction of the afternoon and vital to the maintenance of the playhouses' contact with popular entertainment. As David Wiles has sensitively indicated, Tarlton's extraordinary success was founded on atavism. He reminded his urban audience of the anarchic peasant who was their ancestor:

The character of Tarlton's clown emerged in response to post-medieval social conditions. The majority of Tarlton's London audience must have been visitors or first-generation immigrants. Tarlton tapped spectators' anxieties about the rustic boor latent within themselves.[24]

There is no doubt, from the scattering of comments and anecdotes that survive, that Tarlton was an electric performer. In an unpublished play called *Spindle-Shank Em*, John Pilkington has pieced together these shreds of documentation to recreate the detail and impact of his style:

Maybe he'd do his drunken man act; or maybe he'd start his jig, dance a step or two, then stop dead on his heels, and speak a rhyme. And people started to laugh – and as soon as they did, he was dancing again till they stopped, so that by then he was ready with his next rhyme. And maybe he'd call out for them to shout something at him – and he'd conjure up a verse about it, in that instant. Then, when he'd got them started, he'd do his faces. And the crowd was alight! He'd start with the corners of his mouth, which were loose, and could stretch like wet leather. Then he'd stick his tongue out and wiggle it about … then the nose would start to twitch, and the squinty eyes to roll … and then: he'd turn about, shake his arse, and back towards the apron of the stage – and you'd hear them roar, thinking he'd fart at them. But instead, he'd blow a blast on his pipe, and he was off into another jig before you'd time to take breath![25]

The jig Platter saw may have included such a one-man turn, but was evidently fashioned around the conventional foursome of an adulterously inclined wife and her female servant (transvestite roles encouraging hilarity) and a duped husband and would-be adulterer. It may be that Will Kempe was the central performer. If so, it is the last glimpse we have of him with the Chamberlain's Men. I think it highly likely that the received text of *As You Like It* is a version rewritten after Kempe's departure. The original play would have had no Touchstone, a worldly-wise clown of the kind Shakespeare consistently wrote for Kempe's successor, Robert Armin. Instead, the role which now belongs to William was more substantial, giving scope for Kempe to play one of his much-loved simpletons. I agree with David Wiles that the (cut-down and renamed) role of William is a deliberate reference to *William* Kempe:

When Armin/Touchstone declares: 'It is meat and drink to me to see a clown' (v.i. 10), he reminds the audience that it is his – Armin's –

livelihood. The other clown's name – 'William' – is repeated three times, so that the audience will not miss the contrast between the departed company clown, William Kemp [sic], and the new fool/clown. The traditional simple-minded rustic clown is symbolically dismissed from the new Globe stage.[26]

Even the touch of malice was probably intentional. Having seen the company through the difficult years of 1597 and 1598, Kempe sold his share and left just as the most glorious decade in the company's history had begun. It is hard to believe that professional disputes, with Shakespeare among others, were not the real cause of his departure. The Curtain audiences had loved the jigs of their supreme jig-maker – Kempe may have returned there in the winter of 1599–1600 – but there is a strong possibility that the Chamberlain's Men voted against importing their ribaldry to the Globe. The inexorable move towards 'high' art was beginning, even before the death of Elizabeth I and the succession of the culturally proprietorial James. Kempe's subsequent career can be briefly sketched, most outstandingly in his famous Morris dance to Norwich during the 1600 closure of the London theatres for Lent. He recorded that trip himself, revealing an enviable gift for self-advertisement. Probably he took on the promised challenge of dancing across the Alps to Italy before returning to London as one of the Earl of Worcester's Men at the Boar's Head playhouse. He may also have made the German tour, so profitable to English clowns. However tempting it may be to speculate on a career in decline once he had parted with Shakespeare, the greater likelihood is that Kempe broke free from restrictions in leaving the Chamberlain's Men, and spent his last years as a triumphant representative of carnival jollity. We do not know whether he is the 'Kempe, a man' who was buried in Southwark on 2 November 1603.

Censorship of literature reached a new extremity in June 1599, when John Whitgift was in his seventeenth year as Archbishop of Canterbury. By a Star Chamber decree of 1586, only the Archbishop and the Bishop of London had the power to license the publication of books. The formalities were rarely observed, but the right remained, and in ordering the burning

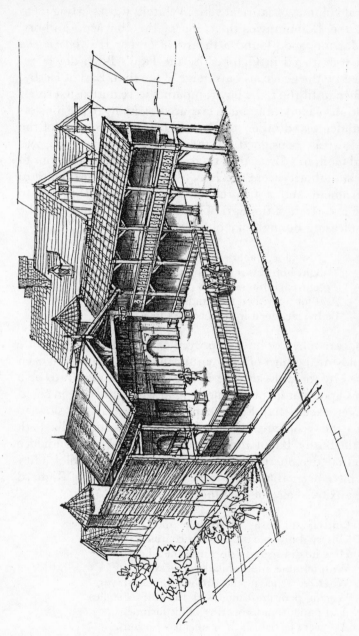

17 C. Walter Hodges has here proposed a reconstruction of the Boar's Head into a permanent playhouse. Compare the earlier stage illustrated on page 56.

of several volumes of satirical verse, Whitgift was asserting it 'to protect the Commonwealth'. One of the 'burned' authors, John Marston, soon found a theatrical outlet. His *Antonio and Mellida* was staged in October by the Paul's Boys, newly re-activated by the generous patronage of the sixth Earl of Derby. From then until 1607, the boy companies were mistrusted rivals of the adult players, and much favoured by many of the inns-of-court students and other privileged playgoers. Another of the satirical works consigned to the flames in June 1599 was Everard Guilpin's *Skialetheia* (1598), whose frequent allusions to figures in authority were precisely of the kind to give offence to a government and a Church on the defensive. We owe to Guilpin a portrait of the Earl of Essex which links him with the crowd-pleasing Bolingbroke of Shakespeare's *Richard II*:

> Signior Machiavel
> Taught him this mumming trick, with courtesy
> To entrench himself with popularity,
> And for a writhen face and body's move
> Be barracadoed in the people's love.[27]

Shakespeare may not have approved of the political uses made of his play at the turn of the century, but he cannot have been surprised by them. Essex, like Bolingbroke, was known to be a courter of popular favour, something at which the Queen could no longer excel; and Essexite propaganda was not slow to compare the sycophantic counsellors who surrounded Elizabeth I with the Bushy, Bagot and Green of long ago. For an audience of habitual decipherers, the parallels were irresistible. They would have been able to hear, in the jealous words of Richard II, the anxious voice of the Queen:

> Ourself and Bushy, Bagot here and Green
> Observ'd his courtship to the common people,
> How he did seem to dive into their hearts
> With humble and familiar courtesy,
> What reverence he did throw away on slaves,
> Wooing poor craftsmen with the craft of smiles
> And patient underbearing of his fortune,
> As 'twere to banish their affects with him.

Off goes his bonnet to an oyster-wench;
A brace of draymen bid God speed him well,
And had the tribute of his supple knee,
With 'Thanks, my countrymen, my loving friends';
As were our England in reversion his,
And he our subjects' next degree in hope.   (I.iv.23–36)

Elizabeth I's famous comment to William Lambarde, after the collapse of the Earl of Essex's rebellion, 'I am Richard II, know ye not that?', has been generally half-understood. The Queen was fearful, certainly, of attempts to depose her, but she was also aware of the common slander that she surrounded herself, like Richard II, with pampered favourites. That, she was explaining to Lambarde, is what people say of me. In courtly parlance, to be a 'King Richard II's man' was to be a deceiving flatterer, a parasite at Court. Sir Francis Knollys, writing as long ago as January 1578 about the Queen's sequestration of Edmund Grindal, gave his view that 'if the bishop of Canterbury shall be deprived, then up starts the pride and practice of the papists. And then King Richard the Second's men will flock into Court apace and will show themselves in their colours.'[28] Shakespeare's *Richard II* was political dynamite, not only because of the deposition scene, but because it permitted Essexites to debate the dangers of a Court crammed with evil counsellors. Essex himself had been despatched to Ireland in March 1599, to tame the rebellious Earl of Tyrone. In direct defiance of the Queen's instructions, he there appointed the Earl of Southampton his Master of Horse and knighted eighty of his men during the inglorious campaign that ended in September with a surrender masquerading as a truce. The story of the Earl of Essex's headlong ride to justify himself to Elizabeth I at Nonsuch Palace, their confrontation in her bedchamber and the two subsequent audiences prior to his year-long house arrest has all the excesses of a historical melodrama, played out by the country's two leading actors. That Christmas, the Earl of Southampton divided his time between sympathetic residence near his imprisoned mentor at Essex House and regular visits to plays. Public sympathy for the fallen Earl grew dangerously strong, despite conciliatory statements from the Privy Council.

Amid the turmoil, the Chamberlain's Men performed twice at Court, as did Nottingham's Men, and then again at Shrovetide, this time sharing the honour with the Earl of Derby's Men from the Boar's Head in Whitechapel. So quickly had the Privy Council forgotten its determination to restrict the number of licensed theatre companies to two.

By 1600, Shakespeare had been living for some time in the liberty of the Clink, close to the Globe. His literary status had been dubiously celebrated on the title page of *The Passionate Pilgrim*, an anthology of amatory poems probably gathered and certainly published in 1599 by William Jaggard. It contains two of Shakespeare's sonnets and several poems identifiably not his. *England's Parnassus* (1600), a commonplace book of quotations collected by Robert Allot, contains ninety-five excerpts from Shakespeare's work, less than a quarter of Spenser's 386 and less than a half of Drayton's 225, but more than any other writer whose professional interest was in the drama. Shakespeare had a hand in neither publication. He may, though, have approved and advised on the tolerable quarto versions of *A Midsummer Night's Dream*, *The Merchant of Venice*, *Henry IV Part Two* and *Much Ado about Nothing* that were published in 1600. This unprecedented resort to print is hard to interpret. The Chamberlain's Men sometimes tried to forestall illicit publication by recording a title in the Stationers' Register, but they would normally release a playhouse copy only to provide a corrected version of a text previously published in mangled form. There was small point in publishing a play that had no audience appeal; but why risk diminishing that audience appeal by publishing it? Do the 1600 publications indicate a company decision to sell Shakespeare's plays because of a falling away of audiences at the Globe? And if so, was the decline associated in any way with the company's known, or suspected, affiliation to the Essex party. The Earl's fall from grace can have done nothing for their confidence. If *Henry V* was still in the repertoire, it would have been played with a section of the Act Five chorus judiciously cut. The passage, originally inserted for a summer performance in 1599, compares Henry's triumphant return to London after the Battle of Agincourt with

the welcome that would surely greet Essex's victorious return
from Ireland:

> But now behold
> In the quick forge and working-house of thought,
> How London doth pour out her citizens,
> The mayor and all his brethren in best sort,
> Like to the senators of the antique Rome,
> With the plebeians swarming at their heels,
> Go forth and fetch their conquering Caesar in:
> As, by a lower but loving likelihood,
> Were now the general of our gracious empress –
> As in good time he may – from Ireland coming,
> Bringing rebellion broached on his sword,
> How many would the peaceful city quit
> To welcome him! much more, and much more cause,
> Did they this Harry.

However qualified by references to 'our gracious empress' and
by insistence that Henry V's triumph was incomparably
greater, these lines, when spoken in the Globe, were designed as
a rallying cry to elicit cheers from admirers of the Earl of Essex:
and there is no getting away from the fact that Essex is
compared to a King of England. Statements much less overt
had been 'deciphered' as *lèse majesté* in Elizabethan England.
Just how close the group of plays from *Richard II* to *Henry V* may
have come to constituting a career crisis for Shakespeare and the
Chamberlain's Men can be illustrated by the fate of Dr John
Hayward. In February 1599, Hayward published his *First part
of the life and reign of King Henry the IIII*, with an ecstatic Latin
dedication to the Earl of Essex. Its principal subject was the
deposition and death of Richard II, and it is unlikely that the
book would have proved so popular or been thought so
dangerous had it not invited its readers to draw contemporary
parallels. By the standards of the time, Hayward was a serious
enough historian, concerned, as Shakespeare was, to instruct
through historical precedent and not scrupling to borrow
sentences from other writers or to allocate to the period under
his scrutiny events that he knew to have happened in other
periods. When the book was published, Essex was not evidently

out of favour. Sixteen months later, with the Earl confined to York House, Hayward was questioned by the Star Chamber and imprisoned in the Tower of London under suspicion of treason. He remained there for nearly a year in constant fear of execution. He was almost exactly the same age as Shakespeare and his 'crime' was to have written about Richard II and Bolingbroke in such a way as to allow analogies to be drawn. Just how differently placed was Shakespeare?

The Chamberlain's Men had lost William Kempe and replaced him with Robert Armin, not a people's clown but a philosophical fool with musical skills and an actor's ability to disguise himself a little in the part he was playing. The shift in Shakespeare's comic characters from Dogberry to Feste, from clown to fool, marks the differences between Kempe and Armin. *Twelfth Night* almost certainly belongs to the 1600–1 season. Leslie Hotson's eccentric proposal that it was first played before the Queen on Twelfth Night in 1601 retains much of its attraction nearly forty years after it was first made,[29] but the play must, I think, have had a public airing in 1600. In March 1600, the company performed for their patron at his request *Henry IV* (Part 2, I suspect, for reasons already indicated), when he entertained the Flemish Ambassador at his home. That summer, the Privy Council again gave instructions that the number of playhouses be restricted to two, this time adding that the number of playing days per week be restricted to two, also. No one took any notice. Henslowe and Alleyn met some local resistance to their plans to build a new playhouse to be called the Fortune, just north of the Cripplegate in the liberty of Finsbury, but they received local support in equal measure. By November 1600, the new house was ready for occupation by the Earl of Nottingham's (Admiral's) Men. The Fortune was built square, a first exception to the polygonal style of the Globe and its predecessors, but its inner dimensions were modelled on those of the Globe. The contract calls for three galleries and a covered stage, forty-three feet by about twenty-five feet, with gentlemen's rooms and twopenny galleries of the kind already in use at the Globe. There is no information about access to the stage, which leaves the two wide doors recorded in the De

Witt/Van Buchell drawing of the Swan as our only visual evidence on this crucial matter. Nor is there any mention of an upper area, or 'above', for use by the actors, an amenity called for in many stage directions of the period. We would no longer expect reference to an 'inner stage', an amenity invented by theatre historians unable to envisage a stage without a proscenium frame somewhere on it. It is the lack of detail on the number and dimensions of the doors that led from the tiring-house onto the platform that is the saddest deficiency.

With the opening of the Fortune, London's theatreland had reached its final Elizabethan state. Regularly active amphitheatres numbered three – the Globe for the Chamberlain's Men south of the river, the Fortune for the Earl of Nottingham's Men north of the city wall and the Boar's Head for the Earl of Derby's and then the Earl of Worcester's Men to the east of the wall. Inside the city stood two indoor playhouses, one in a building adjoining St Paul's Cathedral and used by the Paul's Boys, the other in the Blackfriars Parliament Chamber, sub-leased from Richard Burbage for the Children of the Revels. Still standing, but used erratically for the performance of plays, were the Curtain in Shoreditch and the Rose and the Swan on the Bankside. The Newington theatre had probably been demolished at some time during the 1590s.

For the Chamberlain's Men, the year 1601 began in deceptive calm. They were called to perform at Court on St Stephen's Day and Twelfth Night. The Earl of Essex was not in the audience. Although set free, he had been banned from Court. Always extravagant, he was now impoverished, and surrounded by friends in the same condition. It was an open grievance for all of them that they had lost their wealth in the Queen's service. Dependent on Crown patronage for their income, they now found themselves without either. The situation was impossibly galling for the Earl of Essex, whom many people at home and abroad looked to as the leader of radical Protestantism in England. There was, indeed, a devout element in his complex make-up, but it was as a political malcontent that he now assembled what amounted to a court-in-exile to which even Catholics could buy access with a grievance. The Earl's loyalty

18 John de Critz the Elder's portrait of the Earl of Southampton and cat in the Tower of London.

to his Queen remained a boasted possession. Only in the heat of the moment would he have questioned the political dogma that the monarch could do no wrong, and it was not the Queen who was now the object of his hatred but her evil counsellors, her 'King Richard's Men' – Robert Cecil, Walter Raleigh, the new Lord Cobham. Essex could persuade himself that his true object should be not to *depose* the Queen, but to save her and, by doing so, to save the country. It was his destiny to be the leader of an English revival. The month of January was spent in desultory plotting against a confused background of patriotism and poverty. Bluster and Dutch courage both abounded, and it is unclear when brave words moved the malcontents decisively towards action. The moment may have come when a small group of Essexites took a wherry across the Thames to attend a performance at the Globe on the afternoon of Friday 6 February. Their request, backed up with an offer of £2 guarantee against loss, that the Chamberlain's Men stage a revival of *Richard II* the next day was not, surely, a spur-of-the-moment inspiration, but it marked out the point of no return. It was part of the complex sign-making of Elizabethan domestic politics. But why did the Chamberlain's Men accede to the request? The possibility of an armed uprising was concealed from them, no doubt, but to present Shakespeare and his colleagues as innocent victims of aristocratic duplicity would be to defy belief. Shakespeare, even if he did not know the detail of Dr Hayward's fate, was well aware of the Court's sensitivity to the whole subject of Richard II's reign. The agreement to stage the play on Saturday 7 February was an open statement by a company of players that they supported the maligned Earl of Essex. When, on Sunday 8 February, Essex's discontent broke out into rebellion, such support was no longer easily distinguishable from treason. What actually happened was a fiasco, although it is possible that, had the Earl led his small force against the ill-protected Court instead of riding the opposite way into the city to rally the popular support he had been promised, the outcome would have been very different. In the event it was Essex's old enemy the Earl of Nottingham, patron of the Admiral's Men, who accepted the surrender of the noble rebels.

While the Earl of Essex languished in the Tower, in the company of the Earl of Southampton and with spiritual comfort provided by his Puritan chaplain, what was the condition of the Chamberlain's Men? Some of them were subjected to questioning, perhaps to torture – Shakespeare may, I suppose, have

skipped town to avoid being one – and the deposition of
Augustine Phillips was among the evidence assembled for the
Earl's trial. Phillips was, perhaps, a good enough actor to get
away with his disingenuous plea that the actors 'were determined to have played some other play, holding that play of
King Richard to be so old and so long out of use that they should
have small or no company at it', but were persuaded by the
inducement of forty shillings. No one asked him to explain how
they could stage, within twenty-four hours, a play that,
according to his own deposition, was no longer in the repertoire.
His answer to that question would have had to be clever; and it
might, furthermore, have provided us with valuable insights
(however garbled by special pleading) into playhouse practices.
The Earl of Essex's behaviour in captivity was erratic. He had
burned incriminating documents before his arrest, and at his
trial, on 19 February 1601, confined himself to wayward self-
justification and loyal acceptance of his fate. Only after he had
been sentenced, and only in pious discourse with his chaplain,
did he betray his associates, virtually condemning to death each
man as he named him. It was the Queen who decided the fate
of the Chamberlain's Men. Her witty punishment was to
pardon them and to summon them to perform at Court on 24
February, the day before Essex's execution. They had performed for the Earl on the eve of his rebellion. Let them now
perform for her on the eve of his death. No actor in England had
a better sense of theatrical timing than the old Queen.

The rebellion, though, had hit her hard. She had a little over
two years to live, and her skittishness, if it ever had been
attractive, was no longer so. Sir John Harington, one of Essex's
Irish knights and godson to the Queen, ventured to Court in the
autumn of 1601 In a letter to a friend, he described his
godmother's continuing reaction to the Earl's defection and
death. Harington was, inevitably, a partial observer, but
Elizabeth's erratic behaviour in her sad last years is well
attested:

I feared her Majesty more than Tyrone, and wished I had never
received my Lord of Essex's honour of knighthood. She is quite
disfavoured and unattired, and these troubles waste her much. She

disregardeth every costly cover, and taketh little but manchet and succory pottage. Every new message from the City doth disturb her, and she frowns on all the ladies. I had a sharp message from her, brought by my Lord Buckhurst namely thus: *Go, tell that witty fellow, my godson, to get home; it is no season now to fool it here.* I liked this as little as she doth my knighthood, so took to my boots and returned to the plough in bad weather. I must not say much even by this trusty and sure messenger, but the many evil plots and designs have overcome all her Highness's sweet temper. She walks much in her Privy Chamber, and stamps with her feet at ill-news, and thrusts her rusty sword at times into the arras in great rage. My Lord Buckhurst is much with her, and few else since the City business. But the dangers are over, and yet she always keeps a sword by her table.[30]

'It is no season now to fool it here' has a Shakespearean ring, and the association of the Earl of Essex with the city of London indicates the Queen's increasing sense of alienation from her subjects. In her vigorous days, she would have met it with a self-assertive Royal Progress. Now she was too tired. It was not to thrusting young courtiers that she turned, but to men like the Earl of Nottingham and her ageing Lord Treasurer, Buckhurst, a last link with the years of Burghley's guidance. It had been a supple juggling act to contain faction by keeping the question of the succession unsettled during the early decades of her reign; by the end, it was exclusively a source of political tension. The politics of succession determine the events of the play Shakespeare may have written in the months following the Essex rebellion, *Hamlet*. The claims that he was uniquely disengaged from the tumults of contemporary politics cannot be sustained, although it is true that, unlike Marlowe and Jonson, he rarely burned his fingers. His detachment from the ill-tempered 'war of the poets', in which Jonson, Marston, Dekker and others were engaged between 1599 and 1602 suggests a distaste for professional quarrels, but even a yearning for peace was a political act during the succession crisis.

Shakespeare was no less conscious than his fellow-professionals of the particular challenge mounted by the boy companies, to which he famously alludes in *Hamlet*. There is an unmistakable fastidiousness in the dialogue about the boys between Rosencrantz and Hamlet (II.ii.361–87). It is as if

Shakespeare is trying, but failing, to understand what all the fuss is about, whilst at the same time appealing, on behalf of the company, for help from the spectators in the Globe to bring back the deluded boy-lovers who have abandoned the adult players. The popularity of *Hamlet* must have meant a lot to the Chamberlain's Men at a time when their morale was under threat. Shakespeare incorporates them in his play as the visiting players from the city, paying a delicate tribute to their versatility and skills as he does it. It is generous, even touching, and professionally apt. There is some uncharacteristic self-assessment in all this. I have a strong impression that 1601 was a year in which Shakespeare took stock of his career so far. The death of his father in September would have enforced some reflection. For one thing, it made him rich, by contemporary standards. His inheritance would have included the double house in Henley Street as well as some of the substantial agricultural holdings that John Shakespeare maintained to the end.

By the end of 1601, the Chamberlain's Men had recovered whatever ground they lost at the beginning of the year. They were called three times to Court that Christmas and probably performed for their patron when he entertained the Queen in his Blackfriars residence on 31 December. We have no record of what was staged on any of these occasions. The difficulties of dating Shakespeare's plays in the period from 1600 to 1605 are considerable. *Troilus and Cressida*, which probably belongs to 1602, is a particularly puzzling case. It was, according to an anonymous preface in the 1609 Quarto edition, 'a new play, never stal'd with the Stage, never clapper-clawd with the palmes of the vulgar'. The sentence certainly contains one lie – *Troilus and Cressida* was entered in the Stationers' Register six years before this edition was published – and probably contains two, but the abundance of legalistic debate in the text has encouraged some scholars to propose that it was prepared specially for performance in one of the inns of court. It would run strangely counter to Shakespeare's professional practice if *Troilus and Cressida* were confined to a single private performance, but it is possible that the play failed to attract either the Chamberlain's Men or their audience. It has no easy theatrical charm and few roles for virtuoso actors. If *All's Well that Ends Well* was also in the making in 1602, we can speculate that Shakespeare's usual facility in the penning of plays was temporarily halted. It was at about this time that he moved from the Bankside to the north-west area of the city, to lodge with a Huguenot wigmaker called Christopher Mountjoy. In May he made his purchase of 100 acres of arable land in Old Stratford. To try to make too much of these transactions is risky, but speculation is excusable. An actor would certainly think twice before putting a maze of city streets and the expanse of the Thames between himself and his place of work. Was it at this time that Shakespeare ceased to act, on a regular basis at least? And if so, was it because he was hoping to spend more time in Stratford now that his elder daughter was well into her marriageable years? He was fast turning her into a bourgeois heiress and could hardly be blamed for wanting to be on the spot to vet her suitors. He cannot have earned less than £250 per annum from his income as a sharer in the Globe, a playwright and a property owner. It must, at the very least, have been a temptation to divide his year more equitably between London and Stratford.

Despite her failing health, the Queen commanded a full round of Christmas entertainments in 1602. The Chamberlain's Men were called to perform on St Stephen's Day and again on 2 February, during the last Shrovetide celebrations of the old reign. The atmosphere at the Court, as the imminence of the Queen's death could no longer be doubted, is vividly, and no more than a little fancifully, recorded in the *Memoirs* of the Lord Chamberlain's brother, Robert Carey. It was he who made the amazing ride to Scotland in the desperate hope of mending his fortunes by being the first to inform James VI of the Queen's death. From Carey's account emerges a last cameo of Elizabethan England. The Queen lies on her deathbed, with one hand under the covers and the other free to make whatever feeble signs she wishes. She has lost her power of speech, but 'signed' for the Archbishop of Canterbury to be sent to her. And so old John Whitgift, who will himself be dead within a year, kneels beside her to pray until his knees are weary. Then he blesses her and makes to rise. But no, the Queen wants him to keep praying:

He did so for a long half hour after, and then thought to leave her. The second time she made sign to have him continue in prayer. He did so for half an hour more ...[31]

More than anything else, it was the efficiency of Robert Cecil's scheming and the rapidity with which he put his plans into action that averted the threat of civil wars. The major professional impact on the Chamberlain's Men of the Queen's passing was in the style of patronage favoured by the new King. Assessment of that change will necessitate a step back before we can go forward to Shakespeare's end.

CHAPTER 6

Of Queen, Chamberlains, Admiral and King

In a supremely ill-judged couplet of his elegy for the Queen, *Englands Mourning Garment* (1603), Henry Chettle urges Shakespeare to:

> remember our Elizabeth,
> And sing her rape done by that Tarquin death.

It is, perhaps, surprising that no gracious tribute from Shakespeare survives. He was greatly in the dead Queen's debt, not only because of her direct patronage, but also for the implicit support given to the idea of a theatre by the whole manner of her reign. The cult of Elizabeth was founded on the theatrical metaphor expounded by Jaques in *As You Like It* ('all the world's a stage') and illustrated on the flag that flew over the Globe during performances there. The legend beneath its picture of Hercules carrying the world was 'Totus mundus agit histrionem' (all the world acts the actor). It is a metaphor that pervades Lacey Baldwin Smith's elegant biography, *Elizabeth Tudor* (1976):

The entire production – lighting, props, lines, cast and even censorship – was directed to a single dramatic end: the illusion of majesty by which to captivate an entire kingdom ... no aspect of the Queen's performance is better documented than her unerring dramatic instinct for displaying her majesty ... the hours that went into producing the apparently effortless rhetoric that transformed autocracy into majesty and wrapped it in a mantle of mystification so rich and colourful that no one could say exactly what she meant but everybody agreed it was worth listening to.[1]

Elizabeth was wholly conscious of the aptness of the metaphor: 'We Princes are set as it were upon stages in the sight and view of the world' was her own comment. One French Ambassador observed that 'She is a prince who can act any part she pleases.' Inevitably, she inspired histrionic competition. Mary, Queen of Scots reminded the judges at her trial that 'the theatre of the world is wider than the realm of England', and she would have been pleased to perceive in the Spanish invasion of 1588 a fitting dramatic sequel to her own execution. She was not the last British monarch to die inside the metaphor. It is as a 'Royal Actor' that Andrew Marvell presents Charles I at his beheading in 'An Horatian Ode upon Cromwel's return from Ireland'. Peter Levi, referring to the impoverished theatricality of Court life after the death of the last Tudor, calls Charles I's execution 'the only Stuart masque in which something really happened'.[2] But it was not only with fellow-monarchs that Elizabeth competed. Her courtiers were performers too, familiar with Seneca's much-quoted observation that 'it is with life as it is with a play – it matters not how long the action is spun out, but how good the acting is'. Sir Walter Raleigh, who described the Court as the great theatre of the kingdom, was one of its most accomplished actors, with a characteristic concern for costume well enshrined in the cloak-and-puddle legend. Courtiers played their parts in carefully selected clothes; jewelled hats, white satins, tawny velvets, orange taffetas. And the Queen, who liked to keep them strutting in their plumes and finery, contemplated her competing peacocks with the sceptical eye of a chameleon.

The performance of drama *at* Elizabeth's Court was part of the drama *of* Elizabeth's Court. Like the courtiers, the actors were dependent on their sovereign not only for their financial survival, but also for the simple ability to continue functioning. If Elizabeth I had shown no more interest in plays and the whole ceremony of courtly performance than have many of her successors, the London theatres would certainly have been closed and the household players dispersed. As it was, the actors brought sufficient prestige to their noble patrons to compensate for the accompanying risk of displeasure or even disgrace. A

19 The Procession portrait places the godlike Queen above her subjects. Among the easily identified are the bald-headed Earl of Worcester, standing closest of all to us, the viewers, and the line of three who lead the eye from the chair of state off to the left of the picture: the round-faced Earl of Cumberland, the second Lord Hunsdon, holding the hilt of his sword with his left hand and the Chamberlain's staff of office in his right and the already-aged Lord Admiral glancing back with hand on hip.

proper concern with the rise and social significance of the 'common' player should not blind us to the alternative prospects of the 'courtly' player. In the event, these prospects were insufficient to split the profession, but that cannot have seemed inevitable in the 1590s. More than anything else, it was the poverty of the Queen and her nobles that inhibited the development of a Court theatre in England. Ironically, it was not only the cost of wars and the inadequacies of the land laws that emptied aristocratic pockets, but also the constant demand for conspicuous expenditure on highly theatrical displays. Responsibility for the mundane and ceremonial well-being of the Court rested primarily with the three senior household officials, the Lord Chamberlain (an office distinct from that of the largely functionless Lord Great Chamberlain, hereditarily the possession of the Earls of Oxford), the Lord Steward and the Master of the Queen's Horse. The significance of the last of these three was greatly enhanced, not only by the taste for tournaments, but also by the illustriousness of Elizabeth's appointees, in 1559 Robert Dudley, soon to become Earl of Leicester, and in 1590 Robert Devereux, Earl of Essex. The Lord Steward carried the responsibility for life below stairs: kitchen, scullery, buttery, cellar, bakehouse, laundry and so on. As chief adviser to the Chamberlain, he might also hope to be consulted on the more eye-catching activities in the upstairs 'Chamber'. This fact is of particular interest in the period under review here because the Lords Steward were successively the Earl of Leicester (1585–8), the Earl of Derby (1588–93) and, after nearly four years without a formally appointed Steward, the Lord Admiral, now Earl of Nottingham (1597–1615). In other words, three of the five leading professional theatre companies of Elizabeth I's reign, Leicester's Men, Strange's Men and the Admiral's Men, could have been guaranteed support for selection to play at Court from the Lord Steward of the day. The other two would not have needed it, since one was under the direct patronage of the Queen and the other under that of the Lord Chamberlain. The Chamberlain was ultimately responsible for all Court ceremonies and entertainments, as well as for the routines of daily conduct, although he was assisted by

Masters of the Revels, Tents, Robes, Jewels etc. and Grooms of
the Privy Chamber and Bedchamber. Elizabeth's Chamberlains
were, successively, the first Lord Howard of Effingham (1558–
72), Thomas Howard, third Earl of Suffolk (1572–83), whose
company of players briefly flourished during his period of office,
the second Lord Howard of Effingham (1583–5, later Lord
High Admiral and Earl of Nottingham as well as Lord
Steward), the first Lord Hunsdon (1585–96), Lord Cobham
(1596–7) and the second Lord Hunsdon (1597–1603).

It has become customary to measure the status of Elizabethan
theatre companies by the frequency of their appearances at
Court; but it is hard not to raise an eyebrow when you compare
a list of named companies with a list of the current officers of the
royal household. E. K. Chambers's Court Calendar for the five-
year period from Christmas 1597 to Shrovetide 1603, when
Lord Hunsdon was Chamberlain and the Lord Admiral was
Steward, lists forty-three visits to Court by troupes of players.
The division of the spoils makes provocative reading:

Chamberlain's Men	18
Admiral's Men	14
Derby's Men	3
Worcester's Men	1
Hertford's Men	1

The remaining six are Boy Companies, the Children of the
Chapel Royal (4) and the Boys of St Paul's (2).[3] We will never
know whether quality of performance was the *only* criterion for
selection, but we have reason to note again the closeness and
interdependence of the Queen's courtiers. It may have been to
raise the standard of acting and staging that the Queen
instructed Edmund Tilney, Master of the Revels, to 'choose out
a companie of players for her maiestie'. The Queen's Men,
spearheaded by the outrageous talent of Richard Tarlton, were
dominant from 1583 until Tarlton's death in 1588, but quickly
faded after that. I find it surprising that they were permitted to
retain a formal title to royal patronage for the remaining years
of the Queen's life, and can only assume that their provincial

tours were considered an acceptable embassy to parts of the country that Elizabeth I rarely or never saw fit to visit.[4] Their place at the top was taken by Lord Strange's Men and by those of the Lord Admiral; only after 1594 by the new company of which Shakespeare was part and whose influential patron was Lord Hunsdon. Since it is one of the aims of this book to give theatrical patronage its due, we should pay some attention to this man.

Henry Carey was born in about 1524 and was, through his mother Mary Boleyn, first cousin to Queen Elizabeth. Because Mary Boleyn was one of Henry VIII's mistresses, it has to be recognised that the relationship might have been even closer. The Queen had other near relatives, but Carey was one of the few who never gave her cause to worry. No one ever proposed him as a serious rival claimant to the throne, and the young Elizabeth's confidence in him was quickly expressed when she created him Lord Hunsdon in 1559. In the Whitehall joust of that year (5 November), he shared with Robert Dudley the honour of being the Queen's appointed challenger. His determined opposition to Dudley, after the favourite's elevation to the Earldom of Leicester, had not yet declared itself. It would mark him out as a man capable of fearless independence, somewhat tarnished by envy. Hunsdon House was in Hertfordshire, and it may have been there that Carey assembled his first company of players in about 1564, the year of Shakespeare's birth. It seems probable that James Burbage was a member of Hunsdon's Men during these early years, perhaps until the company was disbanded on its patron's appointment as Warden of the East Marches and Governor of Berwick-upon-Tweed in 1568. It was this appointment that led to his one moment of undoubted glory. The 1569 rebellion of the Northern Earls was, despite the panic it caused in London, a tepid affair. The only military engagement of note was that in which Hunsdon's army defeated the troops of Leonard Dacre. Hunsdon's skills as a general were rarely tested and never proved thereafter, but this single victory allowed him a reputation as a soldier which he never relinquished. It is this achievement that Spenser celebrates in a dedicatory sonnet to *The Faerie Queen*:

> Here eke of right have you a worthie place,
>   Both for your nearnes to that Faerie Queene,
>   And for your owne high merit in like cace,
>   Of which, apparaunt proofe was to be seene,
> When that tumultuous rage and fearfull deene
>   Of Northerne rebels ye did pacify,
>   And their disloiall powre defaced clene,
>   The record of enduring memory.

Like many an old soldier, Hunsdon grumbled at the military incompetence of the Earl of Sussex and of Sussex's successor as Lord President of the North, the Earl of Huntingdon. Even his appointment as Lord Chamberlain in 1585 was insufficient to reassure Hunsdon that he was adequately valued. Writing to Lord Burghley in 1587, he protested at his appointment as the Earl of Huntingdon's Lieutenant in the North:

I have been her majesty's lieutenant myself, when I should a gone to win Edinburgh castle, and now to be a lieutenant under one that never saw any service, nor knows in any respect what appertains to be a captain, much less to be a lieutenant, I am offered greater wrong than I did think would a been offered me by that lord: but I perceive it is a great matter to be an earl.[5]

The accents are those of a cantankerous Fluellen rather than of a dignified officer of the royal household. Sir Robert Naunton's brief description of Hunsdon's character fills out the picture:

he was a fast man to his Prince, and firm to his friends and servants; and though he might speak big, and therein would be born out, yet was he not the more dreadfull, but lesse harmfull, and far from the practise of my Lord of *Leicesters* instructions, for he was down-right; and I have heard those that both knew him well, and had interest in him, say merrily of him, that his Latine and his dissimulation were both alike: and that his custome of swearing, and obscenity in speaking, made him seem a worse Christian than he was, and a better Knight of the Carpet than he should be: As he lived in a ruffling time, so he loved sword and buckler men, and such as our Fathers were wont to call men of their hands; of which sort, he had many brave Gentlemen that followed him; yet not taken for a popular and dangerous person.[6]

Here is a portrait of a courtier who is neither a people's favourite nor a flattering 'King Richard's man', foul-mouthed among men, but with a well-known eye for the ladies (a Knight of the Carpet). He was certainly sexually active. As well as his ten legitimate children, he fathered several bastards, one of whom became Bishop of Exeter, with the emended west-country surname of Carew. For A. L. Rowse, much the most significant of his extra-marital relationships was that with the musical Emilia Lanier, whom Rowse considers indisputably 'the dark lady of the sonnets'. It is also his view that the child Emilia bore in 1593 was Lord Hunsdon's. The Chamberlain was then in his seventieth year. No wonder Rowse calls him 'a very masculine type'.[7]

Only a hunger for recognition would have reconciled this military hero (he was appointed Commander of the Queen's Bodyguard in the Armada year of 1588) to the domesticities of the Chamberlainship, but he seems to have taken the ceremonial side of the job, at least, seriously. He supported his own players in their disputes with the city authorities and was a constant friend at Court for London's professional companies. Unusually among Elizabeth's courtiers, he grew richer in office, shrewdly exploiting his powers of patronage and husbanding his granted monopolies on the inspection of soap and the barrelling of butter for transport into and out of London. He was able to live well, with a London residence at Somerset House in addition to the family home in Hertfordshire. As a provincial grandee, he speculated in land; as a Londoner, he speculated in property. Early in her reign, Elizabeth I granted him the Paris Garden manor, which brought him a tidy income from licence-fees for the Bankside brothels. Hunsdon's own venereal reputation may have been well earned. It was probably to receive the painful mercury treatment for syphilis that he became a patient of the brilliant quack, Simon Forman. His interests in Paris Garden brought him into direct contact with Francis Langley, the least attractive of Elizabethan theatrical speculators. It was Hunsdon's sale, or farming out, of the manor to Langley that enabled the building of the Swan. There is no evidence that Hunsdon himself was involved in the playhouse's construction, but he was certainly associated with James Burbage in the negotiations for an indoor playing-space at the Blackfriars. On becoming Lord

Chamberlain in 1585, Hunsdon had taken over from the playwright John Lyly the two leases on the property. We do not know whether he ever made the leased rooms available to his players, though it was arguably in his power to do so. The Children of the Revels were no longer active in the Blackfriars, and Hunsdon may have invited James Burbage into collusion on plans for an indoor theatre. Surviving documents are exasperatingly unhelpful, and there is no evidence that the Chamberlain was a party to the eventual conversion, in 1596, of the large Parliament Chamber in the Blackfriars. He was, by then, old and infirm, but the weight of suggestive detail leaves an impression of a patron actively engaged in the affairs of his players to the end.

We should not be surprised if this notably bourgeois aristocrat used the actors to whom he granted legitimacy to advance his own prestige at Court. He remained constant to his Queen, mistrusted the Earl of Leicester and was bewildered by the Earl of Essex. Robert Carey, fourth of his seven sons, records in his *Memoirs* that 'I had the happiness to be born of good parents'[8] and the last glimpse we have of the old man is a domestic one. On 19 February 1596, he presided at the wedding of his grand-daughter Elizabeth to Thomas Berkeley. It was a marriage that brought to the Careys the one thing they were short on – ancestry. Six months later, Hunsdon was dead. The Queen granted £800 towards his funeral expenses and a further £400 to his widow and daughters. His will provided for £1,000 to furnish him a tomb in Westminster Abbey.

The title of Lord Hunsdon, together with patronage of the players, was inherited by the oldest son, George Carey. The Queen's favour and written encouragement from Robert Cecil had led him to hope for appointment as Lord Chamberlain as well, but there, temporarily at least, he was disappointed. The post went to his Blackfriars neighbour William Brooke, Lord Cobham. We do not know whether the new Lord Hunsdon was involved in the negotiations, resolved in deference to the Brooke family ancestry, that turned Sir John Oldcastle into Sir John Falstaff, but it seems highly probable that he was. We do know that Hunsdon was one of the protestors against James Burbage's plans to open a playhouse in the Blackfriars. Not too much should be read into that. Hunsdon had just been appointed joint-leader of a commission of enquiry into ways of reforming the Blackfriars precinct. Eager for preferment at Court, he was inevitably disinclined to support an enterprise that threatened increased lawlessness. Even so, it was an ominous start to the relationship of established players to their new patron.

Born in 1547, George Carey was approaching fifty when he inherited his father's title. His marriage to a Spencer of Althorp, the sister of Ferdinando, Lord Strange's wife, had produced only the daughter so recently married to Thomas Berkeley, but his connections at Court could scarcely have been better. His own sister, Katherine, was the wife of the Lord Admiral, formerly Chief Gentlewoman of the Privy Chamber and still a trusted friend to the Queen. Less wayward than his father, he had accumulated considerable wealth from his ownership of coal-mines in Carmarthenshire, tin-mines in Cornwall and the monopoly, granted to him in 1589, on the transporting of wool. Even more significantly, he had made use of his 1582 appointment as Captain-General of the Isle of Wight to amass a private fortune from privateering. As well as his houses in Hertfordshire, the Blackfriars and West Drayton, he leased and had extravagantly fortified, Carisbrooke Castle on the Isle of Wight. His hunger for recognition was quickly gratified by his indulgent cousin and Queen. Lord Cobham died in early 1597, and George Carey, like his father before him, was appointed Lord Chamberlain. A month later, on 23 April 1597, he was invested with the Order of the Garter. His ride to Windsor, with 300 attendants in the orange taffeta of his livery and bearing the Hunsdon emblem of a rampant swan, was a contributory splendour to the gorgeousness of the occasion. The possibility that the ceremony concluded with a specially commissioned performance of *The Merry Wives of Windsor* from Lord Hunsdon's own players has already been mentioned. But his high days did not long continue. In 1600, Hunsdon suffered what may have been a fairly severe stroke. Convalescing in Bath, he received a letter from the Queen, promising that 'you shall find in us a mother and wife to minister unto you'.[9] Her concern was evidently genuine. Elizabeth visited her stricken cousin three times during the year from Christmas 1601 to Christmas 1602, twice in the Blackfriars and once in West Drayton. The first of these visits, on 29 December 1601, is known to have been the pretext for a play, but we know neither what it was nor where it was played. The Chamberlain's Men are certain to have been the players. Like his father, the second Lord Hunsdon seems to have been very ready to bolster his own reputation by use of his acting company. A semi-invalid at risk of losing his Court appointment (he died in September 1603), he presented the vigour of the Lord Chamberlain's Men as a disguise for the weakness of the Lord Chamberlain.

I am less confident of the theatrical involvement of the rival company's patron, Lord Howard of Effingham (Lord High Admiral after 1585 and Earl of Nottingham from 1597). Robert Kenny, his biographer, finds no evidence of interest beyond surviving letters of fairly token support for the players. However, Howard was always ready to speak up for the players in the Privy Council and he remained their patron through the last thirty years of Elizabeth I's reign. He is the only one of the major patrons to have continued in public life under James I. Only twelve years younger than his father-in-law, the first Lord Hunsdon, Howard was born in 1536. Barring those who succumbed to the family tendency to be executed, the Howards were blessed with unusual longevity. Charles was, perhaps, fortunate to belong to a lesser branch, deriving from the second Duke of Norfolk's marriage to his deceased wife's sister. Elizabeth I was great-grand-daughter of the second Duke by the direct line from Elizabeth Tilney. Henry VIII had married twice into the Howards and escaped from both marriages with the assistance of the executioner. Anne Boleyn, Elizabeth I's mother, was one of these victims, something on which the Queen must have reflected when she authorised the execution of her cousin, the fourth Duke of Norfolk, in 1572. Caught up in the dynastic assertiveness of the Howards, he had allowed himself to be drawn into the Ridolfi Plot to secure the Catholic succession through Mary, Queen of Scots. But William, the first Lord Howard of Effingham, had been Elizabeth's protector during the dangerous years of Mary Tudor's reign, and his son inherited her majesty's confidence. He was tall and, in old age, still strikingly elegant, even to the point of being dandified, and although most of his public life was spent in administration, he was more at home with horses and, to a slightly lesser extent, ships. It was probably his 1574 appointment as deputy to the Lord Chamberlain (his Howard uncle, the Earl of Suffolk) that encouraged him to house his own group of liveried players; but there is surely something more than mere formality behind the fact that he remained patron of a company, almost without a break, throughout the last thirty years of Elizabeth's reign. If he was less actively engaged than the Hunsdons, it may have been because his company was supervised by the socially ambitious Edward Alleyn and the busily entrepreneurial Philip Henslowe. Their theatrical enterprises were always tied in with bulls, bears, brothels and usury, and they may have been more often keen to divert the attention of their patron than to attract it.

Howard was not, temperamentally, a tycoon, although he exploited his office as Lord Admiral to enhance his income, for example from privateering. He would have demanded his tenth share of the prize money from most of the 299 vessels captured and brought into English ports between 1589 and 1591.[10] It was his good fortune to be England's Lord Admiral at the height of the maritime wars with Spain. It was his misfortune to be overshadowed in the major naval campaigns of his life by such charismatic popular heroes as Sir Francis Drake and the Earl of Essex. He was valuable to Elizabeth I because he lacked imagination, was loyal and governable. His political caution chimed with that of Lord Burghley and Robert Cecil and led to inevitable clashes with the volatile Earl of Essex. More a public servant than a statesman, he earned and, for the most part, justified the Queen's continuing trust. The puzzle, as Robert Kenny indicates, is that an effective and honourable Elizabethan should so quickly have declined into a venal Jacobean:

Under Elizabeth he was a diligent, loyal, somewhat cautious administrator and commander who merited the affection of his country and carried his honors with dignity and grace; to James he was no less loyal, but his administration became flaccid and self-serving, completely blind to the corruption it was helping to create. In the life of perhaps no other man is the change in the nature of government that came with the change of dynasty so clearly reflected.[11]

It is the effect of that change of dynasty on Shakespeare's professional career that is the remaining concern of this book. For Howard, it was a doubly melancholy time. His wife, close friend to the Queen, died exactly a month before her. Before the end of the year, at the age of sixty-seven, he had married again. His new wife, only nineteen, was a Scottish heiress, sister to the Earl of Moray and already well-placed in the Court of the new King. Such marriages invite ribald responses, and Howard was never free of ribaldry for the rest of his long life. He was eighty-one when his young wife bore their last child. There were rumours that the true paternity belonged to a young page with whom the Countess of Nottingham was often in company. These rumours were in no way weakened when, a year after the Earl's death at the age of eighty-eight, his widow married the page.

We should not readily accept the sentimental view that the Queen's death plunged her beloved country into deep mourning. Her politic rejection of policy and her meanness accentuated by poverty had led Court and country into disarray by the end of the century. Economic crisis has always a variety of causes. The vast cost of the wars with Spain was a major factor, as was the long run of foul weather, leading to bad harvests. Population growth exacerbated shortage and impeded the necessary adjustment to new market forces, particularly with regard to England's staple trade in cloth. And over all hung the dark cloud of the succession. It was, perhaps, lucky that the Earl of Essex's stutter of rebellion was still echoing while the Queen was dying, since it enabled Robert Cecil to carry the Privy Council with him into compromise. James I could not have asked for a more auspiciously timed death than the old player-Queen's; and he would have been hard-pressed to devise for himself a more bungled entrance onto the stage of England than the one he made. It is a matter of fundamental contrast that the new King should so little have relished public appearances. His patronage of actors, though genuine, seemed covert, even covetous. It was Elizabeth I's gift to deck out private avarice as public munificence. James, by contrast, was munificent in private and publicly a niggard. He was certainly the most generous patron that Shakespeare's company ever had, and if the death of the Queen raised fears for the future, those fears were quickly dispelled with the proclamation of the new monarch's letters patent on 19 May 1603:

Knowe yee that Wee of our speciall grace, certeine knowledge, & mere motion have licenced and authorized and by theise presentes doe licence and aucthorize theise our Servauntes Lawrence Fletcher, William Shakespeare, Richard Burbage, Augustyne Phillippes, John Heninges, Henrie Condell, William Sly, Robert Armyn, Richard Cowly, and the rest of their Assosiates freely to use and exercise the Arte and faculty of playinge Comedies, Tragedies, histories, Enterludes, moralls, pastoralls, Stage-plaies, and Suche others like as theie have alreadie studied or hereafter shall use or studie, aswell for the recreation of our lovinge Subjectes, as for our Solace and pleasure when wee shall thincke good to see them, during our pleasure.

We do not know which Polonius supplied the King with the catchall list of dramatic kinds, but the proclamation must have brought great satisfaction to Shakespeare. To be able to count the King as one's patron was, in a fiercely hierarchical society, a proof of quality. Furthermore, the wording of the proclamation promised a release from the tired fiction that 'public' performances were rehearsals for court performances. The new licence permitted the presentation of plays 'aswell for the recreation of our lovinge Subjectes, as for our Solace and pleasure'. Nor did it end there. The letters patent went on to confirm the right of the King's Men:

to shewe and exercise publiquely to their best Commoditie, when the infection of the plague shall decrease, aswell within theire nowe usual howse called the Globe within our County of Surrey, as alsoe within anie towne halls or Moute halls or other conveniente places within the liberties and freedome of anie other Cittie, universitie, towne, or Boroughe whatsoever within our said Realmes and domynions.

For the former players of the dying Lord Chamberlain, the death of the Queen was surely a cause for rejoicing.

They had barely a week to celebrate in public. On 26 May 1603, a notified rise in plague-deaths brought about the closure of the London playhouses. From the wording of the Proclamation, it would seem that some were already closed. The King's Men took to the road, evidently still unseen by their royal patron. Not until 2 December 1603, when James summoned them to perform before him at Wilton House, the home of the Earl of Pembroke, can we be certain that the King witnessed his Men in action. He rewarded them lavishly with £30 in payment, but we do not know what play was chosen. Not surprisingly, the company was anxious to please James, so that the choice of repertoire had a new urgency and Shakespeare in particular a new responsibility. It is not at all clear what he did about it. *Measure for Measure* probably belongs to 1603–4. It is a play that treats with some earnestness the question of good government, and it might reasonably have been addressed to a King who had pondered more deeply on the rights and duties of a ruler than any other in the whole history of the British monarchy: but the play's mood is too mottled to pass for flattery. James I had not yet presented himself to the people of London because fear of the plague was prolonging his absence from the capital. Would it not have been singularly tactless to present *Measure for Measure* at Wilton, a play which displays the tyrannising of a puritanical deputy over the people of a capital city during the unnecessary absence of the rightful ruler? *Measure for Measure* advertises Shakespeare's awareness that good government demands more than well meaning, and it is, in subtle ways, an 'interregnum' play, but it is certainly not a politic thank-you for prompt and generous patronage. On the available evidence, the King seems to have done more for the playwright than the playwright for the King. For the delayed Coronation celebrations (the Coronation had taken place in comparative seclusion in July 1603) in March 1604, he provided each of the nine named King's Men with $4\frac{1}{2}$ yards of red cloth from the Great Wardrobe, so that they could wear his livery without needing to skimp in the making. He had already called them for seven further performances over Christmas and Shrovetide, amply compensating them for the continuing closure of the Globe. One year after the death of the Queen, the King's Men had still no cause to bemoan the change of patronage.

*　　*　　*

At this mid-point in his membership of the Chamberlain's/ King's Men, Shakespeare remained sensitive to the needs of his colleagues. It is no longer the youthful Romeo that Burbage is invited to personate, but the mature Othello, Macbeth, Antony, Leontes, and the old Prospero and Lear. The diptych of player and king, in which the *Theatrum Mundi* found its supreme expression, maintained its hold on Shakespeare's imagination. Even on the heath, King Lear is also Burbage in a startling costume. From *Hamlet* onwards, the heroic gesture is impeded, not only by mundane circumstance, but also by the inbuilt sense of its theatricality. This is nowhere clearer than in the intrusion of the rustic Clown, bringing the killing asp ('the worm's an odd worm') and a confusion of malapropisms, as a reductive prelude to Cleopatra's apotheosis in suicide. It is only with difficulty, and after a negotiation protracted beyond her wishes, that Cleopatra can progress towards her *Liebestod*:

CLOWN: But this is most fallible, the worm's an odd worm.
CLEO: Get thee hence; farewell.
CLOWN: I wish you all joy of the worm.
CLEO: Farewell.
CLOWN: You must think this, look you, that the worm will do his kind.
CLEO: Ay, ay; farewell.
CLOWN: Look you, the worm is not to be trusted but in the keeping of wise people; for indeed there is no goodness in the worm.
CLEO: Take thou no care; it shall be heeded.
CLOWN: Very good. Give it nothing, I pray you, for it is not worth the feeding.
CLEO: Will it eat me?　　　　　(*Antony and Cleopatra*, v. ii. 257–71)

All of Shakespeare's later protagonists stand at a critical distance from their own moral imperatives: and that distance is widened from 'below' by the invention of the alienated Fool – Touchstone, Feste, Thersites, Lavache, Lear's Fool, perhaps

Cloten and Caliban, certainly Autolycus. This unplaced character, admitted everywhere but belonging nowhere, was Shakespeare's intuitive response to the qualities of Kempe's successor, Robert Armin. He is a cultural commentator on the new uncertainties of Stuart England, to which the whole company had now to be responsive.

CHAPTER 7

Servant to the King: 1603–1616

Once assured of the new King's active support for his players, Shakespeare might reasonably, in his fortieth year, have elected to consolidate a professional career that had been pronounced successful. It would be surprising if his colleagues did not invite him, or he volunteer, to provide an appropriate prologue for the company's first performance before their royal patron at Wilton House in December 1603, but none survives. He may have made the additional 'gesture' of returning to his old profession of acting: he is certainly listed among the performers in Ben Jonson's *Sejanus*, which received an ill-fated production at Court that first Christmas of the new reign. Jonson, whose professional career both contrasts and compares with Shakespeare's, would have had high hopes after the summer of 1603. The new Queen's progress from Scotland, accompanied by the young Prince Henry, had included a welcome rest at Althorp. Her host there was Sir Robert Spencer, brother-in-law to the sickly Lord Hunsdon and to the long-dead Ferdinando, Lord Strange. Ben Jonson was there as well, brought in to write and supervise the presentation of an outdoor pastoral, which he called *The Satyr*. The composition of this short piece may have offered Jonson a welcome distraction: his seven-year-old son had just died of the plague in London. The contrivances of *The Satyr* combine courtly compliment with what we might now call *kitsch* in ways that need surprise no student of Elizabeth I's progresses. As Queen Anne and Prince Henry were driven along the woodland drive to Althorp House, welcoming fanfares were played, but the coach was halted when a satyr jumped from behind a bush to enquire into the cause of such revelry. The explanation was then given by Queen Mab, whose attendant fairies provided music and dance to greet the royal guests. At the end of Jonson's play, a jewel was given to James's Queen, and the eldest son of the Spencers, in archaic huntsman's attire, was presented to her. Two deer were then released – and shot – and the royal coach continued its stately way to the house. Two days later, the royal guests were entertained by amateurs of the Althorp district with music, dance, and what Jonson contemptuously called 'a morris of the clowns thereabout, who most officiously presented themselves'.[1] The present Princess of Wales, herself a Spencer, has cause to reflect, when watching obscure folk-plays in far-flung corners of England's lost empire, on this ancestral greeting of a travel-worn Danish Queen.

Unlike Shakespeare, Jonson had, by 1603, abandoned the struggle for survival in London's theatre-world. From the generous patronage of Sir Robert Townsend, he had moved on to live under the protection of James I's cousin Esme Stuart, Seigneur d'Aubigny. He considered *Sejanus* 'the first fruit of his retirement'. Its presentation by the King's Men was, as the outcome proved, a tactical error. To an unwary modern reader the play may seem innocuous, but the portrayal of bitter factions at court, by a man rightly suspected of being a Catholic, invited hostile reactions and could almost have been guaranteed to provoke them. Jonson took the blame that might equally have been taken by the King's Men. His chief antagonist was a Howard, the learned and scheming Earl of Northampton, who was a politician first and a Catholic second. It seems to have been at his instigation that Jonson was summoned before the Privy Council to answer charges of 'popery and treason'. However farfetched these imputations may be, it should be remembered that, before 1603 was out, two Catholic plots against the King had been uncovered. At the unmasking of the great Gunpowder Plot two years later, it would emerge that Jonson had dined with the arch-conspirator, Robert Catesby, less than a month before. Indeed, the whole story of Jonson's life under the Stuarts is astonishingly chequered. Celebrated by many as the great writer of masques, he remained for others a marked man. It is only in contrast to this great contemporary that Shakespeare's ability to keep his head down can be fully appreciated. Shakespeare may have envied Jonson the patronage of d'Aubigny; Jonson almost certainly envied Shakespeare his ability to get away with murder. The *Sejanus* affair did no lasting damage to the King's Men, but it has an interesting coda. In his prefatory Epistle to the readers of the 1605 Quarto, Jonson writes:

> I would inform you that this book, in all numbers, is not the same with that which was acted on the public stage, wherein a second pen had good share: in place of which I have rather chosen to put weaker (and no doubt less pleasing) of mine own, than to defraud so happy a genius of his right by my loathed usurpation.

There is veiled contempt for the 'genius' whose poetry is 'more pleasing' than Jonson's own, and scholars have been unwilling to admit the probability that the second pen was Shakespeare's, but it has to be said that there is no better candidate. The scholars' favourite, George Chapman, is not best characterised as 'pleasing'. It would be an obviously diplomatic gesture for the company playwright, two years after that company has lambasted Jonson in Dekker's *Satiromastix*, to collaborate in a new commission. According to the most widely accepted dating of his plays, Shakespeare's productivity was meagre in the years from 1603 to 1605, just when the King's Men were in most need of him. If he spent the latter part of 1603 trying to satisfy Ben Jonson, his ill-timed slowness is understandable.

I underline this probability partly because the play which is generally placed at this point in the Shakespearean canon, *Measure for Measure*, has a Jonsonian anxiety to punish wrongdoing. Seen in the context of James's first full year on the English throne, it is nothing short of a *caveat Rex* from the nation's leading playwright to the new monarch. Through Isabella, devout and politically disengaged Catholicism is commended. Through Angelo, the excesses of Puritanism are pilloried. Through the Duke, the ruler is decorously reminded of his people's need of him. Jonathan Goldberg has argued, with some subtlety, that *Measure for Measure* links politics and literature through 'the principle of representation that prescribes a single law for the state and the theater. In this relationship, the king, the author and the text of the play all have a part.'[2] This is something more than a restatement of the commonplace that 'all the world's a stage'. I am not suggesting that Shakespeare laid his career on the line in *Measure for Measure*, but I cannot see how an open-minded reading of this play leaves room for a belief that Shakespeare, sublimely or not, was removed from the religious and political discourse of his day. Goldberg is one among recent Shakespearean scholars who have been arguing that our inability to place Shakespeare politically is a result, not of his disengagement, but of his radical instability. It is an intelligent reading of a writer who embodies, and by embodying tests, the ideas of the age, but who will not adopt exclusively any one of them. To such a man, the crowning of a new and very different sovereign is an invitation to speculate. Catholicism is only peripherally his concern in the Vienna/London of *Measure for Measure*. The Puritan upsurge is more central. In January 1604, James I received the Millenary Petition of leading Puritans at the Hampton Court Conference. The outcome was a setback for radical Puritans. The King had some difficulty in containing his impatience. When the bachelor Dr Reynolds objected to the inclusion in the marriage service of the phrase, 'with my body I thee worship', James's riposte was, 'Many a man speaks of Robin Hood who never shot in his bow.'[3] It would be too much to suggest that Angelo is Dr Reynolds in office, but it is not inappropriate to perceive in Shakespeare's probing of his conduct a humane inquisition of Puritan precepts. Far more significant, though, is the play's investigation of the royal prerogative, an investigation of which was already the dominant topic in James's first House of Commons.

Parliament met in March 1604, with its most radical Puritans still feeling the sting of the Hampton Court Conference. They would have been relieved to hear the King make open acknowledgement of parliamentary privilege, something which it had become the Queen's custom in her last Parliaments to trammel with curbs and constraints. But James's mental flexibility could be deceptive. The most important of Parlia-

ment's privileges, as was immediately apparent in his dispute
with the Commons over the Buckinghamshire election, was its
privilege of agreeing with the King. In May, his dander up,
James summoned the lower House to Whitehall and tongue-
lashed them for wasting parliamentary time on issues of privilege
instead of conducting more urgent business. After a short period
of reflection, and perhaps after hearing that the House intended
to respond by preparing an 'Apology' which would not defend
but justify their actions, the King tried to dispel the hurt feelings
of the elected members, but it was too late. The *Apology* was
prepared and read to the House. The heart of the matter was
still the question of privilege. Against James's claim that
parliamentary privilege was dependent on royal grace and
favour, the Commons committee argued that it was a right,
duly acknowledged by the sovereign. In the event, the *Apology*
was never fully recorded in the transactions of the House, but it
remained in the memories of its members. Even so early, the first
salvo of the Civil War was fired.[4] It is in this historical context
that the Duke of *Measure for Measure* reflects on the condition of
his people and King Lear undergoes his enlightenment on the
heath. The 1604 *Apology* sets out to establish those areas in
which the voice of the people's representatives is the voice of
God: 'no human wisdom, how great soever can pierce into the
particularities of the rights and customs of [the] people ... but
by tract of experience and faithful report of such as know
them'.[5] The world observed by the Commons committee, and
discovered by the Duke and King Lear, was one in which 'the
prerogatives of princes may easily and do daily grow; the
privileges of the subject are for the most part at an everlasting
stand'.[6]

Measure for Measure was performed at Court on 26 December
1604. Earlier that year, Shakespeare had sold twenty bushels of
malt to Philip Rogers, a Stratford neighbour. When Rogers
defaulted on payment, Shakespeare sued him. I mention this
now, partly because it is not the action of an unworldly man and
partly to show how consistently Shakespeare maintained his
foothold in Stratford. If he had wished to cut his links with wife
and daughters, he would have bought a house in London. He

was, by now, quite rich enough to buy two, but he preferred to continue in lodgings with the Mountjoys. In August of 1604, he was probably one of the King's Men who attended the Spanish Ambassador, Juan Fernandez de Velasco, at Somerset House. The purpose of Velasco's visit was to sign the treaty of perpetual peace with Spain that was the diplomatic evidence of James I's pacific intentions. There were many in high places who saw and resented the Catholic Howards' influence in the new policy towards Spain. The Earldom of Northampton was Henry Howard's reward for his contribution to the negotiations, together with a secret pension of £1,000 from Philip III of Spain. Sir Walter Raleigh, who had written to the King to advise against making peace with the old enemy, was quickly removed from the scene. Together with Lord Cobham and others, he was tried for treason, accused of complicity in a Spanish-inspired plot against James I, found guilty and locked in the Tower under threat of execution. For what the Attorney-General termed his 'Machiavellian policy', Raleigh was the most loathed man in England during the first years of James's reign:

> Damnable fiend of Hell,
> Mischievous Machiavel![7]

but he was not alone in pointing out the inconsistency of a government that exposed Spanish plots and then made peace with Spain. One of the King's most prized assets, the ten-year-old Prince Henry, was trotted out to grace the ball given on the eve of Velasco's departure at the end of August 1604:

After a little while the Prince was commanded by his parents to dance a galliard, and they pointed out to him the lady who was to be his partner; and this he did with much sprightliness and modesty, cutting several capers in the course of the dance. The Earl of Southampton then led out the Queen, and three other gentlemen their several partners, who all joined in dancing a *brando*. In another, her Majesty danced with the Duke of Lennox. After this they began a galliard ... and in it a lady led out the Prince, who then led out another lady whom their Majesties pointed out to him. After this a *brando* was danced, and that being over, the Prince stood up to dance a *correnta*, which he did very gracefully. The Earl of Southampton was now again the Queen's partner, and they went through the *correnta* likewise. Hereupon the ball ended, and all then took their places at the windows of the room which looked out upon a square, where a platform was raised, and a vast crowd had assembled to see the King's bears fight with greyhounds. This afforded great amusement. Presently a bull, tied to the end of a rope, was fiercely baited by dogs. After this certain tumblers came who danced upon a rope, and performed various feats of agility and skill on horseback. With this ended the entertainment.[8]

Whether the King's Men were among those who performed feats of agility is not recorded. The Spanish Ambassador woke the next morning with a touch of lumbago.

The capacity of the King's Men to give offence, demonstrated with *Sejanus* late in 1603, was again evident during the Christmas season of 1604–5. It arose this time out of what I can only assume was intended straightforwardly to flatter James I, already notorious for the surprisingly unintelligent delight he took in straightforward flattery. An unknown author (there is no reason why it should not have been Shakespeare) had written a play about the events of 1600, when Alexander Ruthven, brother of the Earl of Gowry, had attempted to assassinate James, then King of Scotland only. A letter from that great source of gossip, John Chamberlain, takes up the story:

The tragedy of Gowry, with all the Action and Actors, hath been twice represented by the King's players, with exceeding Concourse of all sorts of People. But whether the matter or manner be not well handled, or that it be thought unfit that Princes should be played on the Stage in their Life-time, I hear that some great Counsellors are much displeased with it, and so 'tis thought shall be forbidden.

The disappearance of this play is very regrettable, not least because it would allow us to measure the lengths Shakespeare and his colleagues were prepared to go to gratify or offend the King. The lengths he went to assist them are apparent from the Court calendar over Christmas 1604–5. Between 1 November and 12 February, they had plays commanded eleven times. The titles are listed, and offer us as clear a picture of Shakespeare's primacy as any record of the period. It is also a useful indication of the company's current repertoire:

1 November	*Othello*
4 November	*The Merry Wives of Windsor*
26 December	*Measure for Measure*
28 December	*The Comedy of Errors*
7 January	*Henry V*
8 January	*Every Man out of His Humour* (Jonson)
c. 9 January	*Love's Labour's Lost*
2 February	*Every Man in His Humour* (Jonson)
10 February	*The Merchant of Venice*
11 February	*The Spanish Maze* (author unknown)
12 February	*The Merchant of Venice*

It is a list that raises a number of unanswerable questions. Was the lost *Spanish Maze* an attack on Spanish deviousness? Why was *The Merchant of Venice* performed twice, with only a day's interval? What motivated the Earl of Southampton (if it was he) to choose *Love's Labour's Lost* for presentation to the Queen? (We have seen that he was her favoured dancing partner.) Had all these plays been regularly in the repertoire or did they have to be revived and relearned to meet the royal command? I find it hard to believe that so unrelenting a piece of Jonsonian improvisation as *Every Man out of His Humour* had retained its popular appeal for the five years since its first performance, but there are few plays so hard to memorise in the whole history of English drama. If this piece was revived in a hurry, that was an astonishing feat. One can have nothing but admiration for the versatility and resourcefulness of a company that could meet the demands of such a schedule.

The keenness of the new Court to see revivals of his old plays probably gave Shakespeare a breathing-space. From now on, he seems to have written at his own pace rather than according to any actual or notional contract. But 1604 is the year of *Othello*, the first of the great sequence of tragedies. We cannot be sure whether this concentration on tragedy was a response to popular demand or peer-group pressure or whether it was the outcome of a mature writer's confidence in his ability to create the taste by which he would be enjoyed. It is clear, though, that the King's Men could now call on at least one remarkable boy actor. Shakespeare did not write Desdemona and Cordelia, let alone Cleopatra, to have some squeaking whipper-snapper boy their greatness. The vital interaction of playwright and players continued to the end. One new recruit to the King's Men was John Lowin, who would remain in this uniquely stable company for forty years. Thomas Pope, who had been a founder of the re-formed Chamberlain's Men in 1594, had retired from acting some time before his death in 1604, but in May 1605, Augustine Phillips died in harness. This was the harshest loss that Shakespeare suffered in his professional life. Phillips was at the social centre of the King's Men, a musician, almost certainly an acrobat and the author of at least one jig as well as being a reliable actor. His will is that of someone who was, first and foremost, a company man. There were gifts of £5 to be shared among the hired men, twenty shillings for five of his fellow-shareholders, thirty-shilling gold pieces for Shakespeare and Condell, and silver bowls worth £5 for his three executors, Richard Burbage, John Heminges and William Sly. It is clear that Shakespeare's professional career was enhanced by good fellowship and reasonable to assume that he wrote a tribute for a memorial performance in honour of Augustine Phillips.

The Court saw entertainments other than plays during the Christmas festivities of 1604–5. On 6 January, a masque was performed to celebrate the creation of the boy Prince Charles as Duke of York. The author was Ben Jonson and the setting (Jonson calls it the 'bodily part') was by the brilliant young Court architect Inigo Jones. Compared with some of the later collaborations of Jonson and Jones, *The Masque of Blackness* was a modest affair. *Oberon, Prince of Fairy* (1611) cost a defiant £2,100 at a time when James I, as we shall see, had just fallen foul of his Parliament on the issue of the royal debt. The splendour of such Jacobean occasions is not recoverable by a reading of the texts, which are mostly limp and sycophantic. It is not easy to recognise in them the exemplary innovation of the age. Jacobean masques were closer to performance art than to drama, and gave the King and Queen an ideal opportunity for

the display and conspicuous expenditure in which they delighted. Not that masques were a new invention, but the
lavishness of their staging at James's Court turned what had
been an elegant diversion into a declaration of both Classicist
and Mannerist taste. As Keith Sturgess rightly emphasises, 'in
its iconographic power and allegorical mode the masque was
supremely able to make clear statements about royal prerogative and the magical, mystical power of the divinely
appointed ruler'.[9] Shakespeare could not have wholly ignored
the fashion for display embodied in the Court masques. Nearly
all the plays he is known to have written after 1606 are touched
by it. He did not live to see the collaboration of Jonson and
Jones come to grief. The history of the English theatre is littered
with examples of spectacle's triumph over language. The
wordsmith, on this occasion, took his revenge in a poetic
'Expostulation with Inigo Jones':

> O Shows! Shows! Mighty shows!
> The eloquence of masques! What need of prose
> Or verse or sense t'express immortal you?
> You are the spectacles of state! 'Tis true
> Court hieroglyphics! and all arts afford
> In the mere perspective of an inch board!
> You ask no more than certain politic eyes,
> Eyes that can pierce into the mysteries
> Of many colours! read them! and reveal
> Mythology there painted on slit deal!
> Oh, to make boards to speak! There is a task –
> Painting and carpentry are the soul of masque.

By the time he wrote that, in 1631, Jonson had been many
times the beneficiary of Jacobean and Caroline taste. For
composing a masque – a far lesser undertaking than the crafting
of a full-length play – he could hope to receive as much as £40.
James I's lavishness was in calculated contrast to Elizabeth I's
notorious thrift. The old Queen had set herself the task of saving
sufficiently on the ordinary expenditure of her Court to cover
the extraordinary costs of war against Spain. On inheriting the
throne, James I immediately squandered on spectacle the
money saved by the cessation of hostilities with Spain. Auth-

orised expenditure on Elizabeth's funeral came to £17,000 and
for the Coronation to £20,500. On a smaller scale, but no less
excessive, was the £617 6s 8d that the Great Wardrobe had to
find to pay for parliamentary robes for the King and Prince
Henry.[10] And all this before the end of 1603! Even after these
occasions for national display were over, James I's ordinary
expenditure remained well over double that of his predecessor.
A contributory factor was the maintenance of three separate
Courts, his own, the Queen's at Somerset House and Prince
Henry's in Richmond. In addition, the King requisitioned and
enlarged a number of hunting lodges, where he could indulge
both his love of the ancient sport of killing animals ('The
manner', Sir John Harington commented, 'made me devise the
beasts were pursuing the sober creation') and his need for
seclusion. As a contemporary ballad makes clear, James I's
dislike of the perpetual public eye was no reflection of a
Garboesque desire to be alone:

> At Royston and Newmarket
> He'll hunt till he be lean.
> But he hath merry boys
> That with masques and toys
> Can make him fat again.[11]

It was a new and very different world that Shakespeare held
under review as the Gunpowder Plotters formulated their plans.

King Lear, whether or not it was performed in 1605, must certainly have been in the making. It belongs to the mid-point between Shakespeare's first professional commitment to the Lord
Chamberlain's Men in 1594 and his death in 1616. Enhanced
by the richest dramatic poetry Shakespeare ever produced, it
nevertheless predicates the transition from the old feudal role of
kingship to a new accommodation of the King's subjects ('Oh!
I have ta'en too little care of this'). Reduced to nothing but a
retrospect on kingship, Lear offers food for thought to a reigning
monarch whose narrow escape from being blown up in the
House of Commons was the sensation of 1605. The Gunpowder
Plot lifted James I to a height of popularity that he was too in-
flexible to maintain. Its inevitable aftermath was a wave of anti-

Catholic feeling. Ben Jonson, under pressure from the Privy Council, promised to seek out 'a certain priest' with an offer of safe conduct should the priest agree to furnish the Council with information, but, like his fellows throughout England, Jonson's contact had gone to ground. 'The party will not be found', reported the probably frightened playwright, who had recently spent another term in prison for his part in the writing of *Eastward Ho!* (1605).[12] The trial of the Jesuit priest, Henry Garnet, in March 1606 was one of the saddest postludes to the Gunpowder Plot. Father Garnet's prosecutors centred their case on the Jesuit licence to equivocate. An outright lie was outlawed by their theology, but an oracular statement, susceptible to more than one interpretation, was a permissible alternative. Equivocation excited an indignation much greater than a self-defending lie would have done, even adding to the language the abusive adjective 'jesuitical' to describe duplicitous behaviour. Today's alternative, a marrying of diplomacy with the politics of power, is to be 'economical with the truth', which is presumed to be justifiable whenever state secrets, however distantly, are at issue. Garnet's economy with the truth found its immediate way into Marston's *Sophonisba* and Shakespeare's *Macbeth*.

Macbeth represents Shakespeare's most strenuous attempt to flatter James I. Both the King's Scottish ancestry and his known interest in witchcraft are prudently accommodated. Furthermore, James's interest in the doctrine of equivocation was public knowledge, even if his incognito attendance at Garnet's trial was privileged information. All in all, *Macbeth* presents with particular vividness the two lives of a Jacobean play. When performed at the Globe, where Simon Forman saw it as late as 20 April 1611, it offered an occasion for tumultuous public engagement in the life of the mighty at the level of political fantasy. Presented to the King at Hampton Court, it provided an opportunity for sophisticated courtesy, addressed directly to the royal spectator. The last of the parade of kings in Act Four Scene One holds a mirror:

> And yet the eighth appears who bears a glass
> Which shows me many more (IV.i. 119–20)

On the public stage, the effect is minimal: what can be seen by the actor cannot be seen by the audience. In Court, with the King centrally placed in his chair of state, the dumb-show actor can hold the glass in such a way as to allow James to see his own reflection – the latest and greatest of Banquo's line surveying his own present in the play's future. As a writer for the King's Men, Shakespeare could not have avoided a consciousness of each new play's double life. For those who wish to seek it out, it is present in all his known work, although it is in *Macbeth* that he makes his plainest bid, perhaps in rivalry with Jonson, for the role of Court playwright.

No company in the history of the theatre has survived on a diet of tragedies alone. If Shakespeare was confining himself to that genre in the years from 1604 to 1608, it must have been with the agreement of his colleagues, but they would all have been on the look-out for comedies. If 1606 was the year of *Macbeth* and *King Lear* (which we know to have been performed at Court on 26 December 1606), it was also the year of *Volpone*, the finest of all Jacobean comedies, and probably of *The Revenger's Tragedy*, the decade's supreme depiction of courtly decadence. Despite another plague-haunted closure of the theatres in July, the King's Men should have ended 1606 in good heart. There is small likelihood that Shakespeare was on the road with them in the late summer. Probably he returned to Stratford, where his elder daughter, Susanna, was being wooed by a local physician and herbalist, John Hall. They married on 5 June 1607. Shakespeare, at about this time, was re-reading Sir Thomas North's translation of Plutarch's *Parallel Lives*. The Shakespeare Memorial Trust possesses a copy that once belonged to the Stanley family, and it has sometimes been argued that the 'William' to whom Lord Strange's widow gave it was Shakespeare himself. He must, certainly, have owned a copy. It had been the source for *Julius Caesar* and would once again lie open beside him as he wrote his next plays, *Antony and Cleopatra* and *Coriolanus*. Shakespeare regularly makes no more changes to North's English than are necessary in the translation of prose to verse. It is an alchemy that turns plagiarism into original creation, and the possibility that Shakespeare's reading of Plutarch links back to the early patronage of Ferdinando, Lord Strange is a pleasing one. Peter Levi has recently argued that the poetic effusions, commissioned in 1607 by the former Lady Strange, are by Shakespeare.[13] The occasion for the verses seems to have been the engagement of the Lady Alice's eldest daughter to Lord Chandos, and the fourteen stanzas addressing in sequence fourteen noble ladies are allusive, after the fashion of the time, graceful and not particularly interesting. It is quite possible that Shakespeare wrote them. He was a professional in constant search for aristocratic buttering on his bread. Six years later he would be paid forty-four shillings for composing an impresa for the Earl of Rutland in readiness for a tournament at Belvoir Castle.

The summer of 1606 had brought the Queen's brother, King Christian IV of Denmark, to London. The King's Men were twice called to Greenwich to perform for the royal brothers-in-law, but were absent from the orgy at Theobalds, hilariously described by Sir John Harington.[14] The performance in Robert Cecil's fine house of the masque of *Solomon and the Queen of Sheba* disintegrated into a fiasco of vomit and spilled cakes. The trouble began when the player-Queen of Sheba tripped on the steps to the royal thrones and deposited her gifts of food in Christian IV's lap:

His Majesty then got up and would dance with the Queen of Sheba; but he fell down and humbled himself before her, and was carried to an inner chamber and laid on a bed of state; which was not a little defiled with the presents of the Queen which had been bestowed on his garments; such as wine, cream, jelly, beverage, cakes, spices and other good matters. The entertainment and show went forward, and most of the presenters went backward, or fell down; wine did so occupy their inner chambers.

For Cecil, the sober host, the occasion was a grim reminder of the shortcomings of the increasingly bibulous monarch, whose vexed relationship with his Parliament Cecil was trying vainly to make smooth. By the summer of 1607, it was clear that James I's extravagance was unstemmable. One of the King's earliest acts on his accession was to create Robert Cecil Earl of Salisbury, thus removing him from the House of Commons, where he might more easily have tempered the wilder spirit of resistance. As Secretary of State and Lord Privy Seal, he continued to serve the King with the same combination of zeal and deviousness which had characterised his service to Elizabeth I. David Mathew neatly encapsulates the ambiguity of Cecil's role in Jacobean England when he describes him as 'an overwhelming political personality whose influence was not traceable in its entirety'.[15] Where cajolement failed, he was not averse to using bribery, and even if his methods did not instigate the widespread corruption in James I's Court, they did not contradict it. An overlapping of generosity and duplicity may be apparent even in Cecil's gift to the King of the house and estate of Theobalds. The occasion was marked, on 22 May 1607, by the performance of another of Ben Jonson's indoor entertainments wrapped in scenery and effects by Inigo Jones. The spectacular possibilities of indoor staging, so soon to become available to the King's Men on a regular basis at the Blackfriars, are exemplified in this event in the long gallery at Theobalds. The opening was marked by the drawing of a traverse to reveal the Genius of the House lit by a single candle; but this gloomy scene was 'suddenly' transformed into a brightly lit 'glorious place' with a distant prospect of clouds in perspective. Even though not present, the King's Men would certainly have heard accounts of the show during their thirteen performances at Court over the Christmas of 1607–8.

Jonson was now at the height of his fame as a masque-maker, a much more lucrative occupation than writing plays for the public theatres. It is a field in which Shakespeare seems to have offered no competition, and I find this hard to explain. He had, to be sure, a tolerably stable income, but he had never any aversion to adding to it, and I simply do not believe that he was too high-minded to wish to soil his genius with ephemeral pieces designed to suit the purposes of aristocrats. It is more probable that Jonson was possessive and in a strong position to seek out opportunity. Robert Cecil, who was a generous patron to both Jones and Jonson, commissioned another work from them in the early summer of 1608. The occasion this time was Cecil's appointment as Lord Treasurer, an office about as grateful to a Jacobean as that of the manager of an out-of-form football team in the 1990s. Jonson and Jones each received £20 for their work on this piece, whose total cost was limited by the prudent Cecil to £170. It is of considerable theatrical interest that the great Edward Alleyn was tempted out of retirement to take a part, for which he too received £20. Such prizing of a single actor is testimony to the growing status of the profession.

For Shakespeare and his colleagues, the summer of 1608 was notable for a quite different reason. The world of the boy companies had crashed suddenly about their ears. As recently as 1606, the Children of Paul's had performed, for King Christian IV, the double-play (one comedy and one tragedy) of *Abuses*, but *The Puritan* of the same year had gravely offended the increasingly powerful Puritans of London. Its publication in 1607–8 became the pretext for a blistering sermon from William Crashawe, preached at Paul's Cross on St Valentine's Day, 1608. Crashawe's generalised condemnation of plays was in no way new, nor even his selective attack on those who trained the boy players ('hee that teacheth children to play, is not an instructor, but a spoiler and destroyer of children'), but his singling out of *The Puritan* was rare in its particularity.[16] The Children of Paul's did not long survive Crashawe's sermon. The fortunes of the Children of the Revels at the Blackfriars plummeted soon afterwards. Their staging of Chapman's two-part play, *The Conspiracy and Tragedy of Charles Duke of Byron* had gravely offended the French Ambassador. The events to which it referred were very recent, Byron himself having visited Elizabeth I in 1601, and the *Gowry* debacle of 1604 had demonstrated the sensitivity of statesmen in such instances. Worse still, the managers of the company defied the ban on performance, trusting, as had become common practice with the boys, that notoriety would augment audiences. Cecil was quick to support the French Ambassador and James I huffily issued an order that 'no play be henceforth acted in London'. The adult companies seem to have bribed this order into ineffectiveness, but the Children of the Revels were ruined. Forced to abandon the Blackfriars, they took refuge in the

lawless Whitefriars and struggled on for a few more years. For
the King's Men, the Blackfriars' dream was on the edge of
coming true. In August, though without abandoning the Globe,
they took out a lease on the Blackfriars playhouse. The
signatories of the lease were Richard and Cuthbert Burbage,
Shakespeare, Heminges, Condell, William Sly and the scrivener
Henry Evans, to whom Richard Burbage had sub-let the
Blackfriars in 1600. A week later Sly was dead, probably a
victim of the plague that continued throughout the mild winter
of 1608–9, thus preventing the King's Men from taking full
possession of their new prize until late in 1609. It may even be
that their first full Blackfriars performance was delayed until
February 1610.

In February 1608, Shakespeare's grand-daughter Elizabeth
was born in Stratford. In August, as the Blackfriars negotiations
were being completed, he sued John Addenbrooke, a dealer in
starch licences in Warwickshire, for the recovery of £6 plus 24
shillings damages. In September, his mother died in the Henley
Street house. We must presume that he was in Stratford for her
burial on 9 September. He was probably writing, alone or in
collaboration, the startlingly original *Pericles* towards the end
of the year. The move from tragedy to the essentially uncat-
egorisable 'last plays' has, inevitably, been associated with the
King's Men's occupation of the Blackfriars, but the matter is of
great theatrical complexity. There is no doubt that indoor
playing, as we have seen in the Theobalds entertainment,
offered new scope for spectacle, and the last plays are capable of
exploiting it in performance. In addition, the indoor theatres
were traditionally hospitable to music, and the last plays made
use of the talents of the gifted lutanist, Robert Johnson. Nearly
all the foreign visitors who have left a record of their travels in
England under Elizabeth and James refer to the excellence of
the music they heard. Paul Hentzner, for example, notes that
'They excel in dancing and music, for they are active and lively,
though of a thicker make than the French.' (Hentzner moved
among meat-eaters.) But music in the open-air theatres was
always threatened by another feature of the English to which
Hentzner refers, their vast fondness for great noises 'such as the

firing of cannon, drums, and the ringing of bells'.[17] The music that charms life out of the statue of Hermione in *The Winter's Tale* sounds like a Blackfriars speciality, and the noises of which Caliban's isle is full are not the street-cries and church bells of London or the maritime hum of the busy River Thames, which must have been constantly audible from the Globe. It is not at all surprising that Shakespeare should have proved himself able to adapt his style to new circumstances. Only Ben Jonson among contemporaries excelled him as an incorporator of theatrical fact in his dramatic fictions. But we should never forget that the Globe remained open. Plays were not like masques. They could be performed in any number of places. The greater significance of the Blackfriars is that it increased the personal prosperity and social status of every one of the King's Men. Shakespeare was a man of substance at the beginning of 1608. By the end of it, he had a prospect of great riches.

Squabbles over ambassadorial precedence delayed until February Jonson's 1609 Court entertainment, *The Masque of Queens*. This was one of the most elaborate of the Jonson/Jones collaborations and it cost over £3,000. The interests of various members of the royal family were separately served. An anti-masque of witches was designed to please the King. The Queen acted the part of Bel-Anna, presenting no more than herself, 'the worthiest queen...possessed [of] all virtues'. The third of the dances she led ended in a formation carefully contrived to spell out the name of the eight-year-old Prince Charles. His older brother was an involved spectator, who gratified Jonson with a request for an annotated copy of the text. After long labour, Jonson presented him with the copiously documented 450-line manuscript that is now in the British Library. The demonstrative scholarship is as characteristic of Jonson as was the gracious request of Prince Henry. The heir to the throne reached the age of fifteen in the month that saw the performance of *The Masque of Queens*:

He was of a comely tall middle stature, about five foot and eight inches high, of a strong, streight, well-made Body (as if Nature in him had shewed all her cunning) with somewhat broad shoulders, and a small waist, of an amiable Majestick Countenance, his hair of an Auborne

Collour, long faced and broad forehead, a piercing, grave eye, a most gracious smile with a terrible frowne, courteous, loving.[18]

The cult of Prince Henry was carefully nurtured, by Robert Cecil among others, and Shakespeare was well aware of the hopes invested in this exemplary youth. There had been nothing like it since the palmy days of the cult of Elizabeth I. Utterly unlike his father, Henry revelled in public show and despised the weak, piping time of peace into which James I was leading the kingdom. The Court which he assembled was devoted both to the arts and to the mathematical sciences. Horsemanship and the skills of the tilt featured there, and, although he was nominal patron of the former Admiral's Men, masques were more to the Prince's taste than plays. The ambience of his Court was a very decent, *mens sana in corpore sano* one. Attendance at sermons was obligatory and anyone heard swearing was fined. Two centuries later, Dr Thomas Arnold would have been pleased to elect Henry head of School House at Rugby. There was, though, one major blight on the Prince's happiness. James I's vision of himself as an international statesman rested on his determination to marry his two older children into the great continental royal families, one Protestant and one Catholic. Henry was not consulted. Once the match was made between his sister Elizabeth and the Protestant Elector Palatine, he was destined to take a Catholic bride, despite his fervent Protestantism and his personal resolution that 'two religions should never lie in his bed'.[19] Because he had been trained to obedience, a sexless marriage was probably more likely than no marriage at all, but there is enough of the relationship between Prince Henry and King James in that of Prince Florizel and King Polixenes to suggest that Shakespeare was intrigued by the London rumours during his writing of *The Winter's Tale*.

The plague continued its death march through most of 1609, and the theatres remained closed. Shakespeare could afford to work slowly, perhaps on *Cymbeline*. The most significant event of his year may have been the publication by Thomas Thorpe of the *Sonnets*. I have nothing whatsoever to add to the inventive speculations on the autobiographical provenance of these intricate poems. A man as fertile in his fictions as Shakespeare was would not have been constricted by fact, of course, but there is, in many of the sonnets, a felt life of friendship and sexual betrayal which may date from the poet's involvement with the Earl of Southampton around the time of the dedications to *Venus and Adonis* and *The Rape of Lucrece*. We do not know how the *Sonnets* came to be published, nor what gossip they excited. If Mrs Shakespeare read them as curiously as modern critics have, there must have been domestic tensions in New Place, but there is no reason to assume she did. If they tell a story at all, it is an old story. Shakespeare may have approved their publication in 1609, confident that the past was another country and the wenching dead, or he may have known nothing about it. The dominant view is that Thorpe went ahead without authorisation, perhaps paying Shakespeare a customary £2 in tactical retrospect or out-of-court compensation. Compensation for the King's Men, after a hard year on the road, came with the royal command for thirteen plays at Court over the Christmas period. Shakespeare must have had a voice in the decision to buy *Philaster* from the new-generation writers, Francis Beaumont and John Fletcher, to re-stage the old favourite *Mucedorus* and to commission *The Alchemist* from Ben Jonson. Little else is known of his activities in 1609, a year which ended with the King's Men at their indoor theatre in the Blackfriars.

The following year began in London with high political hopes and ended with many hopes shattered. The hopes were focussed on Prince Henry, the disappointments on his father. The heir was to be made Prince of Wales in the year 1610, and there were carefully orchestrated celebrations throughout the country. One of the most interesting took place in the Banqueting Hall at Whitehall on Twelfth Night. On 31 December, the Prince (as Meliadus, Lord of the Isles) had delivered a challenge at Court. He and six attendants would fight a combat on foot at barriers against fifty-six adversaries. There were to be *Speeches at Prince Henry's Barriers* by Ben Jonson, with scenery designed by Inigo Jones. Jonson took as his theme the revival of chivalry in the person and conduct of Prince Henry, who was presented as the rightful successor of King

Arthur. This combination of masque and tournament was a peculiarly apt monument to the athletic heir. It is to such occasions that Shakespeare alludes through Vernon's description of the army of Prince Henry's namesake in *Henry IV Part One*:

> All furnish'd all in arms;
> All plum'd like estridges, that with the wind
> Bated like eagles having lately bath'd;
> Glittering in golden coats, like images;
> As full of spirit as the month of May
> And gorgeous as the sun at midsummer;
> Wanton as youthful goats, wild as young bulls.
> I saw young Harry with his beaver on,
> His cushes on his thighs, gallantly arm'd,
> Rise from the ground like feathered Mercury,
> And vaulted with such ease into his seat
> As if an angel dropp'd down from the clouds
> To turn and wind a fiery Pegasus,
> And witch the world with noble horsemanship.

(IV.i.97–110)

Tournament and masque were, in Jacobean England, about equidistant from drama, and the brilliant Prince Henry was a leader in both.

While the Prince was making himself yet more friends in 1610, his father was adding to his store of enemies. Cecil, as Lord Treasurer, was forced to appeal to Parliament 'to relieve his majesty's necessity'. Despite his extra income from the unabashed sale of knighthoods, the King had built up a debt of at least £600,000. Cecil was now appealing to the House of Commons for that sum, together with the acceptance of an increase in the annual 'ordinary' award to £200,000. He recognised the need to bargain, and had persuaded James I to offer to relinquish his rights in purveyance (the provision of goods to Court at a discount) and the lucrative Wardships (a system which vested in the Crown the land of those who inherited as minors) in return for the required financial concessions. For Cecil, these negotiations were immensely delicate, but by July, when Parliament was prorogued, he seemed to have won his case. Both King and subjects were given

20 Portrait by Daniel Mytens of James I, looking uncommonly like 'the wisest fool in Christendom'.

time to reflect before the opening of the next parliamentary session in October, and the result of their reflections was a dangerous shift from negotiation to confrontation. The eventual vote, on 7 November 1610, was overwhelmingly to reject James I's demands. It was the beginning of the end of the first Stuart Parliament. The House of Commons, the King told Cecil, was the 'rotten seed of Egypt', and he dissolved Parliament in January 1611. Its short-lived successor, known to historians as the Addled Parliament, would not meet until the spring of 1614. For Cecil, more than for any other individual, the November vote was a calamity. It marked the end of his effective damage limitation. One of James's first acts, when he began his 'personal rule', was to create his then-favourite, the handsome but ductile Robert Carr, Viscount Rochester. Whatever the intention, Cecil was bound to read the decision as a snub to him. Shakespeare's response to the events of 1610 is unknown, and it may be of no more than coincidental interest that the two plays of this period, *The Winter's Tale* and *The Tempest*, have at their centre rulers who are given ample time to reflect on past mistakes.

Despite the acquisition of the Blackfriars, the King's Men continued to perform at the Globe. Ludwig Friedrich, Prince of Württemberg saw *Othello* there on 30 April 1610. His travelling companion and scribe makes no comment on the performance, but is presumably recording a half-understood explanation made to him when he calls the Globe 'the usual place for acting plays'.[20] *The Alchemist* and the new Beaumont and Fletcher piece, *The Maid's Tragedy*, were probably in the repertoire before plague-deaths brought about another closure of the theatres on 12 July. This succession of summer interruptions did nothing to increase Shakespeare's productivity. *The Winter's Tale* may have been completed in time for the 1610 season, but it probably stands alone. Even for an established playwright, it is not easy to keep working without the promise of an audience. Possession of his past plays was still precious to the King's Men, but for the future they were looking to Beaumont, Fletcher and, perhaps, Jonson. Shakespeare was aware of the shifting sands. The mood of his last plays is uniquely retrospective. What

21 In Wenceslaus Hollar's *Long view of London* (1647), the Second Globe is mistakenly labelled 'Beere bayting'.

Henry James perceived in *The Tempest* – 'the momentous conjunction ... between his charged inspiration and his clarified experience' – might equally be said of *The Winter's Tale*. The sense is of something (a professional career?) ending.

It has often, and intelligently, been argued that Shakespeare's active association with the King's Men ended with the production of *The Tempest* in 1611 and that he spent most of the rest of his life with his family in Stratford. It seems more likely, though, that he continued in full membership of the company until 1613, writing in collaboration with his heir apparent, John Fletcher. The lost *Cardenio* (1612), as well as *Henry VIII* (1613) and *The Two Noble Kinsmen* (1613) are likely products of this collaboration. Shakespeare was certainly in London in the early summer of 1612, when he was before the Court of Records as a witness to a domestic wrangle involving the Mountjoy family, in whose house he had been a lodger. The suit was heard while Robert Cecil lay dying, worn out by his attempts to temper the excesses of King and Commons. His death in May spared him the political pain of Prince Henry's sudden death in October of the same year. The new heir, who would accede to the throne as Charles I, was not quite thirteen and had just over thirty-five years to wait for his beheading. The Prince of Wales's death delayed his sister's wedding, but the celebrations, when they came in the new year of 1613, included fourteen plays by the King's Men. For their part in the marriage celebrations, the company received £153 6s 8d. Some of Shakespeare's share went towards the purchase of a lease on a gatehouse in the Blackfriars. There is no evidence that he ever lived in it, and the purchase may have been a simple investment in real estate, but its proximity to the company's indoor playhouse would have made it a good base for a working playwright. It may, after all, have been the burning of the Globe on 29 June 1613 that released Shakespeare into retirement. The occasion was a performance of *Henry VIII*, whose sub-title *All Is True* is alluded to in the refrain of a contemporary street-ballad:

> This fearful fire began above,
> A wonder strange and true,
> And to the stage-house did remove

As round as tailor's clew,
And burned down both bean and snag
And did not spare the silken flag.
Oh sorrow, pitiful sorrow,
And yet all this is true.

The ballad goes on to mention Burbage, Condell and Heminges, but not Shakespeare.[21]

The variability of a playwright's career can be nicely illustrated from the standpoint of 1613. Shakespeare was certainly rich enough to afford retirement in 1613. So was the gentlemanly Francis Beaumont. But Thomas Dekker began a six-year stint in a debtors' prison. After the burning of the Globe, Shakespeare may have advised his colleagues to cut their losses and confine themselves to the Blackfriars. He seems to have sold his interest in the Globe when his colleagues set about rebuilding it ready for opening inside a year. This, I think, is when he determined to return to Stratford. His last remaining brother had died in February 1613, leaving only himself and his sister Joan of John Shakespeare's eight children. There is no reference to theatrical shares in Shakespeare's will, and he may have sold his portion to the three fellow-actors to whom he left £1 6s 8d each to enable them to buy a memorial ring, Burbage, Heminges and Condell. The last two would, in 1623, give him the greater memorial of the First Folio. Shakespeare's evident concern in the time that remained to him was with property. For several months from September 1614, he was peripherally involved in William Combe's attempts to enclose the common fields in Welcombe; some of his land would have been affected. The sparse surviving documentation allows the impression that he followed the old Stanley family policy of waiting to see who won, Combe or commoners. His last weeks of life were not, as they might have been, made happier by his daughter Judith's marriage to Thomas Quiney, whose family had been closely linked with the Shakespeares for many years and three generations. The couple married on 10 February 1616. On 26 March, Thomas was in the ecclesiastical court of Stratford, confessing to fornication with a certain Margaret Wheeler. Childbirth had accounted for mother and baby earlier in the month. The fornicator escaped with a fine of five shillings.

In January 1616, Philip Henslowe, most enduring of play-house-owners, died full of years. In March, Francis Beaumont, who had retired from a career as a playwright on his marriage in 1613, died in his early thirties. Towards the end of April, after altering his will to protect his daughter Judith from the unreliable Thomas Quiney, Shakespeare followed where Henslowe and Beaumont had led. It was Ben Jonson's year, not his. On 1 February, the King's granting of a life pension made Jonson an *avant la lettre* Poet Laureate, a professional recognition that ought to have gratified Shakespeare. On its way through William Stansby's presses was the impressive Folio of Jonson's *Works*, which would stand alone until 1623, when Heminges and Condell completed their monument to Shakespeare's professional career.

Notes

1 SHAKESPEARE AND STRATFORD

1 There is considerable variation in population statistics. I have taken this one from A. L. Beier, 'The social problems of an Elizabethan country town: Warwick, 1580–90', in Clark (ed.), *Country Towns in Pre-Industrial England*, p. 54.

2 See Clark, *The English Alehouse*, p. 110.

3 Ibid., p. 127.

4 Thomas R. Forbes, 'By what disease or casualty: the changing face of death in London', in Webster (ed.), *Health, Medicine and Mortality*, p. 139.

5 Roger Schofield and E. A. Wrigley, 'Infant and child mortality in England in the late Tudor and early Stuart period', in Webster (ed.) *Health, Medicine and Mortality*, p. 95.

6 Once again statistics vary. Schoenbaum cites Malone as his authority for the figure of 200 and pitches the population at between 1, 200 and 1, 400. See *William Shakespeare*, p. 24. J. F. D. Shrewsbury prefers 176 out of a total population of 800. See *A History of Bubonic Plague*, p. 202. We can only guess how many died for reasons other than the plague.

7 Paul Slack, 'Mortality crises and epidemic disease in England, 1485–1610', in Webster, p. 43.

8 Slack, 'Mortality crises', p. 57.

9 Andrew B. Appleby, 'Diet in sixteenth-century England: sources, problems, possibilities', in Webster, pp. 108–12.

10 See Clark (ed.), *Country Towns*, p. 59.

11 See, for example, Appleby in Webster, pp. 97–116 and Beier, *Masterless Men, passim*.

12 Willett (ed.), *Brecht on Theatre*, p. 192.

13 See Philip Styles, 'The borough of Stratford-upon-Avon', in *Victoria County History of the County of Warwick* (London, 1945), vol. 3, p. 249.

14 Clark, *The English Alehouse*, p. 126.

15 Beier, *Masterless Men*, p. 110.

16 Ibid., p. 16. (Clark, in *The English Alehouse*, p. 129, gives a figure of 80,000 vagrants during the land and housing shortages of the 1550s, 1590s and 1620s.)

17 These examples are from Beier, *Masterless Men*, p. 114.

18 See *Masterless Men*, p. 6.

19 To plead 'benefit of clergy' was to seek the shelter of a mediaeval escape clause for clerics arraigned in a secular court. Having proved themselves genuine clerics by reading a Latin verse from the Bible (usually the opening of the 51st Psalm), they could claim the privilege of being tried by a spiritual court, which did not pass death sentences. In late Tudor England, the process was much abbreviated, and a successful plea of 'benefit of clergy' meant a simple exemption from punishment for a first offence.

20 The reference here is to the use by country landowners of new-fangled coaches to carry them to London – away from their traditional local hospitality.

21 From *London and the Countrey Carbonadoed*, quoted in Wilson, *Life in Shakespeare's England*, pp. 286–7.

22 Quoted by E. G. R. Taylor, 'Leland's England', in Darby (ed.), *An Historical Geography of England*, p. 340.

23 Quoted by Styles in 'The borough of Stratford-upon-Avon', p. 239.

24 See Beier, *Masterless Men*, p. 75.

25 See, for example, Bristol, *Carnival and Theater*.

26 Charles Phythian-Adams has proposed a division of the communal year into two parts, a 'ritualistic' period from 24 December to 24 June and a 'secular' period from 25 June to 23 December. The regular ceremonies, he believes, all took place during the ritualistic period. See his 'Ceremony and the citizen: the communal year at Coventry, 1450–1550', in Clark and Slack (eds.), *Crisis and Order*.

27 The Feast of Corpus Christi, instituted in 1311, took place on the Thursday following Trinity Sunday. It was variously practised in the Catholic countries of Western Europe. In Britain, the formal procession escorting the Host gave an opportunity for the trade guilds to display their own distinctiveness, and the Church fostered the development of scripturally based plays as an extension of this display. Surviving Mystery (or Miracle) plays give evidence of the sophistication and inventiveness of the communal response to the opportunities provided by the Feast of Corpus Christi.

28 See Honigmann, *Shakespeare: the 'Lost Years'*, p. 118. I have not read the paper by D. L. Thomas and N. E. Evans to which he there refers.

29 The standard work on Shakespeare's education remains Baldwin's *William Shakespeare's 'Small Latine & Lesse Greeke'*, but readers less inclined to copiousness may prefer the lovingly eccentric style of Fripp, *Shakespeare, Man and Artist*, vol. 1, pp. 82–124.

30 *Ben Jonson*, ed. Herford and Simpson (Oxford, 1925–52), vol. 6, p. 345.

31 These are the chapter headings of McGrath's *Papists and Puritans*.

32 McGrath, *Papists and Puritans*, p. 375.

33 There is an excellent chapter by Patrick Collinson, 'The downfall of Archbishop Grindal and its place in Elizabethan political and ecclesiastical history', in Clark, Smith and Tyacke (eds.), *The English Commonwealth, 1547–1640*, pp. 39–57.

34 The phrase is from the editorial introduction to Clark and Slack, *Crisis and Order in English Towns*, p. 27.

35 Schoenbaum, *William Shakespeare*, p. 39.

36 Quoted in Fripp, *Shakespeare*, vol. 1, p. 164.

37 Levi, *The Life and Times of William Shakespeare*, pp. 18–20.

38 For Honigmann's discussion of the Shakeshafte/Shakespeare identity, see *Shakespeare: the 'Lost Years'*, p. 18. It should be said that Elizabethan spelling is consistent only in its inconsistency. With reference to the religious significance of the locality of Hoghton's residence, I was interested to read, in Claire Cross's *The Puritan Earl*, p. 246, that in 1966 'Preston has the largest number of Catholics in proportion to its population of any town in England.'

39 See Honigmann, *Shakespeare's Impact on his Contemporaries*, pp. 1–14.

40 For a mind-numbing exploration of circumstances that might have precipitated the composition of *The Phoenix and the Turtle*, see Honigmann, *Shakespeare: the 'Lost Years'*, pp. 90–113.

41 See Coward, *The Stanleys*, p. 167.

42 The plot involving Lord Strange has been explored with some ingenuity in Devlin, *Hamlet's Divinity*.

43 Rowse, *William Shakespeare*, p. 43.

44 Joel Hurstfield, 'The Elizabethan people in the age of Shakespeare', in Sutherland and Hurstfield (eds.), *Shakespeare's World*, p. 36.

45 Ralph Brooke's character and conduct are interestingly described in Willoughby, *A Printer of Shakespeare*, pp. 143–6.

46 See Holderness (ed.), *The Shakespeare Myth*, p. 205.

2 ESTABLISHING A CAREER: OF PATRONS AND PROVINCES

1 Sheavyn, *The Literary Profession*, p. vii.

2 See Thomas, *Cardigan*, pp. 123–7.

3 The examples are from Bristol, *Carnival & Theater*, pp. 202 and 211.

4 The rumours were, at best, half-true. The Norfolk uprising was activated by discontents voiced at the annual gathering in Wymondham on 7 July for the Feast of the Translation of St Thomas Becket. It was on 8 July that a number of those who attended the Feast, which featured a pageant or play about Becket, set off to uproot Sir John Flowerdew's enclosing fences. It is, none the less, the clear view of a modern historian of the rebellion that the gathering of so large a number of people for the Feast of St Thomas at Wymondham in 1549 provided the impetus that turned discontent into mutiny. See Land, *Kett's Rebellion*, p. 25.

5 For information about the Stanleys, I am primarily indebted to Coward, *The Stanleys*.

6 See below, pp. 118 and 124.

7 I do not know why the title emanates from the County of Derby rather than from the more appropriate County of Chester. Perhaps Lord Stanley wished to incorporate a punning reference to his estates in West Derby, near Liverpool.

8 For the early history of pawnbroking, see Hudson, *Pawnbroking*, chapter 1.

9 See Cross, *The Puritan Earl*, p. 81.

10 Litigation over the Earl of Huntingdon's Canford estates, succinctly described by Cross, pp. 87–96, is a typical example.

11 This translation of *De Legationibus* is available in the Classics of International Law series (New York, 1924), vol. 2, p. 139.

12 Ibid., p. 140.

13 Horne (ed.), *The Life and Minor Works of George Peele*, p. 233.

14 Quoted in Coward, *The Stanleys*, pp. 94–5.

15 Quoted in Jeayes, *Descriptive Catalogue of Charters and Muniments at Berkeley Castle*, p. 335. I am grateful to David Wiles for this reference.

16 Quoted in Coward, *The Stanleys*, p. 53.

17 Among the nearly 700 pages of Francis Meres's *Palladis Tamia* (1598) are included sixteen pages of 'Comparative discourse of our English Poets, with the Greeke, Latine, and Italian Poets'. Though highly derivative, it is a unique commentary on Elizabethan literary values.

18 Quoted in Gair, *The Children of Paul's*, p. 118.

19 Quoted in Chambers, *The Elizabethan Stage*, vol. 2, p. 127.

20 Quoted in Coward, *The Stanleys*, p. 3.

21 For detailed information on continental tours by English actors, see Limon, *Gentlemen of a Company*.

22 This invaluable series, under the executive editorship of Alexandra Johnston, groups its findings regionally, publishing its thick volumes under the heading of Devon, York etc. The patchwork is by no means complete and will be uncovering new information well into the next century.

23 See Bentley, *The Profession of Player in Shakespeare's Time*, pp. 185–6.

24 Ibid., p. 201.

25 Quoted in Limon, *Gentlemen of a Company*, p. 20.

26 Quoted in Limon, p. 21.

27 Quoted in Limon, p. 13.

28 The alternatives of thirty or forty are discussed in Bentley, *The Profession of Player*, pp. 181–2. He believes that the permitted number was raised in *c.* 1608, but I am not convinced that the numbers were ever so precisely calculated.

29 I have examined the sources, incidence and theatrical effects of plague in more detail in my *Shakespeare's Theatre*, pp. 7–8, from which I am here silently quoting. For fuller explorations of the plague in action, see F. P. Wilson, *The Plague in Shakespeare's London* and Shrewsbury, *A History of Bubonic Plague*.

30 *Henslowe's Diary*, ed. Foakes and Rickert, p. 130. Fond as I am of Elizabethan spelling, I have thought it politic to spare the reader the wilder vagaries of Henslowe's.

31 From *The Bel-man of London*, in *Non-Dramatic Works*, ed. A. B. Grosart (1884–6), vol. 3, p. 81.

32 So, at least, was the custom in Gloucester as recalled by R. Willis in *Mount Tabor* (London, 1639), p. 110.

33 This list is from Fripp (*Shakespeare*, vol. 1, p. 209), who got it from Murray's *English Dramatic Companies*. For a vigorous attack on Murray's multifold errors, see David Galloway, 'Records of early English drama in the provinces and what they may tell us about the Elizabethan theatre', in Hibbard (ed.), *The Elizabethan Theatre VII*, pp. 87–9.

34 See Carson, *A Companion to Henslowe's Diary*, p. 38.

35 This is Carol Rutter's deduction from a record in Henslowe's *Diary* for 8 May 1593 of a loan of £15 to his nephew Francis, 'to laye downe for his share to the Quenes players when they brocke & went into the contrey to playe'. See Rutter (ed.), *Documents of the Rose Playhouse*, p. 70.

36 See Kathleen M. D. Barker, 'An early seventeenth-century provincial playhouse', in *Theatre Notebook* 29 (1975), pp. 81–4 and Mark C. Pilkinton, 'The playhouse in Wine Street, Bristol', in *Theatre Notebook* 37 (1983), pp. 14–21.

37 See Bentley, *The Profession of Player*, p. 188.

3 ESTABLISHING A CAREER: LONDON 1590

1 For details of the lawsuit, see Janet S. Loengard, 'An Elizabethan lawsuit: John Brayne, his carpenter, and the building of the Red Lion theatre', in *Shakespeare Quarterly* 34, no. 3 (Autumn, 1983), pp. 298–310.

2 My population estimates conflate the figures suggested by Clark and Slack in *Crisis and Order in English Towns* and by Wrightson in *English Society*, p. 128.

3 Quoted in Chambers, *The Elizabethan Stage*, vol. 4, pp. 266–7.

4 Bradbrook, *The Rise of the Common Player*, p. 18.

5 The alternative arguments can be followed in *The Elizabethan Stage*, vol. 2, pp. 129–30 and *William Shakespeare*, vol. 1, pp. 277–93.

6 Thomas Nashe, *Works*, ed. R. B. McKerrow (Oxford, 1958), vol. 1, p. 212.

7 Sidney Thomas, 'On the dating of Shakespeare's early plays', in *Shakespeare Quarterly* 39, no. 2 (Summer, 1988), 187–94.

8 Thomas overstates his case here by including in the number *Love's Labour's Lost*, whose writing Honigmann ascribes to the winter of 1592, immediately following Greene's death.

9 Once again Thomas overplays his hand, partly by disguising his own mistrust of Meres and partly by misrepresenting Honigmann. Meres makes no mention of the *Henry VI* plays, which Thomas includes in his count of eleven, as he evidently also includes the mysterious *Love labours wonne* (perhaps assuming that it is *The Taming of the Shrew*). Nor does he acknowledge Honigmann's ascription of *Love's Labour's Lost* to late 1592 and the fact that Meres, writing in 1598, would not have included all the plays that Shakespeare may have added in that year (*Henry V* and *Much Ado* being candidates). Even so, there is substance in his concern about the discrepancy between the productivity of the apprenticeship years up to the end of 1591 (ten plays) and the leanness of the next six years (only six plays) that results from Honigmann's proposals.

10 See Chambers, *The Elizabethan Stage*, vol. 1, p. 309.

11 Nashe, *Selected Writings*, ed. Stanley Wells (London, 1964), p. 245.

12 Johnson, *Southwark and the City*, p. 138.

13 See Burford, *The Orrible Synne*, pp. 178–88.

14 See Johnson, *Southwark and the City*, p. v.

15 *Henslowe's Diary*, ed. Foakes and Rickert, p. 9.

16 Thomson, *Shakespeare's Theatre*, p. 23.

17 In addition to books by Carol Rutter and Neil Carson, already cited, see Bernard Beckerman's chapter on Henslowe in Donohue (ed.), *The Theatrical Manager*.

18 Rutter, *Documents of the Rose*, p. 102.
19 Alleyn married Henslowe's step-daughter, Joan Woodward, on 22 October 1592.
20 Rutter, p. 8.
21 See E. W. Ives, 'The law and the lawyers', in *Shakespeare Survey* 17 (1964), p. 80.
22 Leaflet published by Museum of London (Department of Greater London Archaeology), 1989.
23 See, for example, Orrell, *The Quest for Shakespeare's Globe*, pp. 161–2.
24 Orrell's research has guided the plans for the building of the new Globe on the Bankside. These plans are outlined in Gurr with Orrell, *Rebuilding Shakespeare's Globe*. Orrell and Gurr have given their preliminary responses to the Rose findings in 'What the Rose can tell us', in the *Times Literary Supplement*, June 9–15, 1989, pp. 636 and 649–50.
25 *Rebuilding Shakespeare's Globe*, p. 113.
26 The Fortune contract has been frequently reprinted. See, for example, *Henslowe's Diary*, ed. Foakes and Rickert, pp. 306–10.
27 See Appendix A of *The Quest for Shakespeare's Globe* and *Theatre Notebook* 38(1984), pp. 69–76.

4 A PLAYTEXT AND ITS CONTEXT

1   Dutton, *William Shakespeare*, pp. 27–8.
2   Rutter, *Documents of the Rose*, p. 141.
3   Ibid., p. 91.
4   Quoted in Bentley, *The Profession of Dramatist*, p. 52.
5   See Strong, *The Cult of Elizabeth*, p. 100.
6   James Boaden, *Memoirs of the Life of John Philip Kemble* (London, 1825), vol. 1, p. 193.
7   Carson, *Companion to Henslowe's Diary*, pp. 73–4.
8   There is a useful short account of Phillips's career, together with excerpts from his will in Nungezer, *A Dictionary of Actors*, pp. 180–2.
9   For a commentary on this list, see Carson, *Companion to Henslowe's Diary*, pp. 51–2.
10 Kenny, *Elizabeth's Admiral*, p. 6.
11 *Henslowe's Diary*, pp. 98–9.
12 See Carson, *Companion to Henslowe's Diary*, pp. 37–8.
13 The inventory is in Mathew, *The Jacobean Age*, p. 35.
14 See David Galloway in Hibbard (ed.), *Elizabethan Theatre VII*, p. 99.
15 Gwynne's play flattered the King's learning in two ways. It was in

Latin and it was about witches. *Tres Sibyllae* was performed for James I at Oxford in August 1605. It may have some slight bearing on *Macbeth*.

16 Cook, *The Privileged Playgoers of Shakespeare's London*, p. 272.
17 Gurr, *Playgoing in Shakespeare's London*, pp. 85–97.
18 Ibid., p. 38.
19 Ibid., p. 64.
20 Ibid., p. 150.
21 The quotation is from Gurr, *Playgoing in Shakespeare's London*, p. 150, but the contrast of the two companies is discussed on pp. 147–52.
22 Martin Butler, 'Royal slaves? The Stuart Court and the theatres', *Renaissance Drama Newsletter*, Supplement Two (University of Warwick, 1984), p. 18.

5 SERVANT TO THE LORD CHAMBERLAIN: 1594–1603

1 See Bray, *Homosexuality in Renaissance England*, p. 27 and *passim*.
2 Quoted in Chambers, *The Elizabethan Stage*, vol. 4, pp. 223–4. *The Anatomie of Abuses* was first published in 1583.
3 Nicholas Rowe (ed.), *Works of Shakespeare* (London, 1709), vol. 1, p. x. The 'Italian Eunuchs' were the *castrati* singers, for whom there was a rage.
4 *Henslowe's Diary*, p. 132. *Patient Griselda* was a collaborative work by Dekker, Chettle and Houghton.
5 Rutter, *Documents of the Rose*, p. 171.
6 See *Shakespeare: the 'Lost Years'*, pp. 64ff.
7 For a fuller discussion of this contrast, see Wiles, *Shakespeare's Clown*, pp. 103–7. Wiles's book is rich in new perceptions of the Shakespearean text's playhouse context.
8 William A. Ringler, Jr, 'The number of actors in Shakespeare's early plays', in Bentley (ed.), *The Seventeenth-Century Stage*, pp. 110–34.
9 Richard Mansfield, *The Protean Player*, unpublished Ph.D. thesis in the University of East Anglia, 1989.
10 For a fuller examination of Brome's contract, see Bentley, *The Profession of Dramatist in Shakespeare's Time*, chapter 6.
11 For informed observations on indoor playing in inns, see Wickham, *Early English Stages*, vol. 2, part 2, pp. 99–100.
12 A throne was an essential item of furniture on the Elizabethan stage. Henslowe may have been copying the Theatre in deciding to build in a pulley system which would allow the raising and

lowering of the throne from the roofing canopy, or 'Heavens', over the Rose stage.

13 *Masterless Men*, p. 84.

14 I have been fortunate to read in typescript David Wiles's *Saint Valentine is Past*, a detailed argument that the play was commissioned for this particular wedding. Wiles finds the text peppered with allusions to the Carey/Berkeley match.

15 Strong, *The Cult of Elizabeth*, p. 165. Strong's chapter on the Garter pageantry is highly informative.

16 Ibid., p. 173.

17 Quoted in Bevington, *Tudor Drama and Politics*, pp. 8–9.

18 Nashe, *Works*, vol. 2, p. 182.

19 Carol Rutter's argument that the Privy Council order was not directly connected with *The Isle of Dogs* (see *Documents*, pp. 115–17) is interestingly circumstantial, but not, in my view, conclusive. If it was not *The Isle of Dogs* that galvanised the Privy Council, what was it?

20 Quoted in Fripp, *Shakespeare*, vol. 2, p. 480.

21 Robert Lacey, *Robert, Earl of Essex*, pp. 201ff.

22 W. B. Rye (ed.), *England as seen by Foreigners in the days of Elizabeth and James I* (London, 1865), pp. 104–5.

23 For an explanation of 'benefit of clergy', see note 19 to chapter 1.

24 *Shakespeare's Clown*, p. 23.

25 *Spindle Shank Em* is a long monologue spoken by Emma Ball, a London prostitute in whose house Tarlton died and who bore Robert Greene's son. It has been impeccably researched and is packed with contemporary social detail.

26 *Shakespeare's Clown*, p. 146.

27 Everard Guilpin, *Skialetheia*, is Satire 1 in the Shakespeare Association Facsimiles (London, 1931), vol. 1.

28 Knollys to Wilson, British Library, Harleian MS 6992, no. 44, f.89.

29 Hotson, *The First Night of Twelfth Night*.

30 Sir John Harington, *Nugae Antiquae* (London, 1769), vol. 1, p. 317.

31 *The Memoirs of Robert Carey*, ed. Mares, p. 60.

6 OF QUEEN, CHAMBERLAINS, ADMIRAL AND KING

1 Smith, *Elizabeth Tudor*, pp. 79–82.

2 Levi, *Life and Times*, p. xxii.

3 *The Elizabethan Stage*, vol. 4, pp. 111–16.

4 Elizabeth I never went further north than Coventry.

5 Quoted in Cross, *The Puritan Earl*, p. 214.
6 Sir Robert Naunton, *Fragmenta Regalia*, Arber's *English Reprints* (London, 1870), pp. 46–7.
7 For Rowse's treatment of Lord Hunsdon, see *Simon Forman*, pp. 99ff.
8 Carey, *Memoirs*, p. 3.
9 Quoted in Jeayes, *Descriptive Catalogue of Charters and Muniments*, p. 323.
10 See Andrews, *Elizabethan Privateering Voyages to the West Indies*, pp. 243–65.
11 Robert Kenny, *Elizabeth's Admiral*, p. 2.

7 SERVANT TO THE KING: 1603–1616

1 Quoted in Miles, *Ben Jonson*, p. 74. This excellent biography gives a real sense of Jonson's professional career.
2 Goldberg, *James I and the Politics of Literature*, p. 239. The full discussion of *Measure for Measure* is on pp. 230–9.
3 See Kenyon, *The Stuarts*, p. 33.
4 There is a lucid account of the provenance of the *Apology* in J. H. Hexter, 'The *Apology*', in Ollard and Tudor-Craig (eds.), *For Veronica Wedgwood These*, pp. 13–44.
5 Tanner (ed.), *Constitutional Documents of the Reign of James I*, p. 218.
6 Ibid., p. 222.
7 The full version of this anonymous poem is in Williams, *Sir Walter Raleigh*, p. 185. Williams also includes a fairly full transcript of Raleigh's trial.
8 Rye, *England as seen by Foreigners*, pp. 123–4.
9 Sturgess, *Jacobean Private Theatres*, p. 161.
10 See Elizabeth Read Foster, 'Staging a Parliament in Early Stuart England', in Clark, Smith and Tyacke (eds.), *The English Commonwealth*, p. 139.
11 Bodleian Library, MS Malone 23, 20v.
12 *Eastward Ho!* included two jocular references to James I's Scottish favourites, a subject on which the King was sensitive. Jonson and Chapman, who were both imprisoned, protested that the offensive passages were the work of Marston, who was not imprisoned.
13 See Levi, Appendix 1, pp. 345–58, where the verses are printed in full.
14 See Harington, *Nugae Antiquae*, vol. 1, pp. 349–50.
15 Mathew, *The Jacobean Age*, p. 1.
16 For a fuller account of the *Puritan* affair, see Gair, *The Children of Paul's*, pp. 160–75. The play has been tentatively ascribed to Middleton.

17 Rye, *England as seen by Foreigners*, pp. 110–11.
18 Sir Charles Cornwallis, *The Life of Henry, Prince of Wales* (London, 1641), p.93.
19 The supposed source of this statement was Prince Henry's secretary, Adam Newton. See S. R. Gardiner, *History of England, 1603–1642* (London, 1884), vol. 2, p. 57.
20 Rye, *England as seen by Foreigners*, p. 61.
21 For a full version, see Levi, *Life & Times*, Appendix 10, pp. 378–9.

Bibliography

This is a list of the books I have knowingly used in the writing of my own. It omits many to which I might or should have referred and many more whose views have formed mine beyond my awareness.

Andrews, K. R. *Elizabethan Privateering Voyages to the West Indies, 1588–1595* (Cambridge, 1959).

Aston, Trevor, (ed.) *Crisis in Europe: 1560–1660* (London, 1965).

Baldwin, T. W., *William Shakespeare's 'Small Latine & Lesse Greeke'*, 2 vols. (Urbana, IL, 1944).

Beckerman, Bernard, *Shakespeare at the Globe* (New York, 1962).

Beier, A. L., *Masterless Men* (London, 1985).

Bentley, G. E., (ed.) *The Seventeenth-Century Stage* (Chicago and London, 1968).

The Profession of Dramatist in Shakespeare's Time (Princeton, NJ, 1971).

The Profession of Player in Shakespeare's Time (Princeton, NJ, 1984).

Bevington, David, *Tudor Drama and Politics* (Cambridge, MA, 1968).

Billington, Sandra, *A Social History of the Fool* (Brighton, 1984).

Bloom, J. Harvey, *Shakespeare's Garden* (London, 1903).

Bradbrook, M. C., *The Rise of the Common Player* (Cambridge, 1962).

Bray, Alan, *Homosexuality in Renaissance England* (London, 1982).

Bristol, Michael, *Carnival and Theater* (New York, 1985).

Brooks, Eric St John, *Sir Christopher Hatton: Queen Elizabeth's Favourite* (London, 1946).

Burford, C. J., *The Orrible Synne: London Lechery from Roman to Cromwellian Times* (London, 1973).

Carson, Neil, *A Companion to Henslowe's Diary* (Cambridge, 1988).

Chambers, E. K., *The Elizabethan Stage*, 4 vols. (Oxford, 1923, revised ed., 1951).

William Shakespeare: a Study of Facts and Problems, 2 vols. (Oxford, 1930).

Clark, Peter & Paul Slack (eds.) *Crisis and Order in English Towns, 1500–1700* (London, 1972).

Alan G. R. Smith & Nicholas Tyacke (eds.), *The English Commonwealth, 1570–1640: Essays in Politics & Society presented to Joel Hurstfield* (Leicester, 1979).

(ed.), *Country Towns in Pre-Industrial England* (Leicester, 1981).

The English Alehouse: a Social History, 1200–1830 (London, 1983).

Cook, A. J., *The Privileged Playgoers of Shakespeare's London, 1576–1642* (Princeton, NJ, 1981).

Coward, Barry, *The Stanleys: Lords Stanley and Earls of Derby, 1385–1672* (Manchester, 1983).

Cross, Claire, *The Puritan Earl: the Life of Henry Hastings, 3rd Earl of Huntingdon* (London, 1966).

Darby, H. C., (ed.), *An Historical Geography of England before A. D. 1800* (Cambridge, 2nd ed., 1948).

Devlin, Christopher, *Hamlet's Divinity* (London, 1963).

Dollimore, Jonathan, & Alan Sinfield (eds.), *Political Shakespeare* (Manchester, 1985).

Donohue, Joseph W. Jr (ed.), *The Theatrical Manager in England and America* (Princeton, NJ, 1971).

Dutton, Richard, *William Shakespeare: a Literary Life* (London, 1989).

Eccles, Christine, *The Rose Theatre*, London, 1990.

Eccles, Mark, *Shakespeare in Warwickshire* (Madison, WI, 1961).

Foakes, R. A., & R. T. Rickert (eds.) *Henslowe's Diary* (Cambridge, 1961).

Fox, Levi, *The Borough Town of Stratford-upon-Avon* (Stratford, 1953).

Fripp, Edgar, *Shakespeare, Man and Artist*, 2 vols. (London, 1938).

Gair, Reavley, *The Children of Paul's: the Story of a Theatre Company, 1553–1608* (Cambridge, 1982).

Goldberg, Jonathan, *James I and the Politics of Literature* (Baltimore, 1983).

Graves, R. B., *English Stage Lighting, 1575–1642*, unpublished Ph.D. thesis in Northwestern University, 1976.

Gray, Arthur, *A Chapter in the Early Life of Shakespeare* (Cambridge, 1926).

Griffin, Alice, (Venezky) *Pageantry on the Shakespearean Stage* (New York, 1951).

Gurr, Andrew, *The Shakespearean Stage, 1574–1642* (Cambridge, 1970).

Playgoing in Shakespeare's London (Cambridge, 1987).

(with John Orrell) *Rebuilding Shakespeare's Globe* (London, 1989).

Harbage, Alfred, *Shakespeare's Audience* (New York, 1941).

Hattaway, Michael, *Elizabethan Popular Theatre* (London, 1982).

Haynes, Alan, *The White Bear: Robert Dudley, the Elizabethan Earl of Leicester* (London, 1987).

Hibbard, G. R. (ed.), *The Elizabethan Theatre VII* (London, 1981).

Holderness, Graham, (ed.), *The Shakespeare Myth* (Manchester, 1988).

Honigmann, E. A. J., *Shakespeare's Impact on his Contemporaries* (London, 1982).

Shakespeare: the 'Lost Years' (Manchester, 1985).

Horne, David H., *The Life and Minor Works of George Peel* (New Haven, CT, 1952).

Hotson, Leslie, *The First Night of Twelfth Night* (London, 1954).

Hudson, Kenneth, *Pawnbroking: an Aspect of British Social History* (London, 1982).

Hyde, Mary Crapo, *Playwriting for Elizabethans* (New York, 1949).

Jeayes, I. H., *Descriptive Catalogue of Charters & Muniments at Berkeley Castle* (Bristol, 1982).

Johnson, David, *Southwark and the City* (Oxford, 1969).

Kenny, Robert W., *Elizabeth's Admiral: the Political Career of Charles Howard, Earl of Nottingham* (Baltimore, 1970).

Kenyon, J. P., *The Stuarts* (London, 1966).

Lacey, Robert, *Robert, Earl of Essex: an Elizabethan Icarus* (London, 1971).

Land, Stephen K., *Kett's Rebellion* (Ipswich, 1977).

Levi, Peter, *The Life and Times of William Shakespeare* (London, 1988).

Limon, Jerzy, *Gentlemen of a Company* (Cambridge, 1985).

McGrath, Patrick, *Papists and Puritans under Elizabeth I* (London, 1967).

Mansfield, Richard, *The Protean Player*, unpublished Ph.D. thesis in the University of East Anglia, 1989.

Mares, F. H., *The Memoirs of Robert Carey* (Oxford, 1972).

Mathew, David, *The Jacobean Age* (London, 1938).

Mercer, Eric, *Elizabethan Art: 1553–1625* (Oxford, 1962).

Miles, Rosalind, *Ben Jonson: his life and work* (London, 1986).

Murray, J. T., *English Dramatic Companies, 1558–1642* (2 vols., London, 1910).

Nicoll, Allardyce, (ed.), *Shakespeare Survey* 17, 'Shakespeare in His Own Age' (Cambridge, 1964).

Nungezer, Edwin, *A Dictionary of Actors and of Other Persons Associated with the Public Representations of Plays in England before 1642* (New Haven, CT, 1929).

Ollard, Richard, & Pamela Tudor-Craig (eds.), *For Veronica Wedgwood These: Studies in Seventeenth-Century History* (London, 1986).

Orrell, John, *The Quest for Shakespeare's Globe* (Cambridge, 1983).

Parker, Patricia, & Geoffrey Hartman (eds.), *Shakespeare and the Question of Theory* (London, 1985).

Rowse, A. L., *Simon Forman* (London, 1974).

William Shakespeare: a Biography (London, 1963).

Rutter, Carol (ed.), *Documents of the Rose Playhouse* (Manchester, 1984).

Schoenbaum, Samuel, *William Shakespeare: a Documentary Life* (Oxford, 1975).

Sheavyn, Phoebe, *The Literary Profession in the Elizabethan Age*, 2nd ed., revised by J. W. Saunders (Manchester, 1967).

Shrewsbury, J. F. D., *A History of Bubonic Plague in the British Isles* (Cambridge, 1971).

Smith, Lacey Baldwin, *Elizabeth Tudor* (London, 1976).

Stone, Lawrence, *The Crisis of the Aristocracy, 1558–1641* (Oxford, 1965).

Strong, Roy, *The Cult of Elizabeth* (London, 1977).

Sturgess, Keith, *Jacobean Private Theatres* (London, 1987).

Styles, Philip, 'The borough of Stratford-upon-Avon', in the *Victoria County History of the County of Warwick*, vol. 3, 1945.

Sutherland, James, & Joel Hurstfield (eds.) *Shakespeare's World* (London, 1964).

Tanner, J. R., (ed.) *Constitutional Documents of the Reign of James I* (Cambridge, 1930).

Thomas, Donald, *Cardigan: the Hero of Balaclava* (London, 1974).

Thomson, Peter, *Shakespeare's Theatre* (London, 1983).

Trent, Christopher, *Greater London* (London, 1965).

Webster, Charles, (ed.), *Health, Medicine and Mortality in the Sixteenth Century* (Cambridge, 1979).

Wickham, Glynne, *Early English Stages* (London, 1972).

Wiles, David, *Shakespeare's Clown: Actor and Text in the Elizabethan Playhouse* (Cambridge, 1987).

Saint Valentine is Past, typescript awaiting publication.

Willett, John (ed.), *Brecht on Theatre* (London, 1964).

Williams, Norman Lloyd, *Sir Walter Raleigh* (Harmondsworth, 1965).

Willoughby, E. E., *A Printer of Shakespeare* (London, 1934).

Wrightson, K., *English Society, 1580–1680* (London, 1982).

Wilson, F. P., *The Plague in Shakespeare's London* (Oxford, 1963).

Wilson, Jean, *Entertainments for Elizabeth I* (London, 1980).

Wilson, John Dover, *Life in Shakespeare's England* (Cambridge, 1911).

Young, Alan, *Tudor and Jacobean Tournaments* (London, 1987).

General index

'above' (on the Elizabethan stage) 137
Accession Day tournaments 31, 37–40,
   119, 181–2
Act for the Punishing of Vagabonds
   (1572) 25, 44, 48, 54
acting companies 25–8, 33–4, 42–5; (on
   the continent) 45–7, 130; (in the
   provinces) 47–51, 121
actors' apprentices 90–2, 93–4, 112, 170
actors parts 81–3
actors' status 46, 48–9, 62, 78, 108,
   109–10, 126–8, 146–8, 177–8
Admiral's Men 62, 69, 83, 88, 89, 90,
   94, 99, 108, 109, 110, 115, 116, 122,
   124, 128, 134, 136, 137, 139, 148,
   149, 150, 156, 180
Addenbrooke, John (of Stratford) 178
Allen, Giles 122, 126
Allen, William (Cardinal) 18
Alleyn, Edward 46, 49, 50, 51, 58,
   60–1, 61 (illus.), 63, 66, 68, 69, 75,
   78, 82, 92, 103, 108, 109, 115, 125,
   136, 156, 177
Alleyn, Joan (wife of Edward Alleyn)
   66
Allot, Robert (compiler of *England's
   Parnassus*) 134
Althorp House (residence of the Spencer
   family) 162–3
Anne, Queen (wife of James I) 162–3,
   167–8, 172, 175, 179
Apology (of the House of Commons) 166
Arden, Edward 14, 18
Arden family 5, 11, 13–14
Arden, Mary (see Shakespeare, Mary)
Arden, Robert 5
Armada, Spanish 18–19, 108, 146, 152
Armin, Robert 129, 136, 158, 161

Arnold, Dr Thomas 180
Aubrey, John 15
audiences 96–104
Avon, River (in Stratford) 6
Azores, Earl of Essex's expedition to the
   121, 124

Babington Plot (1586) 18
Bacon, Sir Francis 22
Banbury 6; (as 'Geneva') 11
Beaumont, Francis 181, 184, 187, 188
Beeston, Christopher 15, 95
Beeston, William 15
Beier, A. L. 4, 116
Bell Inn, playhouse at 55
Bel Savage Inn, playhouse at 55
Belvoir Castle 175
Berkeley family 11, 12, 116
Berkeley, Henry, Lord 11
Berkeley, Thomas 153, 154
Bingo (play by Edward Bond) 22
Blackfriars gatehouse, Shakespeare's
   purchase of 22, 186
Blackfriars petititon 118, 153–4
Blackfriars playhouse 97–8, 116, 118,
   137, 152–3, 176, 177, 178, 179, 181,
   186, 187
Blackfriars precinct 93, 116, 118, 142,
   153–4, 186
Boar's Head playhouse 43, 45, 55, 56
   (illus.), 123, 130, 131 (illus.), 134,
   137
Bodley, Sir Thomas 84
Boland, Catherine (pauper) 4
Boleyn, Anne 10, 155
Boleyn, Mary 150
Bond, Edward 22
boy companies 132, 141–2, 149, 177

Bradbrook, Muriel C. 58
Brayne, John 52–7, 63, 64
Brecht, Bertolt 3, 124
Brome, Richard 87, 113
Brooke, Henry (8th Lord Cobham)
 138, 167
Brooke, Ralph (York Herald) 20
Brooke, William (7th Lord Cobham)
 28, 117, 118, 149, 153, 154
brothels 65–6, 121, 152
Browne, Robert (actor) 43, 46
Bruce, Lenny 102
Bryan, George (actor) 46, 108, 110
Brydges, Grey (Lord Chandos) 175
Buckingham, Duke of (see Villiers,
 George)
Buckingham, Duke of (under Richard
 III) 25, 29
Bull Inn, playhouse at 55
Burbage, Cuthbert 110, 118, 122, 126,
 128, 178
Burbage, James 55, 63, 64, 69, 75, 99,
 108, 110, 113, 114, 118, 122, 126,
 150, 152–3
Burbage, Richard 63, 92, 103, 104, 108,
 109, 110, 118, 128, 137, 158, 160,
 170, 178, 187
Burghley, Lord (see Cecil, William)
Butler, Martin 100
Byrd, William (composer) 92

Cadiz, Earl of Essex's capture of 117
Calais, Spanish capture of 116
Caludon Castle (residence of Berkeley
 family) 11
Camden, William 2
Campion, Edmund (Jesuit missionary)
 18
Campion, Thomas (composer and poet)
 92
Cardigan, James Brudenell, 7th Earl of
 24
Carey, Elizabeth (daughter of 2nd Lord
 Hunsdon) 116, 153, 154
Carey, George (2nd Lord Hunsdon) 31,
 41, 44, 93, 16, 117, 118–19, 136,
 142, 147 (illus.), 149, 153–5, 162
Carey, Henry (1st Lord Hunsdon) 31,
 41, 44, 66, 107, 108–9, 110–11,
 113–14, 116, 117, 118, 149, 150–3,
 155
Carey, Katherine (daughter of 1st Lord

Hunsdon and wife of Charles
 Howard) 109, 154, 157
Carey, Robert (son of 1st Lord
 Hunsdon) 143–4, 153
Carisbrooke Castle (residence of George
 Carey) 154
Carleton, Dudley 121
carnival 24–5, 130
Carr, Robert 184
Carson, Neil 88
Catesby family 11
Catesby, Robert (Gunpowder Plot
 conspirator) 163
Catherine of Aragon, Queen 10
Catholicism in England 10–16, 18–20,
 163–5, 180
Cecil, Robert (1st Earl of Salisbury) 31,
 42, 43, 109, 117, 125, 138, 144, 153,
 156, 157, 175–7, 180, 182–4, 186
Cecil, William (Lord Burghley) 13, 19,
 31, 41–2, 117, 120, 125, 141, 151,
 156
censorship 130–2, 135–6
Chamberlain, John 121, 168
Chamberlain, office of (see Lord
 Chamberlain)
Chamberlain's Men (King's Men from
 1603) 37, 47, 68, 94, 95–6, 97, 98,
 99, 100, 101, 106–44, 148, 149, 155,
 158–61, 162–87
Chambers, E. K. 58, 60, 61, 62, 149
Chandos, Lord (see Brydges, Grey)
Chapman, George 80, 164, 177
Charles, Prince (future King Charles I)
 4, 146, 170, 179, 186
Chekhov, Anton 92
Chettle, Henry 145
Children of St Paul's (also Paul's Boys)
 43, 132, 137, 149, 177
Children of the Revels (also Children of
 the Chapel Royal) 137, 149, 153,
 177–8
Cholmley, John (Henslowe's business
 partner) 68
Christian IV (King of Denmark) 175,
 177
Christs Teares (pamphlet by Thomas
 Nashe) 120
Cicero 10
Clifford family 30, 45
Clifford, George (3rd Earl of
 Cumberland) 37, 45, 147 (illus.)

Clifford, Margaret (wife of 4th Earl of
   Derby) 32, 35, 45
Clink, Liberty of the 65, 66, 126, 134
Clopton Bridge (in Stratford) 6
Clopton family 11
Clopton, Sir Hugh 6
clothes, extravagance of 35, 36–7, 90,
   146
clowns 101–3, 110, 136
Cobham, Lords (see Brooke, Henry and
   William)
College of Heralds 6, 20
Combe, William (of Stratford) 22, 36,
   187
concordia discors 34
Condell, Henry 111, 158, 170, 178, 187,
   188
Cook, A. J. 96
Copperplate Map 67
Cornelius, Michael (merchant
   moneylender) 35
Corpus Christi plays 9
costume on the stage 35, 46–7, 89–90,
   146, 160
Cottom, John (Shakespeare's
   schoolteacher) 15–16
Covent Garden Theatre 24
Coventry 6, 9, 11, 48
Cowley, Richard 112, 158
Crashawe, William (Puritan preacher)
   177
Critz, John de 138 (illus.)
Cromwell, Thomas 31
Cross Keys Inn, playhouse at 55, 114
Culham Hythe 6
Cumberland, Earl of (see Clifford,
   George)
Curtain playhouse 58, 63, 122, 125,
   126, 130, 137

Dacre, Leonard 150
Davies, Sir John (of Hereford) 62
Dawes, Robert 90
Dekker, Thomas 48, 80, 88, 112, 141,
   164, 187
Derby, Earls of (see Stanley family)
Derby's Men 33–4, 43, 44, 46, 134, 137,
   149
Dethick, William (Garter King-of-
   Arms) 20
Devereux, Robert (2nd Earl of Essex)
   7, 31, 37, 39 (illus.), 40, 109, 117,

121, 124, 132–3, 134–6, 137–41,
   148, 153, 156, 157
De Witt, Johannes 64, 72, 74, 119,
   136–7
dissolution of the monasteries 5
Donne, John 15, 66
Doomsday Book 4
Douai (and Douai 'martyrs') 18
Dowland, John (composer) 92
Dowton, Thomas 88–9
Drake, Sir Francis 156
Drayton, Michael 15, 88, 134
Dudley, Ambrose (Earl of Warwick) 12
Dudley family 11
Dudley, Robert (Earl of Leicester) 8,
   12, 13, 14, 31, 45–6, 48–9, 148, 150,
   151, 153
Dutton, Richard 80

Eagleton, Terry 22
Edward III, King 28
Edward IV, King 29
Edward VI, King 32
Egerton, Sir Thomas (Lord Ellesmere)
   42
Elizabeth, Princess (daughter of James
   I) 180, 186
Elizabeth I, Queen 7, 9, 10–12, 18, 19,
   20, 25–6, 30–1, 35, 36, 37, 50, 54,
   62, 67, 84, 93, 116, 118, 119, 120,
   124, 125, 130, 132–3, 137–50, 147
   (illus.), 153, 154–5, 156, 157–8, 165,
   171, 176, 177, 180
Emerson, Ralph (Jesuit missionary) 18
Englands Mourning Garment (poem by
   Henry Chettle) 145
England's Parnassus (anthology compiled
   by Robert Allot) 134
Essex, Earl of (see Devereux, Robert)
Essex House 133
Evans, Henry 178

Fenner, George 43
Field, Richard 106
fires in timber towns 2, 5, 47
First Folio of Shakespeare's plays 23,
   111, 187
Fleetwood, Edward 19
Fletcher, John 181, 184, 186
Folio of Jonson's *Works* 84, 188
Forbes, Thomas 1
Forman, Simon 152, 173

Fortune playhouse 53, 68, 72, 73, 74, 75, 99, 108, 136–7
foul papers 81
Frederick II (King of Denmark) 46
Friedrich, Ludwig (Prince of Württemberg) 184
Fripp, Edgar 13, 49

Garbo, Greta 172
Garnet, Henry (Jesuit 'martyr') 173
Gentili, Alberico (author of *De Legationibus*) 36–7
George Inn, playhouse at 63
Gilburne, Samuel 89, 92
Globe playhouse 68, 71, 72, 73, 74, 75, 95, 98, 99, 108, 126, 128–30, 134, 136–7, 139, 142, 143, 145, 158, 160, 173, 178, 179, 184, 185 (illus.), 186–7
Goldberg, Jonathan 164–5
Goodere family 15
Gowry, Earl of 168
Gray, Arthur 15
Greene, Robert 17–18, 51, 59, 60, 62, 78, 82, 93, 100, 105
Grindal, Edmund (Archbishop of Canterbury) 11, 55, 133
Guilpin, Everard (author of *Skialetheia*) 132
Gunpowder Plot 163, 172–3
Gurr, Andrew 96–7, 98, 99, 109
Gwynne, Matthew 93

Hall, John (Shakespeare's son-in-law) 174
Hampton Court 173
Hampton Court Conference (1604) 165
Harbage, Alfred 96
Harington, Sir John 140–1, 172, 175
Hastings, Henry (3rd Earl of Huntingdon) 36, 151
Hayley, William (author of *Lord Russel*) 87
Hayward, John 135–6, 139
Helperby 4
Heminges, John 111, 128, 158, 170, 178, 187, 188
Henri III (King of France) 36
Henry IV, King 28, 36, 118, 132, 136
Henry V, King 124, 135
Henry VII, King 25, 29, 30, 32
Henry VIII, King 4, 10, 25, 31, 32, 150, 155

Henry, Prince (son of James I) 162, 167–8, 172, 179–80, 181–2, 186
Henslowe, Philip 35, 48, 50, 51, 57, 59, 65–9, 72, 75–6, 80, 88, 90, 94, 99, 108, 112, 115, 122, 125–6, 128, 130, 156, 188
Henslowe's *Diary* 35, 48, 57, 68
Hentzner, Paul 125, 178–9
Hertford's Men 149
Hesketh, Sir Thomas 15–16
Heywood, Thomas 85
Hock Tuesday Play (Coventry) 9
Hodges, C. Walter 56, 73, 131 (all illus.)
Hoghton, Alexander 15–16
Hoghton, Thomas 15
Holland's Leaguer 66
Hollar, Wenceslaus 67, 185 (illus.)
homosexuality in Elizabethan England 105
Honigmann, Ernst 13, 15–16, 20, 37, 40, 49, 51, 59–60, 93, 109
Hope playhouse 57, 74
hospitality, decline of 5, 25
Hotson, Leslie 136
House of Commons 165–6, 172, 175–6, 182–6
Howard, Charles (2nd Baron of Effingham, Lord High Admiral from 1585 and 1st Earl of Nottingham from 1597) 62, 90, 91 (illus.), 108, 116, 119, 124, 139, 141, 147 (illus.), 148, 149, 154, 155–7
Howard, Henry (1st Earl of Northampton) 163, 167
Howard, Thomas (4th Duke of Norfolk) 12, 28, 155
Howard, Thomas (3rd Earl of Suffolk) 149, 156
Howard, Lord Thomas (1561–1626) 119
Howard, William (1st Baron of Effingham) 149, 155–6
Hunsdon House 150
Hunsdon, Lords (see Carey, George and Henry)
Hunsdon's Men 150
Huntingdon, Earl of (see Hastings, Henry)

indoor performances 114, 177–9
'inner stage' 137

Jaggard, William 23, 134

James I, King 15, 28, 37, 44, 84, 93, 130, 143, 155, 156–60, 164–86
James, Henry 186
Jenkins, Thomas (Shakespeare's schoolteacher) 9, 11, 15
Jesuit 'invasion' 18
jigs 110, 128, 129–30
Johnson, Robert (lutanist) 178
Jones, Inigo 170, 176–7, 179, 181
Jones, Richard 46
Jonson, Ben 9, 10, 15, 21, 79, 84, 85, 94, 97, 120, 121, 122, 125–6, 128, 141, 162–4, 169, 170–1, 173, 174, 176–7, 179, 181, 184, 188

Keats, John 20
Kempe, Will 46, 99, 109, 110, 111 (illus.), 125, 128, 129–30, 136, 161
Kenilworth Castle 9, 13
Kenilworth water-pageant (1575) 8
Kenny, Robert 155, 156
Kett's Rebellion (1549) 25
King's Men (see Chamberlain's Men)
Kitson, Sir Thomas (merchant) 93
Knollys, Sir Francis 133

Lambarde, William 133
land laws, ineffectiveness of 36, 41–2
Langley, Francis 72, 115, 152
Lanier, Emilia (? the dark lady of the sonnets) 152
Latin in schools 9–10
Lee, Sir Henry 119
Leicester, Earl of (see Dudley, Robert)
Leicester's Men 8, 48–9, 55, 148
Leland, John 2
Lestrange, Joan 29
Levi, Peter 13–14, 146, 175
'Liberties' 65
Life and reign of King Henry the IIII, The (by John Hayward) 135
life-expectancy in Elizabethan England 1–3
Limon, Jerzy 46
London Bridge 14, 67–8
Lord Chamberlain, office of 148–9
Lord Mayor of London, opposition to players from 54, 113–14, 117
Lord Russel (play by William Hayley) 87
Lord Steward, office of 148
Lord Strange's Men (see Strange's Men)

Lowin, John 170
Lucy family 11
Lupton, Donald 5
Lyly, John 153

McGrath, Patrick 10–11
malnutrition 2–3, 21
malting, Stratford trade in 7
Manners, Francis (6th Earl of Rutland) 175
'Manors' 65
Mansfield, Richard 112
Marchioness, sinking of (1989) 67
Marlowe, Christopher 60, 79, 103, 109, 126, 141
Marprelate tracts 19
Marshalsea prison 121, 122
Marston, John 83, 132, 141, 173
Marvell, Andrew 146
Mary I, Queen 10, 19, 155
Mary, Queen of Scots 12, 13, 18, 145, 155
masques 146, 162–3, 170–2, 175–7, 179–80, 181–2
Master of the Queen's Horse, office of 148
Master of the Revels, office of 62–3, 69, 122, 149
Mathew, David 176
Mayne, Cuthbert (Jesuit 'martyr') 18
Memoirs (of Robert Carey) 143–4, 153
Meres, Francis (author of *Palladis Tamia*) 42, 60, 79, 123
Millenary Petition (1604) 165
Morley, Thomas (author of *Consort Lessons*) 92
Mosley, Sir Nicholas (merchant moneylender) 35
Mountjoy, Christopher (Shakespeare's landlord) 143, 167, 186
Munday, Anthony 79
Mytens, Daniel 91, 183 (both illus.)

Nashe, Thomas 58, 59, 64, 75, 117, 120–1
Naunton, Sir Robert 151
Neville, Eleanor (sister of the 'Kingmaker') 29
Neville, Richard (Earl of Warwick, known as 'Kingmaker') 29
Newington Butts playhouse 63–4, 108, 137

New Place (Shakespeare's Stratford house) 21, 119, 181
Norfolk, Duke of (see Howard, Thomas)
North, Sir Thomas 174
Northern Earls, revolt of the (1569) 11, 118, 150–1

Oldcastle, Sir John 28, 117, 118, 124, 153
Old Price Riots (1809) 24
Order of the Garter 36, 58–9, 119, 154
Orrell, John 71, 72, 74
Ovid 10, 106, 123
Owen, Nicholas (builder of priestholes) 19
Oxford, Earl of (see Vere, Edward)

Palladis Tamia (by Francis Meres) 60, 79, 123
Palmer, John 87
Parallel Lives of the Greeks and Romans (by Plutarch) 174
Paris Garden Manor 66, 115, 152
Parsons, Robert (Jesuit missionary) 18
Passionate Pilgrim, The (199) 134
patronage 23, 25–8, 33–4, 37, 43–4, 45, 48–9, 106, 148–60, 163, 176–7
Peele, George 37–40
Pembroke's Men 50, 105, 120–1
Philip II (King of Spain) 18–19, 125
Philip III (King of Spain) 167
Phillips, Augustine 89, 92, 108, 110, 128, 140, 158, 170
Phoenix and the Turtle, The 18
Pierce Penilesse (by Thomas Nashe) 58
Pilkington, John (author of *Spindle-Shank Em*) 129
plague 1, 2, 47–8, 55, 60, 69, 105, 106, 158, 159, 162, 174, 178, 180, 184
Platter, Thomas 128, 129
Plautus 10, 78, 123
playwrights' contracts 113
playwrights' practices 79–88
playwrights' status 79–88, 109–10, 112–13, 125–6
'plots' 79, 85–8, 112
Plutarch 174–5
Pope, Thomas 46, 108, 110, 128, 170
Popham, Sir John 121
population (of England) 1, 157; (of London) 54; (of Norwich) 2; (of Stratford) 1–2; (of under-twenties) 1

poverty 2–5, 21–2, 115–16
'prophesyings' 11
proscenium arch 58, 60, 97, 137
publishing of plays 23, 84–5, 108, 111, 134, 187, 188
Puritanism in England 10–14, 19, 47, 165–6, 177

Queen's Men 8, 62, 108, 149–50
Quiney, Thomas (of Stratford) 187–8

Radcliffe, Thomas (3rd Earl of Sussex) 151
Raleigh, Sir Walter 40, 138, 146, 167
Rape of Lucrece, The 17, 80, 105, 106, 107 (illus.), 123, 181
Records of Early English Drama 45
Red Bull playhouse 94
Red Lion playhouse 52–7, 72
rehearsal practices 88–9
Reynolds, John (carpenter) 52–3
Richard II, King 28, 133, 135–6, 139
Richard III, King 25, 29–30, 104
Ridolfi Plot 12, 155
Ringler, William 112
Robin Hood 165
Robinson, Richard (of Alton) 40
Rogers, Philip (of Stratford) 166
Rose playhouse 49, 50, 58, 63–75, 73 (illus.), 83, 94, 99, 108, 115, 122, 128, 137
Rowe, Nicholas 106
Rowse, A. L. 20, 152
Ruthven, Alexander 168
Rutland, Earl of (see Manners, Francis)
Rutter, Carol 68, 69, 80, 83, 109

Saint George, cult of 7, 119
Salisbury, Earl of (see Cecil, Robert)
Sands, James 92
Schoenbaum, Samuel 13
'School of night' 40
Segar, William 38 (illus.)
Seneca 78, 123, 146
Shakespeare, Anne (née Hathaway) 14, 16, 20, 21, 118, 181
Shakespeare coat of arms 6, 20–1, 21 (illus.), 118
Shakespeare, Hamnet (William's son) 14, 37, 117
Shakespeare, Joan (William's sister) 21, 187

Shakespeare, John (William's father) 1, 5–14, 20, 21, 35, 142, 187
Shakespeare, Judith (William's daughter) 14, 21, 37, 187–8
Shakespeare, Mary (William's mother) 5, 21, 178
Shakespeare, Susanna (William's daughter) 14, 21, 22, 143, 174
Shakespeare, William birth, 1–2; boyhood visits to plays, 8–9; education, 9–10; religious upbringing, 9–20; marriage, 16; 'lost years', 14–17; arrival in London, 17, 51; reliance on patronage, 17–18, 43–4, 158–9, 164; purchases coat of arms, 20–1; involved in litigation, 21, 166, 178, 186; purchases property in Stratford, 21–2, 142–3; purchases Blackfriars gatehouse, 22; possible involvement in usury, 17, 35; touring with players, 45–7; as an actor, 62, 93–4; early plays, 59–62, 77–8; publication of plays, 84–5, 108, 111, 134, 188; collaboration with Richard Burbage, 92, 103–4; reltionship with the Earl of Southampton, 17, 50, 105–7, 123–4, 169, 181; sharer with the Chamberlain's Men, 95, 106–42 (*passim*); and the creation of 'character', 103–4; as house playwright, 112–87 (*passim*); death of only son, 117; relationship with the Earl of Essex, 123–4, 132–40; literary reputation, 123, 134; sharer with the King's Men, 158–87 (*passim*); will and death, 187–8
Shaw, Robert 48
Shrewsbury, Earl of (see Talbot, Gilbert)
Sincler, John 111–12
Singer, John 110
Skialetheia (by Everard Guilpin) 132
Sly, William 158, 170, 178
Smith, Lacey Baldwin 145
Somerset House 152, 167, 172
Somerset House Conference 167
Somerville, John (Catholic conspirator) 18
Sommer, John 46
Sonnets, Shakespeare's 18, 105, 117, 123, 134, 180–1

Southampton, Earl of (see Wriothesley, Henry)
Southwark 4, 65–7, 68, 99, 130; September Fair, 67
Spain (war with) 5, 18–20, 116–17, 120, 125, 156, 171; (peace with) 167–8, 171, 180
Speed, John (author of *The Theatre of the Empire of Great Britaine*) 6
Spencer, Alice, of Althorp (wife of Ferdinando Stanley) 41–2, 106, 154, 174, 175
Spencer, Diana, of Althorp (currently Princess of Wales) 163
Spencer, Elizabeth, of Althorp (wife of George Carey) 41, 154
Spencer, Gabriel (actor) 94, 121, 125–6
Spencer, Sir John, of Althorp 41
Spencer, Sir Robert, of Althorp 162
Spenser, Edmund 40, 134, 150–1
Spindle-Shank Em (play by John Pilkington) 129
stage dimensions (of the Red Lion) 52–3; (of the Rose) 71–4
stage directions in actors' parts 82
stage doors 57, 136–7
stage music 92–3
stage tower (or turret) 53–4, 72–3
stage trapdoor 53, 57
Stanislavsky, Constantin 83, 92
Stanley family 16, 19, 28–43, 45, 49, 174, 187
Stanley, Ferdinando (5th Earl of Derby, d. 1594) 16, 17, 19, 33–4, 35, 37–41, 38 (illus.), 42, 43, 106, 108, 109, 154, 162, 175
Stanley, Henry (4th Earl of Derby, d. 1593) 16, 19, 31–7, 40, 41, 45, 148
Stanley, John (1st Earl of Derby, d. 1504) 29–30
Stanley, Sir John (d. 1414) 28
Stanley, Sir John (d. 1437) 28–9
Stanley, Sir Thomas (1st Lord Stanley, d. 1459) 29
Stanley, Sir Thomas (1st Lord Strange) 29
Stanley, Sir William (Catholic conspirator) 41
Stanley, William (6th Earl of Derby) 31, 35, 41–3, 46, 132
Stansby, William 188
Stationers' Register 110, 134, 142
Stone, Lawrence 31

Strange, Lord (see Stanley, Ferdinando)
Strange's Men 16, 19, 33–4, 37, 40–1,
    46, 47, 49–50, 51, 58, 59, 62, 63–4,
    66, 105, 108, 113, 148, 150
Strong, Roy 119
Stuart, Esmé (Seigneur d'Aubigny)
    163–4
Stubbes, Philip 105
Sturgess, Keith 171
Styles, Philip 7
Suffolk, Earl of (see Howard, Thomas)
Sussex, Earl of (see Radcliffe, Thomas)
Sussex's Men 108
Swan playhouse 64, 72, 74, 115,
    119–20, 122, 137, 152

Talbot family 30
Talbot, Gilbert (7th Earl of
    Shrewsbury) 58
Tarlton, Richard 62, 101–3, 102 (illus.),
    104, 128–9, 149; *Tarlton's Jests*,
    101, 103
Tawney, R. H. 30
teatrum mundi ('All the world's a stage')
    9, 36, 101, 145–7, 160, 165
Terence 10, 62
Thames, River 67–8, 75, 126, 127
    (illus.), 139, 143, 179
Thames watermen 67–8
Theatre, the 55–8, 63, 75, 99, 104, 108,
    110, 115, 118, 122, 123, 125, 126, 128
Theobalds (residence of Robert Cecil)
    175, 176, 178
Thomas, Sidney 60
Thorpe, Thomas (publisher of
    Shakespeare's *Sonnets*) 180, 181
Throgmorton family 11
Tilney, Sir Edmund (Master of the
    Revels) 62, 149
tireman 89, 95
tiring house 53, 57
Tower of London 136, 139, 167
Townsend, Sir Robert 163
Tudor bureaucracy 5
Tudor, Margaret (mother of Henry
    VII) 29
Tudor myth 7, 124
Tyrone, Earl of 133, 140

understudies 51

Unfortunate Traveller, The (by Thomas
    Nashe) 64
university wits 78
Unton, Sir Henry 84
usury 34–5, 68–9

vagrancy 4–5, 44, 115–16
Van Buchell, Arend 74, 137
Vanlore, Peter (merchant moneylender)
    35
Velasco, Juan Fernandez de 167–8
Venus and Adonis 17, 50, 105, 106, 110,
    123, 181
Vere, Edward (17th Earl of Oxford) 22,
    31, 41–2
Vere, Elizabeth (his daughter) 41–3
Vice (in morality plays) 103
Villiers, George (Duke of Buckingham)
    28
Visscher, Claes Jan 127 (illus.)

wages 2, 9, 69, 95, 115
Walsingham, Sir Francis 31, 94
war of the poets 141
Wars of the Roses 25, 29
Warwick 2, 6, 11
Warwickshire 6
Warwick's Men 8
Webster, John 94
Wheeler, Margaret (of Stratford) 187–8
Whitgift, John 12, 13, 14, 19, 130, 132,
    143–4
Whitsuntide Pastime (at Stratford) 7, 8
Wilde, Oscar 100
Wiles, David 110, 116, 128–30
Wilton House 159, 162
Winter, Samuel 3 (illus.)
Wolsey, Cardinal 25–6
Woodliffe, Oliver 123
Worcester, Earl of 31, 122, 147 (illus.)
Worcester's Men 8, 122, 130, 137, 149
Wriothesley, Henry (3rd Earl of
    Southampton) 15, 17, 41, 43, 50,
    105–6, 107 (illus.), 123, 133, 138
    (illus.), 139, 167–8, 169, 181

York House 136
youth culture 7–8

Index of plays

Anonymous *Gowry*, 168, 177; *Mucedorus*, 128, 181; *Sir Thomas More*, 113; *The Spanish Maze*, 169

Beaumont, Francis (with John Fletcher) *The Maid's Tragedy*, 184; *Philaster*, 181

Brome, Richard *The Antipodes*, 87

Chapman, George *The Conspiracy and Tragedy of Charles Duke of Byron*, 177; (with Ben Jonson and John Marston) *Eastward Ho!*, 173

Dekker, Thomas (with Michael Drayton) *Civil Wars*, 88–9, 90; (with Drayton and Robert Wilson) *Pierce of Winchester*, 88; *Satiromastix*, 164

Drayton, Michael (with Dekker) *Civil Wars*, 88–9, 90; (with Dekker and Robert Wilson) *Pierce of Winchester*, 88; (with Richard Hathaway, Anthony Munday and Robert Wilson) *Sir John Oldcastle*, 124

Fletcher, John (with Beaumont) *The Maid's Tragedy*, 184; *Philaster*, 181; (with Shakespeare) *Cardenio*, 190; *Henry VIII*, 101, 186–7; *The Two Noble Kinsmen*, 186

Greene, Robert *Orlando Furioso*, 82

Hathaway, Richard (with Drayton, Anthony Munday and Robert Wilson) *Sir John Oldcastle*, 124

Heywood, Thomas *If You Know Not Me, You Know Nobody*, 85; *The Rape of Lucrece*, 85

Johnson, Ben *The Alchemist*, 181, 184; *Althorp Entertainment*, 162–3; (with Chapman and John Marston) *Eastward Ho!*, 173; *Every Man in His Humour*, 94, 128, 169; *Every Man out of His Humour*, 21, 169; (with Thomas Nashe) *The Isle of Dogs*, 120; *The Masque of Blackness*, 170; *The Masque of Queens*, 179; *Oberon, Prince of Fairy*, 170; *The Satyr*, 162–3; *Sejanus*, 162, 163–4, 168; *Speeches at Prince Henry's Barriers*, 181–2; *The Staple of News*, 10; *Volpone*, 174

Marlowe, Christopher *Tamburlaine the Great*, 60

Marston, John *Antonio and Mellida*, 83, 132; (with Chapman and Jonson) *Eastward Ho!*, 173; *Sophonisba*, 173

Middleton, Thomas (?) *The Revenger's Tragedy*, 174

Munday, Anthony (with Drayton, Hathaway and Robert Wilson) *Sir John Oldcastle*, 124

Nashe, Thomas (with Jonson) *The Isle of Dogs*, 120

Shakespeare, William *All's Well that Ends Well*, 143, 161; *Antony and Cleopatra*, 68, 160, 170, 174; *As You Like It*, 32, 128, 145, 161; (with Fletcher) *Cardenio*, 186; *The Comedy of Errors*, 60, 78, 109, 112, 169; *Coriolanus*, 174; *Cymbeline*, 161, 180; *Hamlet*, 81, 86 (illus.), 94, 104, 141–2, 160; *Henry IV Part One*, 116, 117, 118, 119, 182; *Henry IV Part Two*, 66, 118, 119, 134, 136; *Henry V*, 124, 134–5, 169; (with others) *Henry VI*, 20, 58–61, 75, 109; (with Fletcher) *Henry VIII*, 101, 186–7; *Julius Caesar*, 100, 128, 174; *King John*, 20, 60, 112; *King Lear*, 25, 32, 160, 161, 166, 170, 172, 174; *Love's Labour's Lost*, 40, 109–10, 169; *Macbeth*, 32, 160, 173–4; *Measure for Measure*, 66, 100, 121,

159, 164–6; *The Merchant of Venice*, 35, 116, 134, 169; The Merry Wives of Windsor, 10, 119, 154, 169; *A Midsummer Night's Dream*, 8, 42, 82, 104, 115, 116, 134; *Much Ado about Nothing*, 32, 125, 134; *Othello*, 160, 169, 179, 184; (with ? George Wilkins) *Pericles, Prince of Tyre*, 178; *Richard II*, 112, 123, 132–3, 135–6, 139–40; *Richard III*, 30, 60, 101–4, 109, 112, 123; *Romeo and Juliet*, 60, 104, 115; *The Taming of the Shrew*, 60, 104, 109; *The Tempest*, 32, 160, 161, 179, 184, 186; *Titus Andronicus*, 60, 78, 109; *Troilus and Cressida*, 142–3, 161; *Twelfth Night*, 25, 136, 161; *The Two Gentlemen of Verona*, 60, 100, 109; (with Fletcher) *The Two Noble Kinsmen*, 186; *The Winter's Tale*, 8, 160, 161, 179, 180, 184, 186

Tarlton, Richard *The Seven Deadly Sins*, 112

Tourneur, Cyril (see Middleton, Thomas)

Webster, John *The White Devil*, 94

Wilson, Robert (with Dekker and Drayton) *Pierce of Winchester*, 88; (with Drayton, Hathaway and Munday) *Sir John Oldcastle*, 124